143 gogh's starry night

163 dissonance 900 AD?

163— 4 3rds in England 1200AD

THE BRITANNICA GUIDE TO
THEORIES AND IDEAS
THAT CHANGED THE MODERN WORLD

TURNING POINTS IN HISTORY

THE BRITANNICA GUIDE TO

THEORIES AND IDEAS

THAT CHANGED THE MODERN WORLD

EDITED BY KATHLEEN KUIPER, MANAGER, ARTS AND CULTURE

Britannica®
Educational Publishing

IN ASSOCIATION WITH

ROSEN
EDUCATIONAL SERVICES

Published in 2010 by Britannica Educational Publishing
(a trademark of Encyclopædia Britannica, Inc.)
in association with Rosen Educational Services, LLC
29 East 21st Street, New York, NY 10010.

Distributed exclusively by Rosen Educational Services.
For a listing of additional Britannica Educational Publishing titles, call toll free (800) 237-9932.

First Edition

Britannica Educational Publishing
Michael I. Levy: Executive Editor
Marilyn L. Barton: Senior Coordinator, Production Control
Steven Bosco: Director, Editorial Technologies
Lisa S. Braucher: Senior Producer and Data Editor
Yvette Charboneau: Senior Copy Editor
Kathy Nakamura: Manager, Media Acquisition
Kathleen Kuiper: Manager, Arts and Culture

Rosen Educational Services
Jeanne Nagle: Senior Editor
Nelson Sá: Art Director
Matthew Cauli: Designer
Introduction by Holly Cefrey

Library of Congress Cataloging-in-Publication Data

The Britannica guide to theories and ideas that changed the modern world / edited by
Kathleen Kuiper.—1st ed.
  p. cm.—(Turning points in history)
Includes bibliographical references and index.
"In association with Britannica Educational Publishing, Rosen Educational Services."
ISBN 978-1-61530-029-7 (library binding)
1. Civilization, Modern. 2. Intellectual life—History. 3. Science—History. 4. Philosophy,
Modern—History. I. Kuiper, Kathleen.
CB358.B69 2010
901—dc22

2009048166

Manufactured in the United States of America

On the cover: *Nicolaus Copernicus's heliocentric concept of the solar system is but one of the
theories and ideas that have had a profound effect on humankind throughout the ages.* Kean
Collection/Hulton Archive/Getty Images

CONTENTS

29

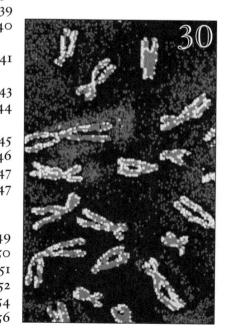

30

82

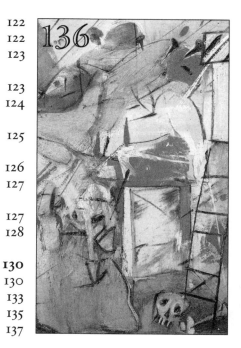

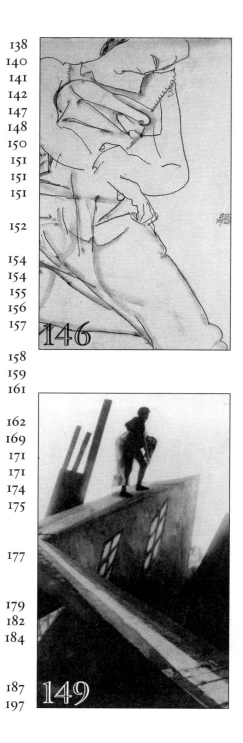

*I*ntroduction

At choice moments throughout time, individuals have posed new ideas or theories that have gone against the grain. Someone decided what is known is not enough and asked—sometimes demanded—that the world look at an issue, circumstance, or traditional method in a whole new way. The story of humanity is rife with such turning points. Some have begun as small changes but reverberated, building in strength until their impact on the world became tremendous. Others were so essential that they were expressed almost immediately on a global scale.

This book examines the theories and ideas that have inextricably altered the foundation of existence—atomic theory, evolution, absolutism, Modernism, and natural law among them. The players behind each concept are highlighted throughout, and each chapter includes information about the climate and cultural perspectives from which each crucial moment sprang.

The biological sciences have engendered any number of theories designed to explain the origin, structure, function, and evolution of living organisms. In this discipline, ideas are continually put to the test through research and experimentation, then challenged and enhanced as new facts come to light. For instance, the ancient Greek belief that life was spontaneously generated gave way to the conceit that every living creature emanated from a fertilized egg.

Although scientists had begun observing and cataloguing various kinds of cells as early as the 1600s, it wasn't until much later that they truly began to understand their nature, how they functioned and reproduced. Cell theory—the notion that all living things are made from cells, and that all vital functions occur within them—was formulated in the 1800s by two German scientists, Theodore Schwann and Matthias Schleiden.

The situation was much the same when it came to germ theory. Since at least 100 BCE, investigators had suspected that disease was cause by tiny invaders. But it wasn't until the 19th century, when Italy's Agostino Bassi showed that a particular silkworm disease was caused by a fungus, that this theory was proved. Such studies underscored the need for stringent sanitary standards to combat the specific bacteria and viruses that threatened the health and well being of humans and animals. French chemist Louis Pasteur took this concept one step further, developing vaccines to contain or prevent the spread of diseases such as anthrax, cholera, and rabies. In this way, cell theory and germ theory helped save untold millions of lives.

Other biological science turning points have centred on the subject of diversity. Evolutionary theory charts the progression of life from a single progenitor, generally moving from simple to complex forms all the while. Evolution makes distinctions among various species. Genetics, on the other hand, concentrates on variations within species. The ability to determine the transmission of individual inherited traits by studying genes — or, in modern times, mapping links on the DNA chain — has yielded life-altering breakthroughs in the way humans grow food, solve crimes, reproduce, and, perhaps most important, treat disease.

The physical sciences have witnessed their fair share of momentous change due to ideas wrought from observation and conjecture. Several well-known, fundamental theories and scientific concepts are associated with the study of nonliving entities: Albert Einstein's theory of relativity ($E = mc^2$); the legend of Isaac Newton getting konked on the head by an apple, which illustrates laws governing the universal force of attraction known as gravity.

Many turning points in human comprehension of the universe have come about through the study of astronomy, a field that itself stemmed from ideas conceived by curious stargazers. Astronomy and mathematics, a field that makes good use of the theoretical in order to solve problems, are closely linked. Ancient astronomers believed the order of the universe was fundamentally mathematical in nature, and used arithmetic to predict celestial movements. As time went by, astronomers (who were also frequently mathematicians by trade) honed equations and progressions to get a more accurate reading of the night sky. The development of calculus in the late 1600s made it possible to gauge area and volume and predict the movement patterns of distant celestial objects. Today calculus is the basic entry point for anyone wishing to study physics, chemistry, biology, economics, finance, or actuarial science.

The arts also lend themselves quite well to new ideas. In fact, finding new and creative ways of expression is the artist's stock in trade. With regard to the fine arts (painting, drawing, sculpting), this spirit of artistic innovation is evident in the various movements that have taken art in a variety of directions.

During the Renaissance—a time of great cultural change throughout Europe—painting and drawing literally took on a new dimension with the advent of perspective. Giving depth to objects in a way that makes them pop off the flat page, perspective was made popular by Filippo Brunelleschi. In his work as an architect and engineer, Brunelleschi reintroduced the concept of the vanishing point, which is a distant spot in a drawing or rendering where parallel lines converge. The eye is drawn to the vanishing point, creating the illusion of depth and three-dimensionality. Several influential Renaissance artists, including Donatello and Fra Angelico, employed perspective in their work.

Other movements in the graphic arts that have served as turning points include Impressionism (accurately recording reality using light and colour) and Expressionism (distorted reality meant to arouse the viewer's emotions). In the 20th century, many artists abandoned realistic portrayals altogether in favour of abstraction. Instead of classic representational methods, abstract art uses lines, texture, and colour, rather than representation or figuration, to convey meaning.

One of the most far-reaching movements in the arts was Modernism. Coming on the heels of World War I, Modernism permeated every facet of the arts. Many creative people—writers, artists, philosophers, composers, and architects—used their creations to make a break with convention. Impressionism and Abstract Expressionism were modernist approaches to art. Modernist literature, exemplified by the works of T.S. Eliot, Virginia Woolf, Gertrude Stein, and James Joyce, among others, experimented with new forms and manners of expression. Dancers abandoned traditional steps for free-form movement, architects embraced clean lines and unadorned facades, and composers experimented with atonality.

Another important milestone, which changed the experience of music, is the incorporation of harmony into vocal and instrumental compositions. Church choirs in the 9th century are credited with the first usage of harmony. The fuller, richer sound afforded by voices rising in intervals was received so favourably by listeners that composers embraced the use of polyphony and favoured it over the unison musical line.

The visual replaces the aural when it comes to a key turning point in motion picture production—the montage.

In its broadest sense, montage means to assemble various elements to make a unified whole. The cinematic definition is a matter of the way in which film is edited to create a cohesive sequence of storytelling. This can be done narratively, by exploring a character or location from several angles or over time; graphically, using a method that links shots by physical appearance; or ideationally, where images are spliced together more or less by topic as a way of solidifying an idea the director is trying to get across in a certain scene. The introduction of montage occurred very early on in the history of filmmaking. Pioneering directors Edwin S. Porter and D.W. Griffith popularized the technique in America, while montage was refined and used to great effect by Russian directors in the early 20th century.

Turning points in the social sciences have sought to clarify and strengthen people's understanding of society and social relationships, why they work and why they fail. They constitute changes that have affected behaviour and human interaction. Mass production and the assembly line greatly altered the role of the worker, negotiations between employers and employees, and even international relations with regard to trade practices.

Other crucial social science turning points include the advent of psychoanalysis, including the study of child behaviour. Psychologists such as Sigmund Freud sought answers much deeper below the surface, revealing that human behaviour is the result of many factors, including repressed memories and desires. Beyond the psyche—or, more accurately, intertwined with it—is the idea that human beings have a conscience that guides their behaviour. The conscience gives rise to the notion of what is good and evil.

Religious concepts that have had an impact on human behaviour include the notions of sin and the soul. The relation of the soul to the body has been a subject of philosophical debate for centuries. The ancient Greek theologian and philosopher Augustine of Hippo claimed that the body and soul were separate and that the latter contained the true essence of a person. In the Middle Ages, Thomas Aquinas contemporized the idea of the soul that had already long been pondered from the time of early Hebrews and ancient Greeks. Modern philosophers have held a number of opinions, anything from the soul being equivalent to the mind to it being merely a justification for the development of ethics.

Throughout history, ethical conceits such as right and wrong have given rise to ideas concerning fair and equal treatment. These include important universal concepts such as human rights and natural law, which is a theory that there is an innate, common set of rules that all people follow simply because of their basic nature as human beings. For instance, people everywhere understand that killing an innocent person is wrong; they don't need a written, man-made law to tell them that. However, societies throughout the world have always thought it was a good idea to institute what is known as "positive laws"—those that are decreed and agreed to by various cultures—as well. Many positive, or man-made, laws have been influenced by natural laws. Those who do not follow natural and positive laws, or otherwise behave in a manner that is contrary to the greater societal good, are subject to punishment.

In general, people follow rules, regulations, and laws that are created to bring about harmony in a society. When the rules are broken, so is the peace. Therein lies one of the most interesting turning points in political and legal thought, the social contract. To live within society, humans give up certain individual rights, entering into an agreement with those in power in order to remain at peace. Great thinkers through the centuries, including Thomas Hobbes and Jean-Jacques Rousseau, have created works about the social contract that defined, and redefined, humans' understanding of their rights and place in society.

There is a common belief that laws should not be designed merely to protect life and property alone. Original ideas must and should be safeguarded as well. This is the theory behind intellectual-property law. Because ideas can be stolen, and can occur to more than one person at once, many societies have established laws to ensure a balanced legal approach to giving credit where credit is due. After a thorough examination of this book's contents, readers are sure to agree that theories and ideas are well worth protecting.

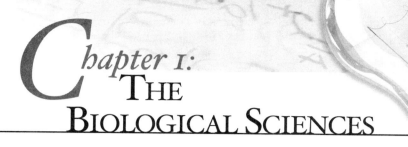

Chapter 1: THE BIOLOGICAL SCIENCES

The probing of the origin of life, cell theory, germ theory, and genetic inheritance, as well as the ideas regarding evolution and ecology—the development of a sense of how living things interact and form a system of relationships—represent profound turning points in human history. This chapter addresses some of the discoveries that have affected the way we think about ourselves, other living things, and life's vital processes.

THE ORIGIN OF LIFE

If a species can develop only from a preexisting species, then how did life originate? Among the many philosophical and religious ideas advanced to answer this question, one of the most popular was the theory of spontaneous generation, according to which living organisms could originate from nonliving matter. With the increasing tempo of discovery during the 17th and 18th centuries, however, investigators began to examine more critically the Greek belief that flies and other small animals arose from the mud at the bottom of streams and ponds by spontaneous generation. Then, when the English physician William Harvey announced his biological theory *ex ovo omnia* ("everything comes from the egg"), it appeared that he had solved the problem, at least insofar as it pertained to flowering plants and the higher animals, all of which develop from an egg. But Antonie van Leeuwenhoek's subsequent disquieting discovery of animalcules demonstrated the existence of a densely populated but previously invisible world of organisms that had to be explained.

A 17th-century Italian physician and poet, Francesco Redi, was one of the first to question the spontaneous origin of living things. Having observed the development of maggots and flies on decaying meat, Redi in 1668 devised a number of experiments, all pointing to the same conclusion: if flies are excluded from rotten meat, maggots do not develop. On meat exposed to air, however, eggs laid by flies develop into maggots. But renewed support for spontaneous generation came from the publication in 1745 of a book, *An Account of Some New Microscopical Discoveries*, by John Turberville Needham, an English Catholic priest; he found that large numbers of organisms subsequently developed in prepared infusions of many different substances that had been exposed to intense heat in sealed tubes for 30 minutes. Assuming that such heat treatment must have killed any previous organisms, Needham explained the presence of the new population on the grounds of spontaneous generation. The experiments appeared irrefutable until Lazzaro Spallanzani, an Italian biologist, repeated them and obtained conflicting results. He published his findings about 1775, claiming that Needham had not heated his tubes long enough nor had he sealed them in a satisfactory manner. Although Spallanzani's results should have been convincing, Needham had the support of the influential French naturalist Buffon; hence the matter of spontaneous generation remained unresolved.

THE DEATH OF SPONTANEOUS GENERATION

After a number of further investigations had failed to solve the problem, the French Academy of Sciences, in January 1860, offered a prize for contributions that would "attempt, by means of well-devised experiments, to throw new light on the question of spontaneous generation." In response to this challenge, Louis Pasteur, who at that time was a chemist, subjected flasks containing a sugared yeast solution to a variety of conditions. Pasteur was able to demonstrate conclusively that any microorganisms that developed in suitable media came from microorganisms in the air, not from the air itself, as Needham had suggested. Support for Pasteur's findings came in 1876 from an English physicist, John Tyndall, who devised an apparatus to demonstrate that air had the ability to carry particulate matter. Because such matter in air reflects light when the air is illuminated under special conditions, Tyndall's apparatus could be used to indicate when air was pure. Tyndall found that no organisms were produced when pure air was introduced into media capable of supporting the growth of microorganisms. It was these results, together with Pasteur's findings, that put an end to the doctrine of spontaneous generation.

When Pasteur later showed that parent microorganisms generate only their own kind, he thereby established the study of microbiology. Moreover, he not only succeeded in convincing the scientific world that microbes are living creatures, which come from preexisting forms, but also showed them to be an immense and varied component of the organic world, a concept that was to have important implications for the science of ecology. Further, by isolating various species of bacteria and yeasts in different chemical media, Pasteur was able to demonstrate that they brought about chemical change in a characteristic and predictable way, thus making a unique contribution to the study of fermentation and to biochemistry.

THE ORIGIN OF PRIMORDIAL LIFE

In the 1920s a Soviet biochemist, A.I. Oparin, and other scientists suggested that life may have come from nonliving matter under conditions that existed on the primitive

Earth, when the atmosphere consisted of the gases methane, ammonia, water vapour, and hydrogen. According to this concept, energy supplied by electrical storms and ultraviolet light may have broken down the atmospheric gases into their constituent elements, and organic molecules may have been formed when the elements recombined.

Some of these ideas have been verified by advances in geochemistry and molecular genetics; experimental efforts have succeeded in producing amino acids and proteinoids (primitive protein compounds) from gases that may have been present on the Earth at its inception, and amino acids have been detected in rocks that are more than three billion years old. With improved techniques it may be possible to produce precursors of or actual self-replicating living matter from nonliving substances. But whether it is possible to create the actual living heterotrophic forms from which autotrophs supposedly developed remains to be seen.

Although it may never be possible to determine experimentally how life originated or whether it originated only once or more than once, it would now seem—on the basis of the ubiquitous genetic code found in all living organisms on Earth—that life appeared only once and that all the diverse forms of plants and animals evolved from this primitive creation.

ANTONIE VAN LEEUWENHOEK
(b. Oct. 24, 1632, Delft, Neth.—d. Aug. 26, 1723, Delft)

The Dutch microscopist Antonie van Leeuwenhoek was the first to observe bacteria and protozoa. In his youth he was apprenticed to a draper; a later civil position allowed him to devote time to his hobby: grinding lenses and using them to study tiny objects. With his simple microscopes—skillfully ground, powerful single lenses of very short focal length, capable of high image quality—he observed what he called "very little animalcules," protozoa in rainwater and pond and well water and bacteria in the human mouth and intestine. He also discovered blood corpuscles, capillaries, and the structure of muscles and nerves, and in 1677 he first described the spermatozoa of insects, dogs, and humans. His research on lower animals argued against the doctrine of spontaneous generation, and his observations helped lay the foundations for the sciences of bacteriology and protozoology.

CELL THEORY

The history of cell theory is a history of the actual observation of cells, because early prediction and speculation about the nature of the cell were generally unsuccessful. The decisive event that allowed the observation of cells was the invention of the microscope in the 17th century, after which interest in the "invisible" world was stimulated. English physicist Robert Hooke, who described cork and other plant tissues in 1665, introduced the term *cell* because the cellulose walls of dead cork cells reminded him of the blocks of cells occupied by monks. Even after the publication in 1672 of excellent pictures of plant tissues, no significance was attached to the contents within the cell walls. The magnifying powers of the microscope and the inadequacy of techniques for preparing cells for observation precluded a study of the intimate details of the cell contents. Leeuwenhoek, beginning in 1673, discovered a number of things such as blood cells and spermatozoa. A new world of unicellular organisms was opened up. Such discoveries extended the known variety of living things but did not bring insight into their basic uniformity. Moreover, when Leeuwenhoek observed the swarming of his animalcules but failed to observe their division, he could only reinforce the idea that they arose spontaneously.

Cell theory was not formulated for nearly 200 years after the introduction of microscopy. Explanations for this delay range from the poor quality of the microscopes to the persistence of ancient ideas concerning the definition of a fundamental living unit. Many observations of cells were made, but apparently none of the observers was able to assert forcefully that cells are the units of biological structure and function.

Three critical discoveries made during the 1830s — when improved microscopes with suitable lenses, higher powers of magnification without aberration, and more satisfactory illumination became available — were decisive events in the early development of cell theory. First, the nucleus was observed by Scottish botanist Robert Brown in 1833 as a constant component of plant cells. Next, nuclei were also observed and recognized as such in some animal cells. Finally, a living substance called protoplasm was recognized within cells, its vitality made evident by its active streaming, or flowing, movements, especially in plant cells. After these three discoveries, cells, previously considered as mere pores in plant tissue, could no longer be thought of as empty, because they contained living material.

German physiologist Theodor Schwann and German biologist Matthias Schleiden clearly stated in 1839 that cells are the "elementary particles of organisms" in both plants and animals and recognized that some organisms are unicellular and others multicellular. This statement was made in Schwann's famous *Mikroskopische Untersuchungen über die*

Robert Brown. Hulton Archive/Getty Images

Übereinstimmung in der Struktur und dem Wachstume der Tiere und Pflanzen (1839; *Microscopical Researches into the Accordance in the Structure and Growth of Animals and Plants*). Schleiden's contributions on plants were acknowledged by Schwann as the basis for his comparison of animal and plant structure.

Schleiden and Schwann's descriptive statements concerning the cellular basis of biologic structure are straightforward and acceptable to modern thought. They recognized the common features of cells to be the membrane, nucleus, and cell body and described them in comparisons of various animal and plant tissues. A statement by Schleiden pointed toward the future direction of cell studies:

Each cell leads a double life: an independent one, pertaining to its own development alone; and another incidental, insofar as it has become an integral part of a plant. It is, however, easy to perceive that the vital process of the individual cells must form the first, absolutely indispensable fundamental basis, both as regards vegetable physiology and comparative physiology in general.

THE PROBLEM OF THE ORIGIN OF CELLS

Schwann and Schleiden were not alone in contributing to this great generalization of natural science, for strong intimations of the cell theory occur in the work of their predecessors. Recognizing that the basic problem was the origin of cells, these early investigators invented a hypothesis of "free cell formation," according to which cells developed *de novo* out of an unformed substance, a "cytoblastema," by a sequence of events in which first the nucleolus develops, followed by the nucleus, the cell body, and finally the cell membrane. The best physical model of the generation of formed bodies then available was crystallization, and their theory was inspired by that model. In retrospect, the hypothesis of free cell formation would not seem to have been justified, however, since cell division, a feature not characteristic of crystallization processes, had frequently been observed by earlier microscopists, especially among single-celled organisms. Even though cell division was observed repeatedly in the following decades, the theory of free cell formation lingered throughout most of the 19th century; however, it came to be thought of more and more as a possible exception to the general principle of the reproduction of cells by division. The correct general principle was affirmed in 1855 by a German pathologist and statesman, Rudolph Virchow, who asserted that "omnis cellula e cellula" ("all cells come from cells").

The inherently complex events of cell division pre-vented a quick resolution of the complete sequence of changes that occur during the process. First, it was noted that a cell with a nucleus divides into two cells, each hav-ing a nucleus; hence, it was concluded that the nucleus must divide, and direct division of nuclei was duly described by some. Better techniques served to create perplexity, because it was found that during cell division the nucleus as such disappears. Moreover, at the time of division, dimly discerned masses, now recognized as chromosomes, were seen to appear temporarily. Observations in the 1870s culminated in the highly accurate description and

Rudolf Virchow. Courtesy of Bildarchiv Preussischer Kulturbesitz BPK, Berlin

interpretation of cell division by German anatomist Walther Flemming in 1882. His advanced techniques of fixing and staining cells enabled him to see that cell reproduction involves the transmission of chromosomes from the parent to daughter cells by the process of mitosis and that the division of the cell body is the terminal event of that reproduction.

Discovery that the number of chromosomes remains constant from one generation to the next resulted in the full description of the process of meiosis. The description of meiosis, combined with the observation that

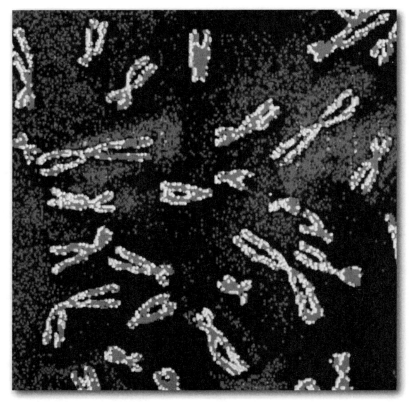

Chromosomes are inside the cells of every living thing. They are so small that they can be seen only through a powerful microscope. © Howard Sochurek/Corbis

fertilization is fundamentally the union of maternal and paternal sets of chromosomes, culminated in the understanding of the physical basis of reproduction and heredity. Meiosis and fertilization therefore came to be understood as the complementary events in the life cycle of organisms: meiosis halves the number of chromosomes in the formation of spores (plants) or gametes (animals), while fertilization restores the number through the union of gametes. By the 1890s "life" in all of its manifestations could be thought of as an expression of cells.

THE PROTOPLASM CONCEPT

As the concept of the cell as the elementary particle of life developed during the 19th century, it was paralleled by the "protoplasm" concept—the idea that the protoplasm within the cell is responsible for life. Protoplasm had been defined in 1835 as the ground substance of living material and hence responsible for all living processes. That life is an activity of an elementary particle, the cell, can be contrasted with the view that it is the expression of a living complex substance—even a supermolecule—called a protoplasm. The protoplasm concept was supported by observations of the streaming movements of the apparently slimy contents of living cells.

Advocates of the protoplasm concept implied that cells were either fragments or containers of protoplasm. Suspicious and often contemptuous of information obtained from dead and stained cells, such researchers discovered most of the basic information on the physical properties—mechanical, optical, electrical, and contractile—of the living cell.

An assessment of the usefulness of the concept of protoplasm is difficult. It was not wholly false; on the one hand, it encouraged the study of the chemical and mechanical properties of cell contents, but it also generated a resistance, evident as late as the 1930s, to the development of biochemical techniques for cell fractionation and to the realization that very large molecules (macromolecules) are important cellular constituents. As the cell has become fractionated into its component parts, *protoplasm*, as a term, no longer has meaning. The word *protoplasm* is still used, however, in describing the phenomenon of protoplasmic streaming—the phenomenon from which the concept of protoplasm originally emerged.

THE CONTRIBUTION OF OTHER SCIENCES

Appreciation of the cell as the unit of life has accrued from important sources other than microscopy; perhaps the most important is microbiology. Even though the small size of microorganisms prohibited much observation of their detailed structure until the advent of electron microscopy, they could be grown easily and rapidly. Thus it was that French chemist and microbiologist Louis Pasteur's studies of microbes published in 1861 helped to establish the principle of biogenesis—namely, that organisms arise only by the reproduction of other organisms. Fundamental ideas regarding the metabolic attributes of cells—that is, their ability to transform simple nutritional substances into cell substance and utilizable energy—came from microbiology. Pasteur perhaps overplayed the relation between catalysis and the living state of cells in considering enzymatic action to be an attribute of the living cell rather than of the catalytic molecules (enzymes) contained in the cell; it is a fact, however, that much of cell chemistry is enzyme chemistry—and that enzymes are one defining attribute of cells. The techniques of microbiology eventually opened the way for microbial genetics, which in turn provided the means for solving the fundamental problems of molecular biology that were inaccessible at first to direct attack by biochemical methods.

The science of molecular biology would be most capable of overthrowing the cell theory if the latter were an exaggerated generalization. On the contrary, molecular biology has become the foundation of cell science, for it has demonstrated not only that basic processes such as the genetic code and protein synthesis are similar in all living systems but also that they are made possible by the same cell components—e.g., chromosomes, ribosomes, and membranes.

In the overlapping histories of cell biology and medicine, two events are especially important. One, the identification in 1827 by Prussian-Estonian embryologist Karl Ernst Ritter von Baer of the ovum (unfertilized egg) as a cell, was important considering the many ways it often differs from other cells. Baer not only laid the foundations for reproductive biology but also provided important evidence for the cell theory at a critical time. The second important event was the promotion in 1855 of the concept of "cellular pathology" by Virchow. His idea that human diseases are diseases of cells and can be identified and understood as such gave an authority to cell theory.

Although biochemistry might have made considerable progress without cell theory, each influenced the other almost from the start. When it was established that all cells share most biochemical phenomena, the cell could be defined by its metabolism as well as by its structure. Cytochemistry, or histochemistry, made a brilliant start in 1869, when Swiss biochemist Johann Friedrich Miescher postulated that the nucleus must have a characteristic chemistry and then went on to discover nucleic acids, which have since been shown to be the crucial molecules of inheritance and metabolism.

Cell theory by itself cannot explain the development and unity of the multicellular organism. A cell is not necessarily an independently functioning unit, and a plant or an animal is not merely an accumulation of individual cells. Fortunately, however, the long controversy centring upon the individuality and separateness of cells has ended. Cell biology now focuses on the interactions and communication among cells as well as on the analysis of the single cell. The influence of the environment on the cell has always been considered important; now it has been recognized that one important part of the environment of a cell is other cells.

Cell theory thus is not so comprehensive as to eliminate the concept of the organism as more than the sum of its parts. But the study of a particular organism requires the investigation of cells both as individuals and as groups.

MARCELLO MALPIGHI

(b. March 10, 1628, Crevalcore, near Bologna, Papal States—d. Nov. 30, 1694, Rome)

In 1661 the Italian physician and biologist Marcello Malpighi identified the pulmonary capillary network, proving William Harvey's theory on blood circulation. He discovered the taste buds and was the first to see red blood cells and realize that they gave blood its colour. He studied subdivisions of the liver, brain, spleen, kidneys, bone, and deeper skin layers (Malpighian layers), concluding that even the largest organs are composed of minute glands. Malpighi also studied insect larvae (especially the silkworm), chick embryology, and plant anatomy, seeing an analogy between plant and animal organization. He is regarded as the founder of microscopic anatomy and may be regarded as the first histologist.

The problem of cancer is an example: a plant or animal governs the division of its own cells; the right cells must divide, be differentiated, and then be integrated into the proper organ system at the right time and place. Breakdown results in a variety of abnormalities, one of which is cancer. When the cell biologist studies the problem of the regulation of cell division, the ultimate objective is to understand the effect of the whole organism on an individual cell.

GERM THEORY

Perhaps the overarching medical advance of the 19th century, certainly the most spectacular, was the conclusive demonstration that certain diseases, as well as the infection of surgical wounds, were directly caused by minute living organisms. This discovery changed the whole face of pathology and effected a complete revolution in the practice of surgery.

The idea that disease was caused by entry into the body of imperceptible particles was of ancient date. It had been expressed by the Roman encyclopaedist Varro as early as 100 BCE, by Fracastoro in 1546, by Athanasius Kircher and Pierre Borel about a century later, and by Francesco Redi, who in 1684 wrote his *Osservazioni intorno agli animali viventi che si trovano negli animali viventi* ("Observations on Living Animals Which Are to Be Found Within Other Living Animals"), in which he sought to disprove the idea of spontaneous generation. Everything must have a parent, he wrote; only life produces life. A 19th-century pioneer in this field, regarded by some as founder of the parasitic theory of infection, was Agostino Bassi of Italy, who showed that a disease of silkworms was caused by a fungus that could be destroyed by chemical agents.

The main credit for establishing the science of bacteriology must be accorded to the French chemist Louis Pasteur. It was Pasteur who, by a brilliant series of experiments, proved that the fermentation of wine and the souring of milk are caused by living microorganisms. His work led to the pasteurization of milk and solved problems of agriculture and industry as well as those of animal and human diseases. He successfully employed inoculations to prevent anthrax in sheep and cattle, chicken cholera in fowl, and finally rabies in humans and dogs. The latter resulted in the widespread establishment of Pasteur Institutes.

From Pasteur, Joseph Lister, an English surgeon, derived the concepts that enabled him to introduce the antiseptic principle into surgery. In 1865 Lister, a professor of surgery at Glasgow University, began placing an antiseptic barrier of carbolic acid between the wound and the germ-containing atmosphere. Infections and deaths fell dramatically, and his pioneering work led to more refined techniques of sterilizing the surgical environment.

Obstetrics had already been robbed of some of its terrors by Alexander Gordon at Aberdeen, Scot., Oliver Wendell Holmes at Boston, and Ignaz Semmelweis at Vienna and Pest (Budapest), who advocated disinfection of the hands and clothing of midwives and medical students who attended confinements. These measures produced a marked reduction in cases of puerperal fever, the bacterial scourge of women following childbirth.

Another pioneer in bacteriology was the German physician Robert Koch, who showed how bacteria could be cultivated, isolated, and examined in the laboratory. A meticulous investigator, Koch discovered the organisms of tuberculosis, in 1882, and cholera, in 1883. By the end of the century many other disease-producing microorganisms had been identified.

DISCOVERIES IN CLINICAL MEDICINE AND ANESTHESIA

There was perhaps some danger that in the search for bacteria other causes of disease would escape detection. Many physicians, however, were working along different lines in the 19th century. Among them were a group attached to Guy's Hospital, in London: Richard Bright, Thomas Addison, and Sir William Gull. Bright contributed significantly to the knowledge of kidney diseases, including Bright's disease, and Addison gave his name to disorders of the adrenal glands and the blood. Gull, a famous clinical teacher, left a legacy of pithy aphorisms that might well rank with those of Hippocrates, a Greek physician often regarded as the father of medicine.

In Dublin Robert Graves and William Stokes introduced new methods in clinical diagnosis and medical training, while in Paris a leading clinician, Pierre-Charles-Alexandre Louis, was attracting many students from America by the excellence of his teaching. By the early 19th century the United States was ready to send back the results of its own researches and breakthroughs. In 1809, in a small Kentucky town, Ephraim McDowell boldly operated on a woman—without anesthesia or antisepsis—and successfully removed a large ovarian tumour. William Beaumont, in treating a shotgun wound of the stomach, was led to make many original observations that were published in 1833 as *Experiments and Observations on the Gastric Juice and the Physiology of Digestion*.

The most famous contribution by the United States to medical progress at this period was undoubtedly the introduction of general anesthesia, a procedure that not only liberated the patient from the fearful pain of surgery but also enabled the surgeon to perform more extensive operations. The discovery was marred by controversy.

Crawford Long, Gardner Colton, Horace Wells, and Charles Jackson, all physicians who pioneered different methods and uses of anesthesia, are all claimants for priority; some used nitrous oxide gas, and others employed ether, which was less capricious. There is little doubt, however, that it was William Thomas Morton who, on Oct. 16, 1846, at Massachusetts General Hospital, in Boston, first demonstrated before a gathering of physicians the use of ether as a general anesthetic. The news quickly reached Europe, and general anesthesia soon became prevalent in surgery. At Edinburgh, the professor of midwifery, James Young Simpson, had been experimenting upon himself and his assistants, inhaling various vapours with the object of discovering an effective anesthetic. In November 1847 chloroform was tried with complete success, and soon it was preferred to ether and became the anesthetic of choice.

Advances at the End of the Century

While antisepsis and anesthesia placed surgery on an entirely new footing, similarly important work was carried out in other fields of study, such as parasitology and disease transmission. Patrick Manson, a British pioneer in tropical medicine, showed in China, in 1877, how insects can carry disease and how the embryos of the *Filaria* worm, which can cause elephantiasis, are transmitted by the mosquito. Manson explained his views to a British army surgeon, Ronald Ross, then working on the problem of malaria, and Ross discovered the malarial parasite in the stomach of the *Anopheles* mosquito in 1897.

In Cuba, Carlos Finlay expressed the view, in 1881, that yellow fever is carried by the *Stegomyia* mosquito. Following his lead, the American physicians Walter Reed, William Gorgas, and others were able to conquer the scourge of

LOUIS PASTEUR

(b. Dec. 27, 1822, Dole, France—d. Sept. 28, 1895, Saint-Cloud, near Paris)

French chemist and microbiologist Louis Pasteur was one of the most important founders of medical microbiology. Early in his career, after studies at the École Normale Supérieure, he researched the effects of polarized light on chemical compounds. In 1857 he became director of scientific studies at the École. His studies of fermentation of alcohol and milk (souring) showed that yeast could reproduce without free oxygen (the Pasteur effect); he deduced that fermentation and food spoilage were due to the activity of microorganisms and could be prevented by excluding or destroying them. His work overturned the concept of spontaneous generation (life arising from nonliving matter) and led to heat pasteurization, allowing vinegar, wine, and beer to be produced and transported without spoiling. He saved the French silk industry by his work on silkworm diseases. In 1881 he perfected a way to isolate and weaken germs, and he went on to develop vaccines against anthrax in sheep and cholera in chickens, following Edward Jenner's example. He turned his attention to researching rabies, and in 1885 his inoculating with a weakened virus saved the life of a boy bitten by a rabid dog. In 1888 he founded the Pasteur Institute for rabies research, prevention, and treatment.

yellow fever in Panama and made possible the completion of the Panama Canal by reducing the death rate there from 176 per 1,000 to 6 per 1,000.

Other victories in preventive medicine ensued, because the maintenance of health was now becoming as important a concern as the cure of disease; and the 20th century was to witness the evolution and progress of national health services in a number of countries. In addition, spectacular advances in diagnosis and treatment followed the discovery of X-rays by Wilhelm Conrad Röntgen, in 1895, and of radium by Pierre and Marie Curie in 1898. Before the turn of the century, too, the vast new field of psychiatry had been opened up by Sigmund Freud. The tremendous increase in scientific knowledge during the 19th century radically altered and expanded the practice of medicine. Concern for upholding the quality of services led to the establishment of public and professional bodies to govern the standards for medical training and practice.

GENETICS

The study of heredity in general and of genes in particular is called genetics. Since the dawn of civilization, humankind has recognized the influence of heredity and has applied its principles to the improvement of cultivated crops and domestic animals. A Babylonian tablet more than 6,000 years old, for example, shows pedigrees of horses and indicates possible inherited characteristics. Other old carvings show cross-pollination of date palm trees. Most of the mechanisms of heredity, however, remained a mystery until the 19th century, when genetics as a systematic science began.

Genetics arose out of the identification of genes, the fundamental units responsible for heredity. Genetics may be defined as the study of genes at all levels, including the ways in which they act in the cell and the ways in which they are transmitted from parents to offspring. Modern genetics focuses on the chemical substance that genes are made of, called deoxyribonucleic acid, or DNA, and the ways in which it affects the chemical reactions that constitute the living processes within the cell. Gene action depends on interaction with the environment. Green plants, for example, have genes containing the information necessary to synthesize the photosynthetic pigment chlorophyll that gives them their green colour. Chlorophyll is synthesized in an environment containing light because the gene for chlorophyll is expressed only when it interacts with light. If a plant is placed in a dark environment, chlorophyll synthesis stops because the gene is no longer expressed.

Genetics as a scientific discipline stemmed from the work of Gregor Mendel in the middle of the 19th century. Mendel suspected that traits were inherited as discrete units, and, although he knew nothing of the physical or chemical nature of genes at the time, his units became the basis for the development of the present understanding of heredity. All present research in genetics can be traced back to Mendel's discovery of the laws governing the inheritance of traits, which he determined using pea plants. The word *gene*, coined in 1909 by Danish botanist Wilhelm Johannsen, has given genetics its name.

Genetics forms one of the central pillars of biology and overlaps with many other areas such as agriculture, medicine, and biotechnology.

ANCIENT THEORIES OF PANGENESIS AND BLOOD IN HEREDITY

Although scientific evidence for patterns of genetic inheritance did not appear until Mendel's work, history shows that humankind must have been interested in heredity long before the dawn of civilization. Curiosity must first have been based on human family resemblances, such as similarity in body structure, voice, gait, and gestures. Such notions were instrumental in the establishment of family and royal dynasties. Early nomadic tribes were interested in the qualities of the animals that they herded and domesticated and, undoubtedly, bred selectively. The first human settlements that practiced farming appear to have selected crop plants with favourable qualities. Ancient tomb paintings show racehorse breeding pedigrees containing clear depictions of the inheritance of several distinct physical traits in the horses. Despite this interest, the first recorded speculations on heredity did not exist until the time of the ancient Greeks; some aspects of their ideas are still considered relevant today.

Hippocrates (c. 460–c. 375 BCE), known as the father of medicine, believed in the inheritance of acquired characteristics, and, to account for this, he devised the hypothesis known as pangenesis. He postulated that all organs of the body of a parent gave off invisible "seeds," which were like miniaturized building components and were transmitted during sexual intercourse, reassembling themselves in the mother's womb to form a baby.

The Greek philosopher Aristotle (384–322 BCE) emphasized the importance of blood in heredity. He thought that the blood supplied generative material for building all parts of the adult body, and he reasoned that blood was the basis for passing on this generative power to the next generation. In fact, he believed that the male's semen was purified blood and that a woman's menstrual blood was her equivalent of semen. These male and female contributions united in the womb to produce a baby. The blood contained some type of hereditary essences, but he believed that the baby would develop under the influence of these essences, rather than being built from the essences themselves.

Aristotle's ideas about the role of blood in procreation were probably the origin of the still prevalent notion that somehow the blood is involved in heredity. Today people still speak of certain traits as being "in the blood" and of "blood lines" and "blood ties." The Greek model of inheritance, in which a teeming multitude of substances was invoked, differed from that of the Mendelian model. Mendel's idea was that distinct differences between individuals are determined by differences in single yet powerful hereditary factors. These single hereditary factors were identified as genes. Copies of genes are transmitted through sperm and egg and guide the development of the offspring. Genes are also responsible for reproducing the distinct features of both parents that are visible in their children.

PREFORMATION AND NATURAL SELECTION

In the two millennia between the lives of Aristotle and Mendel, few new ideas were recorded on the nature of heredity. In the 17th and 18th centuries the idea of preformation was introduced. Scientists using the newly developed microscopes imagined that they could see miniature replicas of human beings inside sperm heads. French biologist Jean-Baptiste Lamarck invoked the idea of "the inheritance of acquired characters," not as an explanation for heredity but as a model for evolution. He lived at a time when the fixity of species was taken for granted, yet he maintained that this fixity was found only in a constant environment. He enunciated the law of use and disuse, which states that when certain organs become specially developed as a result of some environmental need, then that state of development is hereditary and can be passed on to progeny. He believed that in this way, over many generations, giraffes could arise from deerlike animals that had to keep stretching their necks to reach high leaves on trees.

British naturalist Alfred Russel Wallace originally postulated the theory of evolution by natural selection.

However, Charles Darwin, who accumulated evidence showing that evolution had occurred and that diverse organisms share common ancestors, first began to formulate this theory during his circumnavigation of the globe aboard the HMS *Beagle* (1831–36). His expedition provided evidence for natural selection and supported his suggestion that humans and animals shared a common ancestry. Many scientists at the time believed in a hereditary mechanism that was a version of the ancient Greek idea of pangenesis, and Darwin's ideas did not appear to fit with the theory of heredity that sprang from the experiments of Mendel.

THE WORK OF MENDEL

Before Gregor Mendel, theories for a hereditary mechanism were based largely on logic and speculation, not on experimentation. In his monastery garden, Mendel carried out a large number of cross-pollination experiments between variants of the garden pea, which he obtained as pure-breeding lines. He crossed peas with yellow seeds to those with green seeds and observed that the progeny seeds (the first generation, F_1) were all yellow. When the F_1 individuals were self-pollinated or crossed among themselves, their progeny (F_2) showed a ratio of 3:1 (3/4 yellow and 1/4 green). He deduced that, since the F_2 generation contained some green individuals, the determinants of greenness must have been present in the F_1 generation, although they were not expressed because yellow is dominant over green. From the precise mathematical 3:1 ratio (of which he found several other examples), he deduced not only the existence of discrete hereditary units (genes) but also that the units were present in pairs in the pea plant and that the pairs separated during gamete formation. Hence, the two original lines of pea plants were proposed to be YY (yellow) and yy (green). The gametes from these were Y and y, thereby producing an F_1 generation of Yy that were yellow in colour because of the dominance of Y. In the F_1 generation, half the gametes were Y and the other half were y, making the F_2 generation produced from random mating 1/4 Yy, 1/2 YY, and 1/4 yy, thus explaining the 3:1 ratio. The forms of the pea colour genes, Y and y, are called alleles.

Mendel also analyzed pure lines that differed in pairs of characters, such as seed colour (yellow versus green) and seed shape (round versus wrinkled). The cross of yellow round seeds with green wrinkled seeds resulted in an F_1 generation that were all yellow and round, revealing the dominance of the yellow and round traits. However, the F_2 generation produced by self-pollination of F_1 plants showed a ratio of 9:3:3:1 (9/16 yellow round, 3/16 yellow wrinkled, 3/16 green round, and 1/16 green wrinkled; note that a 9:3:3:1 ratio is simply two 3:1 ratios combined). From this result and others like it, he deduced the independent assortment of separate gene pairs at gamete formation.

Mendel's success can be attributed in part to his classic experimental approach. He chose his experimental organism well and performed many controlled experiments to collect data. From his results, he developed brilliant explanatory hypotheses and went on to test these hypotheses experimentally. Mendel's methodology established a prototype for genetics that is still used today for gene discovery and understanding the genetic properties of inheritance.

How the Gene Idea Became Reality

Mendel's genes were only hypothetical entities, factors that could be inferred to exist in order to explain his results. The 20th century saw tremendous strides in the development of the understanding of the nature of genes and how they function. Mendel's publications lay unmentioned in the research literature until 1900, when the same conclusions were reached by several other investigators. Then there followed hundreds of papers showing Mendelian inheritance in a wide array of plants and animals, including humans. It seemed that Mendel's ideas were of general validity. Many biologists noted that the inheritance of genes closely paralleled the inheritance of chromosomes during nuclear divisions, called meiosis, that occur in the cell divisions just prior to gamete formation.

THE DISCOVERY OF LINKED GENES

It seemed that genes were parts of chromosomes. In 1909 this idea was strengthened through the demonstration of parallel inheritance of certain *Drosophila* (a type of fruit fly) genes on sex-determining chromosomes by American zoologist and geneticist Thomas Hunt Morgan. Morgan and one of his students, Alfred Henry Sturtevant, showed not only that certain genes seemed to be linked on the same chromosome but that the distance between genes on the same chromosome could be calculated by measuring the frequency at which new chromosomal combinations arose (these were proposed to be caused by chromosomal breakage and reunion, also known as crossing over). In 1916 another student of Morgan's, Calvin Bridges, used fruit flies with an extra chromosome to prove beyond reasonable doubt that the only way to explain the abnormal inheritance of certain genes was if they were part of the extra chromosome. American geneticist Hermann Joseph Müller showed that new alleles (called mutations) could be produced at high frequencies by treating cells with X-rays, the first demonstration of an environmental mutagenic agent (mutations can also arise spontaneously). In

1931, American botanist Harriet Creighton and American scientist Barbara McClintock demonstrated that new allelic combinations of linked genes were correlated with physically exchanged chromosome parts.

EARLY MOLECULAR GENETICS

In 1908, British physician Archibald Garrod proposed the important idea that the human disease alkaptonuria, and certain other hereditary diseases, were caused by inborn errors of metabolism, providing for the first time evidence that linked genes with molecular action at the cell level. Molecular genetics did not begin in earnest until 1941 when American geneticist George Beadle and American biochemist Edward Tatum showed that the genes they were studying in the fungus *Neurospora crassa* acted by coding for catalytic proteins called enzymes. Subsequent studies in other organisms extended this idea to show that genes generally code for proteins. Soon afterward, American bacteriologist Oswald Avery, Canadian American geneticist Colin M. MacLeod, and American biologist Maclyn McCarty showed that bacterial genes are made of DNA, a finding that was later extended to all organisms.

DNA AND THE GENETIC CODE

A major landmark was attained in 1953 when American geneticist and biophysicist James D. Watson and British biophysicists Francis Crick and Maurice Wilkins devised a double helix model for DNA structure. This model showed that DNA was capable of self-replication by separating its complementary strands and using them as templates for the synthesis of new DNA molecules. Each of the intertwined strands of DNA was proposed to be a chain of chemical groups called nucleotides, of which there were known to be four types. Because proteins are strings of amino acids, it was proposed that a specific nucleotide sequence of DNA could contain a code for an amino acid sequence and hence protein structure. In 1955, American molecular biologist Seymour Benzer, extending earlier studies in *Drosophila*, showed that the mutant sites within a gene could be mapped in relation to each other. His linear map indicated that the gene itself is a linear structure.

In 1958 the strand-separation method for DNA replication (called the semiconservative method) was demonstrated experimentally for the first time by American molecular biologist Matthew Meselson and American geneticist Franklin W. Stahl. In 1961, Crick and South African biologist Sydney Brenner showed that the genetic code must be read in triplets of nucleotides, called codons. American geneticist Charles Yanofsky showed that the positions of mutant sites within a gene matched perfectly the positions of altered amino acids in the amino acid sequence of the corresponding protein. In 1966 the complete genetic code of all 64 possible triplet coding units (codons), and the specific amino acids they code for, was deduced by American biochemists Marshall Nirenberg and Har Gobind Khorana. Subsequent studies in many organisms showed that the double helical structure of DNA, the mode of its replication, and the genetic code are the same in virtually all organisms, including plants, animals, fungi, bacteria, and viruses. In 1961, French biologist François Jacob and French biochemist Jacques Monod established the prototypical model for gene regulation by showing that bacterial genes can be turned on (initiating transcription into RNA and protein synthesis) and off through the binding action of regulatory proteins to a region just upstream of the coding region of the gene.

RECOMBINANT DNA TECHNOLOGY AND THE POLYMERASE CHAIN REACTION

Technical advances have played an important role in the advance of genetic understanding. In 1970, American microbiologists Daniel Nathans and Hamilton Othanel Smith discovered a specialized class of enzymes (called restriction enzymes) that cut DNA at specific nucleotide target sequences. That discovery allowed American biochemist Paul Berg in 1972 to make the first artificial recombinant DNA molecule by isolating DNA molecules from different sources, cutting them, and joining them together in a test tube. These advances allowed individual genes to be cloned (amplified to a high copy number) by splicing them into self-replicating DNA molecules, such as plasmids (extragenomic circular DNA elements) or viruses, and inserting these into living bacterial cells. From these methodologies arose the field of recombinant DNA technology that presently dominates molecular genetics. In 1977 two different methods were invented for determining the nucleotide sequence of DNA: one by American molecular biologists Allan Maxam and Walter Gilbert and the other by English biochemist Fred Sanger. Such technologies made it possible to examine the structure of genes directly by nucleotide sequencing, resulting in the confirmation of many of the inferences about genes originally made indirectly.

In the 1970s, Canadian biochemist Michael Smith revolutionized the art of redesigning genes by devising a method for inducing specifically tailored mutations at defined sites within a gene, creating a technique known as site-directed mutagenesis. In 1983, American biochemist Kary B. Mullis invented the polymerase chain reaction (PCR), a method for rapidly detecting and amplifying a specific DNA sequence without cloning it. In the last decade

GREGOR MENDEL

(b. July 22, 1822, Heinzendorf, Austria—d. Jan. 6, 1884, Brünn, Austria-Hungary)

The Austrian botanist and plant experimenter Gregor Mendel laid the mathematical foundation of the science of genetics. He became an Augustinian monk in 1843 and later studied at the University of Vienna. In 1854, working in his monastery's garden, he began planning the experiments that led to his formulation of the basic principle of heredity. He used the edible pea for his studies, crossing varieties that had maintained constant differences in distinct traits such as height (tall or short) and seed colour (green or yellow). He theorized that the occurrence of the visible alternative traits, in the constant hybrids and in their progeny, was due to the occurrence of paired elementary units of heredity, now known as genes. What was new in Mendel's interpretation of his data was his recognition that genes obey simple statistical laws. His system proved to be of general application and is one of the basic principles of biology. His work was rediscovered in 1900 by three botanists, Carl Erich Correns, Erich Tschermak von Seysenegg, and Hugo de Vries, who independently obtained similar results and found that both the experimental data and the general theory had been published 34 years previously.

of the 20th century, progress in recombinant DNA technology and in the development of automated sequencing machines led to the elucidation of complete DNA sequences of several viruses, bacteria, plants, and animals. In 2001 the complete sequence of human DNA, approximately three billion nucleotide pairs, was made public.

EVOLUTION

All human cultures have developed their own explanations for the origin of the world and of human beings and other creatures. Traditional Judaism and Christianity explain the origin of living beings and their adaptations to their environments—wings, gills, hands, flowers—as the handiwork of an omniscient God. The philosophers of ancient Greece had their own creation myths. Anaximander proposed that animals could be transformed from one kind into another, and Empedocles speculated that they were made up of various combinations of preexisting parts. Closer to modern evolutionary ideas were the proposals of early Church Fathers such as Gregory of Nazianzus and Augustine, both of whom maintained that not all species of plants and animals were created by God; rather, some had developed in historical times from God's creations.

The notion that organisms may change by natural processes was not investigated as a biological subject by Christian theologians of the Middle Ages, but it was, usually incidentally, considered as a possibility by many, including Albertus Magnus, a Dominican friar, and his student Thomas Aquinas, who later became a leading medieval theologian and philosopher.

The idea of progress, especially that of unbounded human progress, was central to the Enlightenment of the 18th century, particularly in France among such philosophers as the marquis de Condorcet and Denis Diderot and such scientists as Georges-Louis Leclerc, comte de Buffon. Belief in progress, however, did not necessarily lead to the development of a theory of evolution. Pierre-Louis Moreau de Maupertuis proposed the spontaneous generation and extinction of organisms as part of his theory of origins, but he advanced no theory of evolution. Buffon explicitly considered—and rejected—the possible descent of several species from a common ancestor. The Swedish botanist Carolus Linnaeus devised the hierarchical system of classification that is still in use. Although he insisted on the fixity of species, his classification system eventually contributed much to the acceptance of the concept of common descent.

The great French naturalist Jean-Baptiste de Monet, chevalier de Lamarck, held that living organisms represent a progression, with humans as the highest form. In the early years of the 19th century, he proposed the first broad theory of evolution. Organisms evolved through eons of time from lower to higher forms, a process still going on, always culminating in human beings. As organisms become adapted to their environments through their habits, modifications occur. Lamarck held that use of a structure reinforces it, whereas disuse leads to obliteration. The characteristics acquired by use and disuse would be inherited. This assumption, later called the inheritance of acquired characteristics (or Lamarckism), did not stand up in the light of later knowledge; however, Lamarck made important contributions to the gradual acceptance of biological evolution.

THE WORK OF CHARLES DARWIN

The founder of the modern theory of evolution, Charles Darwin, is well-known for sailing aboard the HMS *Beagle* on a round-the-world trip that lasted from December 1831 until October 1836. As a naturalist, or a person who studies natural history, Darwin was often able to disembark for extended trips ashore to collect natural specimens.

The discovery of fossil bones from large extinct mammals in Argentina and the observation of numerous species of finches in the Galapagos Islands were among the events credited with stimulating Darwin's interest in how species originate. In 1859 he published *On the Origin of Species by Means of Natural Selection*, a treatise establishing the theory of evolution and, most important, the role of natural selection in determining its course. He published many other books as well, notably the two-volume *The Descent of Man, and Selection in Relation to Sex* (1871), which extends the theory of natural selection to human evolution.

Before Darwin, the origin of Earth's living things had been attributed to the design of an omniscient God. An argument from design seems to be forceful. A ladder is made for climbing, a knife for cutting, and a watch for telling time; their functional design leads to the conclusion that they have been fashioned by a carpenter, a smith, or a watchmaker. Similarly, the obvious functional design of animals and plants seems to denote the work of a Creator. Darwin accepted the facts of adaptation—hands are for grasping, eyes for seeing, lungs for breathing. He showed, however, that the multiplicity of plants and animals, with their exquisite and varied adaptations, could be explained by natural selection, without recourse to any designer agent. This achievement would prove to have profound intellectual and cultural implications.

Darwin's theory of natural selection is summarized in the *Origin of Species* as follows:

> As many more individuals are produced than can possibly survive, there must in every case be a struggle for existence, either one individual with another of the same species, or with the individuals of distinct species, or with the physical conditions of life . . . Can it, then, be thought improbable, seeing that variations useful to man have undoubtedly occurred, that other variations useful in some way to each being in the great and complex battle of life, should sometimes occur in the course

*of thousands of generations? If such do occur, can we doubt
(remembering that many more individuals are born than can
possibly survive) that individuals having any advantage,
however slight, over others, would have the best chance of surviving and of procreating their kind? On the other hand, we
may feel sure that any variation in the least degree injurious
would be rigidly destroyed. This preservation of favourable
variations and the rejection of injurious variations, I call
Natural Selection.*

Natural selection was proposed primarily to account
for the adaptive organization of living beings; it is a process that promotes or maintains adaptation. Evolutionary
change through time and evolutionary diversification
(multiplication of species) are not directly promoted by
natural selection, but they often ensue as by-products of
natural selection as it fosters adaptation to different
environments.

THE DARWINIAN AFTERMATH

The publication of the *Origin of Species* produced considerable public excitement. Scientists, politicians, clergymen,
and notables of all kinds read and discussed the book,
defending or deriding Darwin's ideas. Evolution by natural selection was indeed a favourite topic in society salons
during the 1860s and beyond. But serious scientific controversies also arose, first in Britain and then on the
European continent and in the United States.

One occasional participant in the discussion was the
British naturalist Alfred Russel Wallace, who had hit upon
the idea of natural selection independently and had sent a
short manuscript about it to Darwin. On July 1, 1858, one
year before the publication of the *Origin of Species*, a paper

jointly authored by Wallace and Darwin was presented, in the absence of both, to the Linnean Society in London—with apparently little notice. Greater credit is duly given to Darwin for the idea of evolution by natural selection; he developed the theory in considerably more detail, provided far more evidence for it, and was primarily responsible for its acceptance. Wallace's views differed from Darwin's in several ways, most importantly in that Wallace did not think natural selection sufficient to account for the origin of human beings, which in his view required direct divine intervention.

The most serious difficulty facing Darwin's evolutionary theory was the lack of an adequate theory of inheritance that would account for the preservation through the generations of the variations on which natural selection was supposed to act. Contemporary theories of "blending inheritance" proposed that offspring merely struck an average between the characteristics of their parents. But as Darwin became aware, blending inheritance (including his own theory of "pangenesis," in which each organ and tissue of an organism throws off tiny contributions of itself that are collected in the sex organs and determine the configuration of the offspring) could not account for the conservation of variations. (Such differences between variant offspring would be halved each generation, rapidly reducing the original variation to the average of the preexisting characteristics.)

The missing link in Darwin's argument was provided by Mendelian genetics. About the time the *Origin of Species* was published, Gregor Mendel began his series of experiments with peas. Mendel's paper, published in 1866, formulated the fundamental principles of the theory of heredity, which accounts for biological inheritance through genes inherited from one's parent. Mendel's discoveries remained unknown to Darwin, however, and, indeed, they did not become generally known until 1900, when they were simultaneously rediscovered by a number of scientists on the continent.

THE SYNTHETIC THEORY

The rediscovery in 1900 of Mendel's theory of heredity, by the Dutch botanist and geneticist Hugo de Vries and others, led to an emphasis on the role of heredity in evolution. De Vries proposed a new theory of evolution known as mutationism, which essentially did away with natural selection as a major evolutionary process. According to de Vries (who was joined by other geneticists such as William Bateson in England), two kinds of variation take place in organisms. One is the "ordinary" variability observed among individuals of a species, which is of no lasting consequence in evolution. The other consists of the changes brought about by mutations, spontaneous alterations of genes that result in large modifications of the organism and give rise to new species: "The new species thus originates suddenly, it is produced by the existing one without any visible preparation and without transition."

Mutationism was opposed by many naturalists and in particular by the so-called biometricians, led by the English statistician Karl Pearson. Pearson defended Darwinian natural selection as the major cause of evolution through the cumulative effects of small, continuous, individual variations (which the biometricians assumed passed from one generation to the next without being limited by Mendel's laws of inheritance).

A major breakthrough came in 1937 with the publication of *Genetics and the Origin of Species* by Theodosius

Dobzhansky, a Russian-born American naturalist and experimental geneticist. Dobzhansky's book advanced an account of the evolutionary process in genetic terms and may be considered the most important landmark in the formulation of what came to be known as the synthetic theory of evolution, effectively combining Darwinian natural selection and Mendelian genetics. It had an enormous impact on naturalists and experimental biologists, who rapidly embraced the new understanding of the evolutionary process as one of genetic change in populations. Interest in evolutionary studies was greatly stimulated, and the synthesis of genetics and natural selection soon extended to a variety of biological fields.

The main writers who, together with Dobzhansky, may be considered the architects of the synthetic theory were the German-born American zoologist Ernst Mayr, the English zoologist Julian Huxley, the American paleontologist George Gaylord Simpson, and the American botanist George Ledyard Stebbins. These researchers contributed to a burst of evolutionary studies in the traditional biological disciplines and in some emerging ones—notably population genetics and, later, evolutionary ecology. By 1950 acceptance of Darwin's theory was universal among biologists, and the synthetic theory of evolution had become widely adopted.

MOLECULAR BIOLOGY AND EARTH SCIENCES

The most important line of investigation after 1950 was the application of molecular biology to evolutionary studies. In 1953 the American geneticist James Watson and the British biophysicist Francis Crick deduced the molecular structure of DNA (deoxyribonucleic acid), the hereditary material contained in the chromosomes of every cell's nucleus. The

CHARLES DARWIN

(b. Feb. 12, 1809, Shrewsbury, Shropshire, Eng.—d. April 19, 1882, Downe, Kent)

The British naturalist Charles Darwin formulated the theory of evolution by natural selection, which became the foundation of modern evolutionary studies. The grandson of Enlightenment physician, poet, and botanist Erasmus Darwin and pottery designer and manufacturer Josiah Wedgwood, he studied medicine at the University of Edinburgh and biology at Cambridge. He was recommended as a naturalist on the HMS *Beagle*, a British naval vessel bound on a long scientific survey expedition to South America and the South Seas (1831–36). His zoological and geological discoveries on the voyage resulted in numerous important publications and formed the basis of his theories of evolution. Seeing competition between individuals of a single species, he recognized that within a local population the individual bird, for example, with the sharper beak might have a better chance to survive and reproduce and that if such traits were passed on to new generations, they would be predominant in future populations. He saw this natural selection as the mechanism by which advantageous variations were passed on to later generations and less advantageous traits gradually disappeared. He worked on his theory for more than 20 years before publishing it in his famous *On the Origin of Species by Means of Natural Selection* (1859). The book was immediately in great demand, and Darwin's intensely controversial theory was accepted quickly in most scientific circles; most opposition came from religious leaders. Though Darwin's ideas were modified by later developments in genetics and molecular biology, his work remains central to modern evolutionary theory. His many other important works included *Variation in Animals and Plants Under Domestication* (1868) and *The Descent of Man* ... (1871). He was buried in Westminster Abbey.

genetic information is encoded within the sequence of nucleotides that make up the chainlike DNA molecules. This information determines the sequence of amino acid building blocks of protein molecules, which include, among others, structural proteins such as collagen, respiratory proteins such as hemoglobin, and numerous enzymes responsible for the organism's fundamental life processes. Genetic information contained in the DNA can thus be investigated by examining the sequences of amino acids in the proteins.

Modern laboratory techniques of DNA cloning and sequencing have provided a new and powerful means of investigating evolution at the molecular level. The fruits of this technology began to accumulate during the 1980s following the development of automated DNA-sequencing machines and the invention of the polymerase chain reaction (PCR), a simple and inexpensive technique that obtains, in a few hours, billions or trillions of copies of a specific DNA sequence or gene. Major research efforts such as the Human Genome Project further improved the technology for obtaining long DNA sequences rapidly and inexpensively. By the first few years of the 21st century, the full DNA sequence—i.e., the full genetic complement, or genome—had been obtained for more than 20 higher organisms, including human beings, as well as for numerous microorganisms.

ECOLOGY

The study of the relationships between organisms and their environment is most commonly known as ecology, but it is also called bioecology, bionomics, or environmental biology. Some of the most pressing problems in human affairs—expanding populations, food scarcities, environmental pollution including global warming, extinctions of plant and animal species, and all the attendant sociological and political problems—are to a great degree ecological.

The word *ecology* was coined by the German zoologist Ernst Haeckel, who applied the term *oekologie* to the "relation of the animal both to its organic as well as its inorganic environment." The word comes from the Greek *oikos*, meaning "household," "home," or "place to live." Thus, ecology deals with the organism and its environment. The concept of environment includes both other organisms and physical surroundings. It involves relationships between individuals within a population and between individuals of different populations. These interactions between individuals, between populations, and between organisms and their environment form ecological systems, or ecosystems. Ecology has been defined variously as "the study of the interrelationships of organisms with their environment and each other," as "the economy of nature," and as "the biology of ecosystems."

Ecology had no firm beginnings. It evolved from the natural history of the ancient Greeks, particularly Theophrastus, a friend and associate of Aristotle. Theophrastus first described the interrelationships between organisms and between organisms and their nonliving environment. Later foundations for modern ecology were laid in the early work of plant and animal physiologists.

In the early and mid-1900s two groups of botanists, one in Europe and the other in the United States, studied plant communities from two different points of view. The European botanists concerned themselves with the study of the composition, structure, and distribution of plant communities. The American botanists studied the development of plant communities, or succession. Both plant and animal ecology developed separately until American biologists emphasized the interrelation of both plant and animal communities as a biotic whole.

During the same period, interest in population dynamics developed. The study of population dynamics received special impetus in the early 19th century, after the English economist Thomas Malthus called attention to the conflict between expanding populations and the capability of Earth to supply food. In the 1920s the American zoologist Raymond Pearl, the American chemist and statistician Alfred J. Lotka, and the Italian mathematician Vito Volterra developed mathematical foundations for the study of populations, and these studies led to experiments on the interaction of predators and prey, competitive relationships between species, and the regulation of populations. Investigations of the influence of behaviour on populations were stimulated by the recognition in 1920 of territoriality in nesting birds. Concepts of instinctive and aggressive behaviour were developed by the Austrian zoologist Konrad Lorenz and the Dutch-born British zoologist Nikolaas Tinbergen, and the role of social behaviour in the regulation of populations was explored by the British zoologist Vero Wynne-Edwards.

While some ecologists were studying the dynamics of communities and populations, others were concerned with energy budgets. In 1920 August Thienemann, a German freshwater biologist, introduced the concept of

Konrad Lorenz. Hermann Kacher

trophic, or feeding, levels, by which the energy of food is transferred through a series of organisms, from green plants (the producers) up to several levels of animals (the consumers). An English animal ecologist, Charles Elton (1927), further developed this approach with the concept of ecological niches and pyramids of numbers. In the

CHARLES ELTON

(b. March 29, 1900, Liverpool, Eng. — d. May 1, 1991, Oxford, Oxfordshire)

The English biologist Charles Elton was educated at Liverpool College and at New College, Oxford, and he rebelled against the strong emphasis on comparative anatomy in zoology at that time. Throughout his career, he applied the scientific method to the study of animals in their natural habitats. In 1921 Elton conducted ecological surveys of local animals while assisting Julian Huxley during his expedition to Spitsbergen, an island in the Arctic Ocean and part of Norway, and subsequently returned to the Arctic in 1923, 1924, and 1930. He was later hired as a consultant to the Hudson's Bay Company, where he studied the population dynamics of furbearing mammals. In 1932 Elton became editor of the *Journal of Animal Ecology* and established the Bureau of Animal Population at Oxford. In 1936 Oxford appointed Elton reader, or lecturer, in animal ecology. Elton's first book, *Animal Ecology* (1927), was a landmark for his brilliant treatment of animal communities. The main features of his discussion have remained as fundamental principles ever since. His other important works included *Animal Ecology and Evolution* (1930), *Voles, Mice, and Lemmings* (1942), *The Control of Rats and Mice* (1954), *The Ecology of Invasions of Animals and Plants* (1958), and *The Pattern of Animal Communities* (1966).

1930s, American freshwater biologists Edward Birge and Chancey Juday, in measuring the energy budgets of lakes, developed the idea of primary productivity, the rate at which food energy is generated, or fixed, by photosynthesis. In 1942 American Raymond L. Lindeman developed the trophic-dynamic concept of ecology, which details the flow of energy through the ecosystem. Quantified field studies of energy flow through ecosystems were further developed by a pair of American brothers, Eugene Odum and Howard Odum; similar early work on the cycling of nutrients was done by J.D. Ovington of England and Australia.

The study of both energy flow and nutrient cycling was stimulated by the development of new materials and techniques — radioisotope tracers, microcalorimetry, computer science, and applied mathematics — that enabled ecologists to label, track, and measure the movement of particular nutrients and energy through ecosystems. These modern methods encouraged a new stage in the development of ecology — systems ecology, which is concerned with the structure and function of ecosystems.

*C*hapter 2:
MATHEMATICS
AND THE
PHYSICAL SCIENCES

Turning points in mathematics and the physical sciences include the development of the symbols known as Arabic numerals, which represent a complete break with previous methods of counting, and the development of the fundamental principles of calculus. Ideas that shook the foundations of the physical sciences range in subject from the invisible—the atom and quantum mechanics—to the infinite. Also discussed in this chapter are Einstein's theories of relativity, plate tectonics, and geologic time.

ARABIC NUMERALS

Several different claims, each having a certain amount of justification, have been made with respect to the origin of modern Western numerals, commonly spoken of as Arabic but more accurately Hindu-Arabic. These include the assertion that the origin is to be found among the Arabs, Persians, Egyptians, and Hindus. It is not improbable that the intercourse among traders served to carry such symbols from country to country, so that modern Western numerals may be a conglomeration from different sources. However, as far as is known, the country that first used the largest number of these numeral forms is India. The 1, 4, and 6 are found in the Ashoka inscriptions (3rd century BCE); the 2, 4, 6, 7, and 9 appear in the Nana Ghat inscriptions (Maharashtra) about a century later; and the 2, 3, 4, 5, 6, 7, and 9 are found in the Nashik caves (Maharashtra) of the 1st or 2nd century CE— all in forms that have considerable resemblance to today's, 2 and 3 being well-recognized cursive derivations from the ancient = and ≡. None of these early Indian inscriptions gives evidence of place value or of a zero that would make modern place value possible. Hindu literature gives evidence that the zero may have been known earlier, but there is no inscription with such a symbol before the 9th century.

The first definite external reference to the Hindu numerals is a note by Severus Sebokht, a bishop who lived in Mesopotamia about 650. Since he speaks of "nine signs," the zero seems to have been unknown to him. By the close of the 8th century, however, some astronomical tables of India are said to have been translated into Arabic at Baghdad, and in any case the numeral became known to Arabian scholars about this time. About 825 the mathematician al-Khwārizmī wrote a small book on the subject, and this was translated into Latin by Adelard of Bath (*c.*

AL-KHWĀRIZMĪ

(b. *c.* 780 ce, Baghdad, Iraq—d. *c.* 850)

Muslim mathematician and astronomer Muḥammad ibn Mūsā al-Khwārizmī lived in Baghdad during the golden age of Islamic science and, like Euclid, wrote mathematical books that collected and arranged the discoveries of earlier mathematicians. His *Al-Kitāb al-mukhtaṣar fī ḥisāb al-jabr wa'l-muqābala* ("The Compendious Book on Calculation by Completion and Balancing") is a compilation of rules for solving linear and quadratic equations, as well as problems of geometry and proportion. Its translation into Latin in the 12th century provided the link between the great Hindu and Arab mathematicians and European scholars. A corruption of the book's title resulted in the word *algebra*; a corruption of the author's own name resulted in the term *algorithm*.

1120) under the title of *Liber Algorismi de numero Indorum*. The earliest European manuscript known to contain Hindu numerals was written in Spain in 976.

The advantages enjoyed by the perfected positional system are so numerous and so manifest that the Hindu-Arabic numerals and the base 10 have been adopted almost everywhere. These might be said to be the nearest approach to a universal human language yet devised; they are found in Chinese, Japanese, and Russian scientific journals and in every Western language.

THE CALCULUS

The subject of the calculus was properly the invention of two mathematicians, the German Gottfried Wilhelm Leibniz and the Englishman Isaac Newton. Both men published their researches in the 1680s. Although a bitter dispute over priority developed later between followers of the two men, it is now clear that they each arrived at the calculus independently.

The calculus developed from techniques to solve two types of problems, the determination of areas and volumes and the calculation of tangents to curves. In the early 17th century there was a sharp revival of interest in both classes of problems. The decades between 1610 and 1670, referred to in the history of mathematics as "the precalculus period," were a time of remarkable activity in which researchers throughout Europe contributed novel solutions and competed with each other to arrive at important new methods.

THE PRECALCULUS PERIOD

In his treatise *Geometria Indivisibilibus Continuorum* (1635; "Geometry of Continuous Indivisibles"), Bonaventura

Cavalieri, a professor of mathematics at the University of Bologna, formulated a systematic method for the determination of areas and volumes. As had Archimedes, Cavalieri regarded a plane figure as being composed of a collection of indivisible lines, "all the lines" of the plane figure. The collection was generated by a fixed line moving through space parallel to itself. Cavalieri showed that these collections could be interpreted as magnitudes obeying the rules of Euclidean ratio theory.

Although Cavalieri was successful in formulating a systematic method based on general concepts, his ideas were not easy to apply. The derivation of very simple results required intricate geometric considerations, and the turgid style of the *Geometria Indivisibilibus* was a barrier to its reception.

John Wallis presented a quite different approach to the theory of quadratures in his *Arithmetica Infinitorum* (1655; *The Arithmetic of Infinitesimals*). Wallis, a successor to Henry Briggs as the Savilian Professor of Geometry at Oxford, was a champion of the new methods of arithmetic algebra that he had learned from his teacher William Oughtred. Wallis expressed the area under a curve as the sum of an infinite series and used clever and unrigorous inductions to determine its value. To calculate the area under the parabola,

$$\int_0^1 x^2 dx,$$

he considered the successive sums

$$\frac{0+1}{1+1} = \frac{1}{3} + \frac{1}{6}, \frac{0+1+4}{4+4+4} = \frac{1}{3} + \frac{1}{12}, \frac{0+1+4+9}{9+9+9+9} = \frac{1}{3} + \frac{1}{18}$$

and inferred by "induction" the general relation

$$\frac{0^2 + 1^2 + 2^2 + \cdots + n^2}{n^2 + n^2 + n^2 + \cdots + n^2} = \frac{1}{3} + \frac{1}{6n}.$$

By letting the number of terms be infinite, he obtained 1/3 as the limiting value of the expression. With more complicated curves he achieved very impressive results, including the infinite expression now known as Wallis's product:

$$\frac{4}{\pi} = \frac{3}{2} \cdot \frac{3}{4} \cdot \frac{5}{4} \cdot \frac{5}{6} \cdot \frac{7}{6} \cdots.$$

Research on the determination of tangents, the other subject leading to the calculus, proceeded along different lines. In *La Géométrie* the French philosopher René Descartes had presented a method that could in principle be applied to any algebraic or "geometric" curve — i.e., any curve whose equation was a polynomial of finite degree in two variables. The method depended upon finding the normal, the line perpendicular to the tangent, using the algebraic condition that it be the unique radius to intersect the curve in only one point.

A class of curves of growing interest in the 17th century comprised those generated kinematically by a point moving through space. The famous cycloidal curve, for example, was traced by a point on the perimeter of a wheel that rolled on a line without slipping or sliding. These curves were nonalgebraic and hence could not be treated by Descartes's method. Gilles Personne de Roberval, professor at the Collège Royale in Paris, devised a method borrowed from dynamics to determine their tangents. In his analysis of projectile motion Galileo Galilei, an Italian mathematician and astronomer, had shown that the instantaneous velocity of a particle is compounded of two separate motions: a constant horizontal motion and an increasing vertical motion due to gravity. If the motion of the generating point of a kinematic curve is likewise regarded as the sum of two velocities, then the tangent will lie in the direction of their sum. Roberval applied this idea to several different kinematic curves, obtaining results that were often ingenious and elegant.

In an essay of 1636 circulated among French mathematicians, Pierre de Fermat presented a method of tangents adapted from a procedure he had devised to determine maxima and minima and used it to find tangents to several algebraic curves of the form $y = x^n$. His account was short and contained no explanation of the mathematical basis of the new method. It is possible to see in his procedure an argument involving infinitesimals, and Fermat has sometimes been proclaimed the discoverer of the differential calculus.

Isaac Barrow, the Lucasian Professor of Mathematics at the University of Cambridge, published in 1670 his *Geometrical Lectures*, a treatise that more than any other anticipated the unifying ideas of the calculus. In it he adopted a purely geometric form of exposition to show how the determinations of areas and tangents are inverse problems. He began with a curve and considered the slope of its tangent corresponding to each value of the abscissa. He then defined an auxiliary curve by the condition that its ordinate be equal to this slope and showed that the area under the auxiliary curve corresponding to a given abscissa is equal to the rectangle whose sides are unity and the ordinate of the original curve. When reformulated analytically, this result expresses the inverse character of differentiation and integration, the fundamental theorem of the calculus. Although Barrow's decision to proceed geometrically prevented him from taking the final step to a true calculus, his lectures influenced both Newton and Leibniz.

NEWTON AND LEIBNIZ

The essential insight of Newton and Leibniz was to use Cartesian algebra to synthesize the earlier results and to develop algorithms that could be applied uniformly to a wide class of problems. The formative period of Newton's researches was from 1665 to 1670, while Leibniz worked a few years later, in the 1670s. Their contributions differ in origin, development, and influence, and it is necessary to consider each man separately.

Newton's earliest researches in mathematics grew in 1665 from his study of Descartes's *La Géométrie* and Wallis's *Arithmetica Infinitorum*. Using the Cartesian equation of the curve, he reformulated Wallis's results, introducing for this purpose infinite sums in the powers of an unknown x, now known as infinite series. Possibly under the influence of Barrow, he used infinitesimals to establish for various curves the inverse relationship of tangents and areas. The operations of differentiation and integration emerged in his work as analytic processes that could be applied generally to investigate curves.

Newton first published the calculus in Book I of his great *Philosophiae Naturalis Principia Mathematica* (1687; *Mathematical Principles of Natural Philosophy*). Originating as a treatise on the dynamics of particles, the *Principia* presented an inertial physics that combined Galileo's mechanics and Johannes Kepler's planetary astronomy. It was written in the early 1680s at a time when Newton was reacting against Descartes's science and mathematics.

Newton avoided analytic processes in the *Principia* by expressing magnitudes and ratios directly in terms of geometric quantities, both finite and infinitesimal. His decision to eschew analysis constituted a striking rejection of the algebraic methods that had been important in his own early researches on the calculus. Although the *Principia* was of inestimable value for later mechanics, it would be reworked by researchers on the continent and expressed in the mathematical idiom of the Leibnizian calculus.

Leibniz's interest in mathematics was aroused in 1672 during a visit to Paris, where the Dutch mathematician Christiaan Huygens introduced him to his work on the theory of curves. Under Huygens's tutelage Leibniz immersed himself for the next several years in the study of mathematics. He investigated relationships between the summing and differencing of finite and infinite sequences of numbers. Having read Barrow's geometric lectures, he devised a transformation rule to calculate quadratures, obtaining the famous infinite series for $\pi/4$:

$$\frac{\pi}{4} = \frac{1}{1} - \frac{1}{3} + \frac{1}{5} - \frac{1}{7} + \cdots.$$

Leibniz was interested in questions of logic and notation, of how to construct a *characteristica universalis* for rational investigation. After considerable experimentation he arrived by the late 1670s at an algorithm based on the symbols d and $\int$. He first published his research on differential calculus in 1684 in an article in the *Acta Eruditorum*. In this article he introduced the differential dx satisfying the rules $d(x + y) = dx + dy$ and $d(xy) = xdy + ydx$ and illustrated his calculus with a few examples. Two years later he published a second article in which he introduced and explained the symbol $\int$ for integration. He stressed the power of his calculus to investigate transcendental curves, the very class of "mechanical" objects Descartes had believed lay beyond the power of analysis, and derived a simple analytic formula for the cycloid.

Leibniz continued to publish results on the new calculus in the *Acta Eruditorum* and began to explore his ideas in extensive correspondence with other scholars. Within a few years he had attracted a group of researchers to promulgate his methods, including the brothers Johann and Jakob Bernoulli in Basel and the priest Pierre Varignon

GOTTFRIED WILHELM LEIBNIZ

(b. July 1, 1646, Leipzig, Saxony—d. Nov. 14, 1716, Hannover)

Gottfried Wilhelm Leibniz was a German philosopher, mathematician, inventor, jurist, historian, diplomat, and political adviser. He obtained a doctorate in law at age 20. In 1667 he began working for the elector of Mainz, in which position he codified the laws of the city, among other important tasks. He served the dukes of Braunschweig-Lüneburg as librarian and councillor (1676–1716). In 1700 he helped found the German Academy of Sciences in Berlin and became its first president. His *Theodicy* (1710) sought to reconcile the goodness of God with the existence of evil in the world by asserting that only God is perfect and that the actual world is the "best of all possible worlds." Voltaire, a French Enlightenment writer, essayist, and philosopher, famously mocked this view in his comic novel *Candide*. In mathematics, Leibniz explored the idea of a universal mathematical-logical language based on the binary number system (*De arte combinatoria* [1666]), though all the calculating devices that he later built used the decimal system. He discovered the fundamental theorem of calculus independently of Isaac Newton; the acrimonious dispute over priority left England mathematically backward for more than a generation before Leibniz's superior notation and methods were adopted. He also made important contributions to optics and mechanics.

and Guillaume-François-Antoine de L'Hospital in Paris. In 1700 he persuaded Frederick William I of Prussia to establish the Brandenburg Society of Sciences (later renamed the Berlin Academy of Sciences), with himself appointed president for life.

Leibniz's vigorous espousal of the new calculus, the didactic spirit of his writings, and his ability to attract a community of researchers contributed to his enormous influence on subsequent mathematics. In contrast, Newton's slowness to publish and his personal reticence resulted in a reduced presence within European mathematics. Although the British school in the 18th century included capable researchers, they failed to establish a program of research comparable to that established by Leibniz's followers on the continent. There is a certain tragedy in Newton's isolation and his reluctance to acknowledge the superiority of continental analysis.

THE ATOMIC THEORY

The idea that matter is composed of atoms goes back to the Greek philosophers, notably Democritus, and it has never since been entirely lost sight of, though there have been periods when alternative views were more generally preferred. Newton's contemporaries, Robert Hooke and Robert Boyle, in particular, were atomists, but their interpretation of the sensation of heat as random motion of atoms was overshadowed for more than a century by the conception of heat as a subtle fluid dubbed caloric. It is a tribute to the strength of caloric theory that it enabled the French scientist Sadi Carnot to arrive at his great discoveries in thermodynamics. In the end, however, the numerical rules for the chemical combination of different simple substances, together with the experiments on the conversion of work into heat by Benjamin Thompson (Count Rumford) and James Prescott Joule, led to the downfall of the theory of caloric. Nevertheless, the rise of ether theories to explain the transmission of light and electromagnetic forces through apparently empty space postponed for many decades the general reacceptance of the concept of atoms.

These attempts to describe the basic constituents of matter in the familiar language of fluid mechanics were at least atomic theories in contrast to the anti-atomistic movement at the end of the 19th century in Germany under the influence of Ernst Mach, an Austrian physicist, and Wilhelm Ostwald, a Latvian-born German chemist. An inspection of the success of their contemporaries using atomic models shows why this movement failed. It suffices to mention the systematic construction of a kinetic theory of matter in which the physicists Ludwig Boltzmann of Austria and J. Willard Gibbs of the United States were the two leading figures. To this may be added Hendrik Lorentz's electron theory, which explained in satisfying detail many of the electrical properties of matter; and, as a crushing argument for atomism, the discovery and explanation of X-ray diffraction by Max von Laue of Germany and his collaborators, a discovery that was quickly developed, following the lead of the British physicist William Henry Bragg and his son Lawrence, into a systematic technique for mapping the precise atomic structure of crystals.

While the concept of atoms was thus being made indispensable, the ancient belief that they were probably structureless and certainly indestructible came under devastating attack. J.J. Thomson's discovery of the electron in 1897 soon led to the realization that the mass of an atom largely resides in a positively charged part, electrically neutralized by a cloud of much lighter electrons. A few years later Ernest Rutherford and Frederick Soddy showed how the emission of alpha and beta particles from radioactive elements causes them to be transformed into elements of different chemical properties. By 1913, with Rutherford as the leading figure, the foundations of the modern theory of atomic structure were laid. It was determined that a small, massive nucleus carries all the positive charge whose magnitude, expressed as a multiple of the fundamental charge of the proton, is the atomic number. An equal number of electrons carrying a negative charge numerically equal to that of the proton form a cloud whose diameter is several thousand times that of the nucleus around which they swarm. The atomic number determines the chemical properties of the atom, and in alpha decay a helium nucleus, whose atomic number is 2, is emitted from the radioactive nucleus, leaving one whose atomic number is reduced by 2. In beta decay the nucleus in effect gains one positive charge by emitting a negative electron and thus has its atomic number increased by unity.

The nucleus, itself a composite body, was soon being described in various ways, none completely wrong but none uniquely right. Pivotal was James Chadwick's discovery in 1932 of the neutron, a nuclear particle with very nearly the same mass as the proton but no electric charge. After this discovery, investigators came to view the nucleus as consisting of protons and neutrons, bound together by a force of limited range, which at close quarters was strong enough to overcome the electrical repulsion between the protons. A free neutron survives for only a few minutes before disintegrating into a readily observed proton and electron, along with an elusive neutrino, which has no charge and zero, or at most extremely small, mass. The disintegration of a neutron may also occur inside the nucleus, with the expulsion of the electron and neutrino; this is the beta-decay process. It is common enough among the heavy radioactive nuclei but does not occur with all nuclei because the energy released would be insufficient for the reorganization of the resulting nucleus. Certain nuclei have a higher-than-ideal ratio of protons to

JOHN DALTON

(b. Sept. 5 or 6, 1766, Eaglesfield, Cumberland, Eng.—d. July 27, 1844, Manchester)

The British chemist and physicist John Dalton originated the modern theory of atomic elements. He spent most of his life in private teaching and research. His work on gases led him to develop Dalton's law, which states that the total pressure exerted by a gaseous mixture is equal to the sum of the partial pressures of each individual component in a gas mixture. He devised a system of chemical symbols, ascertained the relative weights of atoms, and arranged them into a table. His masterpiece of synthesis was the atomic theory—the theory that each element is composed of tiny, indestructible particles called atoms that are all alike and have the same atomic weight—which elevated chemistry to a quantitative science.

neutrons and may adjust the proportion by the reverse process, a proton being converted into a neutron with the expulsion of a positron and an antineutrino. The positron resembles the electron in all respects except for being positively rather than negatively charged. It was the first antiparticle to be discovered. Its existence had been predicted, however, by P.A.M. Dirac after he had formulated the quantum mechanical equations describing the behaviour of an electron.

THE ROOTS OF ASTRONOMY

Western astronomy had its origins in Egypt and Mesopotamia. Egyptian astronomy, which was neither a very well-developed nor an influential study, was largely concerned with time reckoning. Its main lasting contribution was the civil calendar of 365 days, consisting of 12 months of 30 days each and five additional festival days at the end of each year.

Babylonian astronomy, dating back to about 1800 BCE, constitutes one of the earliest systematic, scientific treatments of the physical world. In contrast to the Egyptians, the Babylonians were interested in the accurate prediction of astronomical phenomena, especially the first appearance of the new Moon. Using the zodiac as a reference, by the 4th century BCE, they developed a complex system of arithmetic progressions and methods of approximation by which they were able to predict first appearances. The mass of observations they collected and their mathematical methods were important contributions to the later flowering of astronomy among the Greeks.

The Pythagoreans (5th century BCE) were responsible for one of the first Greek astronomical theories. Believing that the order of the cosmos is fundamentally mathematical, they held that it is possible to discover the harmonies of the universe by contemplating the regular motions of the heavens. Postulating a central fire about which all the heavenly bodies including the Earth and Sun revolve, they constructed the first physical model of the solar system. Subsequent Greek astronomy derived its character from a comment ascribed to Plato, in the 4th century BCE, who is reported to have instructed the astronomers to "save the phenomena" in terms of uniform circular motion. That is to say, he urged them to develop predictively accurate theories using only combinations of uniform circular motion. As a result, Greek astronomers never regarded their geometric models as true or as being physical descriptions of the machinery of the heavens.

They regarded them simply as tools for predicting planetary positions.

Eudoxus of Cnidus (4th century BCE) was the first of the Greek astronomers to rise to Plato's challenge. He developed a theory of homocentric spheres, a model that represented the universe by sets of nesting concentric spheres the motions of which combined to produce the planetary and other celestial motions. Using only uniform circular motions, Eudoxus was able to "save" the rather complex planetary motions with some success.

Hipparchus (flourished 130 BCE) made extensive contributions to both theoretical and observational astronomy. Basing his theories on an impressive mass of observations, he was able to work out theories of the Sun and Moon that were more successful than those of any of his predecessors. His primary conceptual tool was the eccentric circle, a circle in which the Earth is at some point eccentric to the geometric centre. He used this device to account for various irregularities and inequalities observed in the motions of the Sun and Moon.

Among Hipparchus's observations, one of the most significant was that of the precession of the equinoxes — i.e., a gradual apparent increase in longitude between any fixed star and the equinoctial point (either of two points on the celestial sphere where the celestial equator crosses the ecliptic). Thus the north celestial pole, the point on the celestial sphere defined as the apparent centre of rotation of the stars, moves relative to the stars in its vicinity. In the heliocentric theory, this effect is ascribed to a change in the Earth's rotational axis, which traces out a conical path around the axis of the orbital plane.

Claudius Ptolemy (flourished 140 CE) applied the theory of epicycles to compile a systematic account of Greek astronomy. He elaborated theories for each of the planets, as well as for the Sun and Moon. His theory generally fitted the data available to him with a good degree of accuracy, and his book, the *Almagest*, became the vehicle by which Greek astronomy was transmitted to astronomers of the Middle Ages and Renaissance. It essentially molded astronomy for the next millennium and a half.

THE SCIENTIFIC REVOLUTION

During the 15th, 16th, and 17th centuries, scientific thought underwent a revolution. Out of the ferment of the Renaissance and Reformation there arose a new view of science, bringing about the following transformations: the reeducation of common sense in favour of abstract reasoning; the substitution of a quantitative for a qualitative view of nature; the view of nature as a machine rather than as an organism; the development of an experimental method that sought definite answers to certain limited questions couched in the framework of specific theories; the acceptance of new criteria for explanation, stressing the "how" rather than the "why" that had characterized the Aristotelian search for final causes.

A PREPONDERANCE OF THEORIES

Although there had been earlier discussions of the possibility of the Earth's motion, the Polish astronomer Nicolaus Copernicus was the first to propound a comprehensive heliocentric theory, equal in scope and predictive capability to Ptolemy's geocentric system. Relying on virtually the same data as Ptolemy had possessed, Copernicus turned the world inside out, putting the Sun at the centre and setting the Earth into motion around it. Copernicus's theory, published in 1543, possessed a qualitative simplicity that Ptolemaic astronomy appeared to lack. To achieve comparable levels of quantitative precision, however, the new system became just as complex as the old.

The reception of Copernican astronomy amounted to victory by infiltration. By the time large-scale opposition to the theory had developed in the church and elsewhere, most of the best professional astronomers had found some aspect or other of the new system indispensable. Copernicus's book *De revolutionibus orbium coelestium libri VI* ("Six Books Concerning the Revolutions of the Heavenly Orbs"), published in 1543, became a standard reference for advanced problems in astronomical research, particularly for its mathematical techniques. Thus, it was widely read by mathematical astronomers, in spite of its central cosmological hypothesis, which was widely ignored. In 1551 the German astronomer Erasmus Reinhold published the *Tabulae prutenicae* ("Prutenic Tables"), computed by Copernican methods. The tables were more accurate and more up-to-date than their 13th-century predecessor and became indispensable to both astronomers and astrologers.

During the 16th century the Danish astronomer Tycho Brahe was responsible for major changes in observation, unwittingly providing the data that ultimately decided the argument in favour of the new astronomy. Using larger, stabler, and better calibrated instruments, he observed regularly over extended periods, thereby obtaining a continuity of observations that were accurate for planets to within about one minute of arc—several times better than any previous observation.

At the beginning of the 17th century, the German astronomer Johannes Kepler placed the Copernican hypothesis on firm astronomical footing. His painstaking search for the real order of the universe forced him finally to abandon the Platonic ideal of uniform circular motion in his search for a physical basis for the motions of the heavens.

In 1609 Kepler announced two new planetary laws derived from Tycho's data: (1) the planets travel around the Sun in elliptical orbits, one focus of the ellipse being occupied by the Sun; and (2) a planet moves in its orbit in such a manner that a line drawn from the planet to the Sun always sweeps out equal areas in equal times. With these two laws, Kepler abandoned uniform circular motion of the planets on their spheres, thus raising the fundamental physical question of what holds the planets in their orbits. In 1618 Kepler stated his third law, which was one of many laws concerned with the harmonies of the planetary motions: (3) the square of the period in which a planet orbits the Sun is proportional to the cube of its mean distance from the Sun.

A powerful blow was dealt to traditional cosmology by Galileo Galilei, who early in the 17th century used the telescope, a recent invention of Dutch lens grinders, to look toward the heavens. In 1610 Galileo announced observations that contradicted many traditional cosmological assumptions. He observed that the Moon is not a smooth, polished surface, as Aristotle had claimed, but that it is jagged and mountainous. Earthshine

Two of Galileo's first telescopes, in the Institute and Museum of the History of Science, Florence. Scala/Art Resource, New York on the Moon revealed that the Earth, like the other planets, shines by reflected light. Like the Earth, Jupiter was observed to have satellites; hence, the Earth had been demoted from its unique position. The phases of Venus proved that that planet orbits the Sun, not the Earth.

NICOLAUS COPERNICUS

(b. Feb. 19, 1473, Toruń, Pol.—d. May 24, 1543, Frauenburg, East Prussia)

Nicolaus Copernicus was a Polish astronomer who proposed a heliocentric model of the solar system. He was educated at Kraków, Bologna, and Padua, where he mastered all the knowledge of the day in mathematics, astronomy, medicine, and theology. Elected a canon of the cathedral of Frauenburg in 1497, he took advantage of his financial security to begin his astronomical observations. His publication in 1543 of *Six Books Concerning the Revolutions of the Heavenly Orbs* marked a landmark of Western thought. Copernicus had first conceived of his revolutionary model decades earlier but delayed publication because, while it explained the retrograde motion of the planets (and resolved their order), it raised new problems that had to be explained, required verification of old observations, and had to be presented in a way that would not provoke the religious authorities. The book did not see print until he was on his deathbed. By attributing to Earth a daily rotation around its own axis and a yearly revolution around a stationary Sun, he developed an idea that had far-reaching implications for the rise of modern science. He asserted, in contrast to Platonic instrumentalism, that astronomy must describe the real, physical system of the world.

GRAVITATIONAL THEORY

Galileo's contributions to the science of mechanics were related directly to his defense of Copernicanism. Although in his youth he adhered to the traditional impetus physics, his desire to mathematize in the manner of Archimedes led him to abandon the traditional approach and develop the foundations for a new physics that was both highly mathematizable and directly related to the problems facing the new cosmology. Interested in finding the natural acceleration of falling bodies, he was able to derive the law of free fall (the distance, s, varies as the square of the time, t^2). Combining this result with his rudimentary form of the principle of inertia, he was able to derive the parabolic path of projectile motion. Furthermore, his principle of inertia enabled him to meet the traditional physical objections to the Earth's motion: since a body in motion tends to remain in motion, projectiles and other objects on the terrestrial surface will tend to share the motions of the Earth, which will thus be imperceptible to someone standing on the Earth.

Descartes's contributions to mechanics in the 17th century were more concerned with problems in the foundations of science than with the solution of specific technical problems. He was principally concerned with the conceptions of matter and motion as part of his general program for science—namely, to explain all the phenomena of nature in terms of matter and motion. This program, known as the mechanical philosophy, came to be the dominant theme of 17th-century science.

Descartes rejected the idea that one piece of matter could act on another through empty space; instead, forces must be propagated by a material substance, the "ether," that fills all space. Although matter tends to move in a straight line in accordance with the principle of inertia, it cannot occupy space already filled by other matter, so the only kind of motion that can actually occur is a vortex in which each particle in a ring moves simultaneously.

According to Descartes, all natural phenomena depend on the collisions of small particles, and so it is of great importance to discover the quantitative laws of impact. This was done by Descartes's disciple, the Dutch physicist Christiaan Huygens, who formulated the laws of conservation of momentum and of kinetic energy.

The work of Sir Isaac Newton represents the culmination of the scientific revolution at the end of the 17th century. His monumental *Principia* solved the major problems posed by the scientific revolution in mechanics and in cosmology. It provided a physical basis for Kepler's laws, unified celestial and terrestrial physics under one set of laws, and established the problems and methods that dominated much of astronomy and physics for well over a century. By means of the concept of force, Newton was able to synthesize two important components of the scientific revolution, the mechanical philosophy and the mathematization of nature.

Newton was able to derive these striking results from his three laws of motion:

1. Every body continues in its state of rest or of motion in a straight line unless it is compelled to change that state by force impressed on it;

2. The change of motion is proportional to the motive force impressed and is made in the direction of the straight line in which that force is impressed; and

3. To every action there is always opposed an equal reaction: or, the mutual actions of two bodies upon each other are always equal.

SIR ISAAC NEWTON

(b. Jan. 4, 1643, Woolsthorpe, Lincolnshire, Eng.—d. March 31, 1727, London)

The English physicist and mathematician Isaac Newton discovered the law of gravity and the principles of calculus. He was educated at Cambridge University (1661–65), where he discovered the work of René Descartes. His experiments passing sunlight through a prism led to the discovery of the heterogeneous, corpuscular nature of white light and laid the foundation of physical optics. He built the first reflecting telescope in 1668 and became a professor of mathematics at Cambridge in 1669. He worked out the fundamentals of calculus, though this work went unpublished for more than 30 years. His most famous publication, *Principia Mathematica* (1687), grew out of correspondence with Edmond Halley, an English astronomer and mathematician who was the first to calculate the orbit of a comet later named after him. Describing his works on the laws of motion, orbital dynamics, tidal theory, and the theory of universal gravitation, it is regarded as the seminal work of modern science. He was elected president of the Royal Society of London in 1703 and became the first scientist ever to be knighted in 1705. During his career he engaged in heated arguments with several of his colleagues, including Robert Hooke (over authorship of the inverse square relation of gravitation) and Gottfried Wilhelm Leibniz (over the authorship of calculus). The battle with Leibniz dominated the last 25 years of his life; it is now well established that Newton developed calculus first, but that Leibniz was the first to publish on the subject.

The second law was put into its modern form $F = ma$ (where a is acceleration) by the Swiss mathematician Leonhard Euler in 1750. In this form, it is clear that the rate of change of velocity is directly proportional to the force acting on a body and inversely proportional to its mass.

In order to apply his laws to astronomy, Newton had to extend the mechanical philosophy beyond the limits set by Descartes. He postulated that there was a gravitational force acting between any two objects in the universe, even though he was unable to explain how this force could be propagated.

By means of his laws of motion and a gravitational force proportional to the inverse square of the distance between the centres of two bodies, Newton could deduce Kepler's laws of planetary motion. Galileo's law of free fall is also consistent with Newton's laws. The same force that causes objects to fall near the surface of the Earth also holds the Moon and planets in their orbits.

Newton's physics led to the conclusion that the shape of the Earth is not precisely spherical but should bulge at the Equator. The confirmation of this prediction by French expeditions in the mid-18th century helped persuade most European scientists to change from Cartesian to Newtonian physics. Newton also used the nonspherical shape of the Earth to explain the precession of the equinoxes, using the differential action of the Moon and Sun on the equatorial bulge to show how the axis of rotation would change its direction.

SPECIAL RELATIVITY

Relativity changed the scientific conception of the universe, which began in efforts to grasp the dynamic behaviour of matter. In Renaissance times, Galileo Galilei moved beyond Aristotle's philosophy to introduce the modern study of mechanics, which requires quantitative measurements of bodies moving in space and time. His work and that of others led to basic concepts, such as velocity, which is the distance a body covers in a given direction per unit time; acceleration, the rate of change of velocity; mass, the amount of material in a body; and force, a push or pull on a body.

The next major stride occurred in the late 17th century, when Isaac Newton formulated his three famous laws of motion. In constructing his system, Newton also defined space and time, taking both to be absolutes that are unaffected by anything external. Time, he wrote, "flows equably," while space "remains always similar and immovable."

Newton's law of gravity was brilliantly successful in explaining the mechanism behind Kepler's laws of planetary motion, which Kepler had formulated at the beginning of the 17th century. Newton's mechanics and law of gravity, along with his assumptions about the nature of space and time, seemed wholly successful in explaining the dynamics of the universe, from motion on the Earth to cosmic events.

LIGHT AND THE ETHER

However, this success at explaining natural phenomena came to be tested from an unexpected direction—the behaviour of light, whose intangible nature had puzzled philosophers and scientists for centuries. In 1873 the Scottish physicist James Clerk Maxwell showed that light is an electromagnetic wave with oscillating electrical and magnetic components. Maxwell's equations predicted that electromagnetic waves would travel through empty space at a speed of almost exactly 3×10^8 metres per second

(186,000 miles per second)—i.e., according with the measured speed of light. Experiments soon confirmed the electromagnetic nature of light and established its speed as a fundamental parameter of the universe.

Maxwell's remarkable result answered long-standing questions about light, but it raised another fundamental issue: if light is a moving wave, what medium supports it? Ocean waves and sound waves consist of the progressive oscillatory motion of molecules of water and of atmospheric gases, respectively. But what is it that vibrates to make a moving light wave? Or to put it another way, how does the energy embodied in light travel from point to point?

For Maxwell and other scientists of the time, the answer was that light traveled in a hypothetical medium called the ether (aether). Supposedly, this medium permeated all space without impeding the motion of planets and stars; yet it had to be more rigid than steel so that light waves could move through it at high speed, in the same way that a taut guitar string supports fast mechanical vibrations. Despite this contradiction, the idea of the ether seemed essential—until a definitive experiment disproved it.

In 1887 the German-born American physicist A.A. Michelson and the American chemist Edward Morley made exquisitely precise measurements to determine how the Earth's motion through the ether affected the measured speed of light. In classical mechanics, the Earth's movement would add to or subtract from the measured speed of light waves, just as the speed of a ship would add to or subtract from the speed of ocean waves as measured from the ship. But the Michelson-Morley experiment had an unexpected outcome, for the measured speed of light remained the same regardless of the Earth's motion. This could only mean that the ether had no meaning and that the behaviour of light could not be explained by classical physics. The explanation emerged, instead, from Albert Einstein's theory of special relativity.

EINSTEIN'S *GEDANKENEXPERIMENTS*

Scientists such as Austrian physicist Ernst Mach and French mathematician Henri Poincaré had critiqued classical mechanics or contemplated the behaviour of light and the meaning of the ether before Einstein. Their efforts provided a background for Einstein's unique approach to understanding the universe, which he called in his native German a *Gedankenexperiment*, or "thought experiment."

Einstein described how at age 16 he watched himself in his mind's eye as he rode on a light wave and gazed at another light wave moving parallel to his. According to classical physics, Einstein should have seen the second light wave moving at a relative speed of zero. However, Einstein knew that Maxwell's electromagnetic equations absolutely require that light always move at 3×10^8 metres per second in a vacuum. Nothing in the theory allows a light wave to have a speed of zero. Another problem arose as well: if a fixed observer sees light as having a speed of 3×10^8 metres per second, whereas an observer moving at the speed of light sees light as having a speed of zero, it would mean that the laws of electromagnetism depend on the observer. But in classical mechanics the same laws apply for all observers, and Einstein saw no reason why the electromagnetic laws should not be equally universal. The constancy of the speed of light and the universality of the laws of physics for all observers are cornerstones of special relativity.

STARTING POINTS AND POSTULATES

The fact that the speed of light is the same for all observers is inexplicable in ordinary terms. If a passenger in a train moving at 100 km per hour shoots an arrow in the train's direction of motion at 200 km per hour, a trackside observer would measure the speed of the arrow as the sum of the two speeds, or 300 km per hour. In analogy, if the train moves at the speed of light and a passenger shines a laser in the same direction, then common sense indicates that a trackside observer should see the light moving at the sum of the two speeds, or twice the speed of light.

While such a law of addition of velocities is valid in classical mechanics, the Michelson-Morley experiment showed that light does not obey this law. This contradicts common sense; it implies, for instance, that both a train moving at the speed of light and a light beam emitted from the train arrive at a point farther along the track at the same instant.

Nevertheless, Einstein made the constancy of the speed of light for all observers a postulate of his new theory. As a second postulate, he required that the laws of physics have the same form for all observers. Then Einstein extended his postulates to their logical conclusions to form special relativity.

RELATIVISTIC SPACE AND TIME

In order to make the speed of light constant, Einstein replaced absolute space and time with new definitions that depend on the state of motion of an observer. Einstein explained his approach by considering two observers and a train. One observer stands alongside a straight track; the other rides a train moving at constant speed along the track. Each views the world relative to his own surroundings. The fixed observer measures distance from a mark inscribed on the track and measures time with his watch; the train passenger measures distance from a mark inscribed on his railroad car and measures time with his own watch.

If time flows the same for both observers, as Newton believed, then the two frames of reference are reconciled by the relation: $x' = x - vt$. Here x is the distance to some specific event that happens along the track, as measured by the fixed observer; x' is the distance to the same event as measured by the moving observer; v is the speed of the train—that is, the speed of one observer relative to the other; and t is the time at which the event happens, the same for both observers.

For example, suppose the train moves at 40 km per hour. One hour after it sets out, a tree 60 km from the train's starting point is struck by lightning. The fixed observer measures x as 60 km and t as one hour. The moving observer also measures t as one hour, and so, according to Newton's equation, he measures x' as 20 km.

This analysis seems obvious, but Einstein saw a subtlety hidden in its underlying assumptions—in particular, the issue of simultaneity. The two people do not actually observe the lightning strike at the same time. Even at the speed of light, the image of the strike takes time to reach each observer, and, since each is at a different distance from the event, the travel times differ. Taking this insight further, suppose lightning strikes two trees, one 60 km ahead of the fixed observer and the other 60 km behind, exactly as the moving observer passes the fixed observer. Each image travels the same distance to the fixed observer, and so he certainly sees the events simultaneously. The motion of the moving observer brings him closer to one event than the other, however, and he thus sees the events at different times.

Einstein concluded that simultaneity is relative; events that are simultaneous for one observer may not be for another. This led him to the counterintuitive idea that time flows differently according to the state of motion and to the conclusion that distance is also relative. In the example, the train passenger and the fixed observer can each stretch a tape measure from back to front of a railroad car to find its length. The two ends of the tape must be placed in position at the same instant—that is, simultaneously—to obtain a true value. However, because the meaning of simultaneous is different for the two observers, they measure different lengths.

To make the speed of light constant, the theory requires that space and time change in a moving body, according to its speed, as seen by an outside observer. The body becomes shorter along its direction of motion; that is, its length contracts. Time intervals become longer, meaning that time runs more slowly in a moving body; that is, time dilates. In the train example, the person next to the track measures a shorter length for the train and a longer time interval for clocks on the train than does the train passenger. The relations describing these changes are

$$L = L_0 \sqrt{1 - \frac{v^2}{c^2}} \text{ and } T = \frac{T_0}{\sqrt{1 - \frac{v^2}{c^2}}},$$

where L_0 and T_0, called proper length and proper time, respectively, are the values measured by an observer on the moving body, and L and T are the corresponding quantities as measured by a fixed observer.

The relativistic effects become large at speeds near that of light, although it is worth noting again that they appear only when an observer looks at a moving body. He never sees changes in space or time within his own reference frame (whether on a train or spacecraft), even at the speed of light. These effects do not appear in ordinary life, because the factor v^2/c^2 is minute at even the highest speeds attained by humans, so that Einstein's equations become virtually the same as the classical ones.

COSMIC SPEED LIMIT

To derive further results, Einstein combined his redefinitions of time and space with two powerful physical principles: conservation of energy and conservation of mass, which state that the total amount of each remains constant in a closed system. Einstein's second postulate ensured that these laws remained valid for all observers in the new theory, and he used them to derive the relativistic meanings of mass and energy.

One result is that the mass of a body increases with its speed. An observer on a moving body, such as a spacecraft, measures its so-called rest mass m_0, while a fixed observer measures its mass m as

$$m = \frac{m_0}{\sqrt{1 - \frac{v^2}{c^2}}},$$

which is greater than m_0. In fact, as the spacecraft's speed approaches that of light, the mass m approaches infinity. However, as the object's mass increases, so does the energy required to keep accelerating it; thus, it would take infinite energy to accelerate a material body to the speed of light. For this reason, no material object can reach the speed of light, which is the speed limit for the universe. (Light itself can attain this speed because the rest mass of a photon, the quantum particle of light, is zero.)

$E = MC^2$

Einstein's treatment of mass showed that the increased relativistic mass comes from the energy of motion of the body—that is, its kinetic energy E—divided by c^2. This is

ALBERT EINSTEIN

(b. March 14, 1879, Ulm, Württemberg, Ger.—d. April 18, 1955, Princeton, N.J., U.S.)

Albert Einstein developed the theory of relativity. Born to a Jewish family in Germany, he grew up in Munich, and in 1894 he moved to Aarau, Switz. He attended a technical school in Zürich (graduating in 1900) and during this period renounced his German citizenship; stateless for some years, he became a Swiss citizen in 1901. Einstein became a junior examiner at the Swiss patent office in 1902 and began producing original theoretical work that laid many of the foundations for 20th-century physics. He received his doctorate from the University of Zürich in 1905, the same year he won international fame with the publication of three articles: one on Brownian motion, which he explained in terms of molecular kinetic energy; one on the photoelectric effect, in which he demonstrated the particle nature of light; and one on his special theory of relativity, which included his formulation of the equivalence of mass and energy ($E = mc^2$). Einstein held several professorships before becoming director of Berlin's Kaiser Wilhelm Institute for Physics in 1913. In 1915 he published his general theory of relativity, which was confirmed experimentally during a solar eclipse in 1919 with observations of the deviation of light passing near the Sun. He received a Nobel Prize in 1921 for his work on the photoelectric effect, his work on relativity still being controversial. He made important contributions to quantum field theory, and for decades he sought to discover the mathematical relationship between electromagnetism and gravitation, which he believed would be a first step toward discovering the common laws governing the behaviour of everything in the universe, but such a unified field theory eluded him. His theories of relativity and gravitation represented a profound advance over Newtonian physics and revolutionized scientific and philosophical inquiry. He resigned his position at the Prussian Academy when Adolf Hitler came to power and moved to Princeton, N.J., where he joined the Institute for Advanced Study. Though a longtime pacifist, he was instrumental in persuading Pres. Franklin Roosevelt in 1939 to initiate the Manhattan Project for the production of an atomic bomb, a technology his own theories greatly furthered, though he did not work on the project himself. Einstein became a U.S. citizen in 1940 but retained his Swiss citizenship. The most eminent scientist in the world in the postwar years, he declined an offer to become the first prime minister of Israel and became a strong advocate for nuclear disarmament.

the origin of the famous equation $E = mc^2$, which expresses the fact that mass and energy are the same physical entity and can be changed into each other.

GENERAL RELATIVITY

Because Isaac Newton's law of gravity served so well in explaining the behaviour of the solar system, the question arises why it was necessary to develop a new theory of gravity. The answer is that Newton's theory violates special relativity, for it requires an unspecified "action at a distance" through which any two objects—such as the Sun and the Earth—instantaneously pull each other, no matter how far apart. However, instantaneous response would require the gravitational interaction to propagate at infinite speed, which is precluded by special relativity.

In practice, this is no great problem for describing our solar system, for Newton's law gives valid answers for objects moving slowly compared with light. Nevertheless, since Newton's theory cannot be conceptually reconciled with special relativity, Einstein turned to the development of general relativity as a new way to understand gravitation.

PRINCIPLE OF EQUIVALENCE

In order to begin building his theory, Einstein seized on an insight that came to him in 1907. As he explained in a lecture in 1922:

> *I was sitting on a chair in my patent office in Bern. Suddenly a thought struck me: If a man falls freely, he would not feel his weight. I was taken aback. This simple thought experiment made a deep impression on me. This led me to the theory of gravity.*

Einstein was alluding to a curious fact known in Newton's time: no matter what the mass of an object, it falls toward the Earth with the same acceleration (ignoring air resistance) of 9.8 metres per second squared. Newton explained this by postulating two types of mass: inertial mass, which resists motion and enters into his general laws of motion, and gravitational mass, which enters into his equation for the force of gravity. He showed that, if the two masses were equal, then all objects would fall with that same gravitational acceleration.

Einstein, however, realized something more profound. A person standing in an elevator with a broken cable feels weightless as the enclosure falls freely toward the Earth. The reason is that both he and the elevator accelerate downward at the same rate and so fall at exactly the same speed; hence, short of looking outside the elevator at his surroundings, he cannot determine that he is being pulled downward. In fact, there is no experiment he can do within a sealed falling elevator to determine that he is within a gravitational field. If he releases a ball from his hand, it will fall at the same rate, simply remaining where he releases it. And if he were to see the ball sink toward the floor, he could not tell if that was because he was at rest within a gravitational field that pulled the ball down or because a cable was yanking the elevator up so that its floor rose toward the ball.

Einstein expressed these ideas in his deceptively simple principle of equivalence, which is the basis of general relativity: on a local scale—meaning within a given system, without looking at other systems—it is impossible to distinguish between physical effects due to gravity and those due to acceleration.

In that case, continued Einstein's *Gedankenexperiment*, light must be affected by gravity. Imagine that the elevator has a hole bored straight through two opposite walls. When the elevator is at rest, a beam of light entering one hole travels in a straight line parallel to the floor and exits through the other hole. But if the elevator is accelerated upward, by the time the ray reaches the second hole, the opening has moved and is no longer aligned with the ray. As the passenger sees the light miss the second hole, he concludes that the ray has followed a curved path (in fact, a parabola).

If a light ray is bent in an accelerated system, then, according to the principle of equivalence, light should also be bent by gravity, contradicting the everyday expectation that light will travel in a straight line (unless it passes from one medium to another). If its path is curved by gravity, that must mean that "straight line" has a different meaning near a massive gravitational body such as a star than it does in empty space. This was a hint that gravity should be treated as a geometric phenomenon.

CURVED SPACE-TIME AND GEOMETRIC GRAVITATION

The singular feature of Einstein's view of gravity is its geometric nature. Whereas Newton thought that gravity was a force, Einstein showed that gravity arises from the shape of space-time. While this is difficult to visualize, there is an analogy that provides some insight—although it is only a guide, not a definitive statement of the theory.

The analogy begins by considering space-time as a rubber sheet that can be deformed. In any region distant from massive cosmic objects such as stars, space-time is uncurved—that is, the rubber sheet is absolutely flat. If one were to probe space-time in that region by sending out a ray of light or a test body, both the ray and the body would travel in perfectly straight lines, like a child's marble rolling across the rubber sheet.

However, the presence of a massive body curves space-time, as if a bowling ball were placed on the rubber sheet to create a cuplike depression. In the analogy, a marble placed near the depression rolls down the slope toward the bowling ball as if pulled by a force. In addition, if the marble is given a sideways push, it will describe an orbit around the bowling ball, as if a steady pull toward the ball is swinging the marble into a closed path.

In this way, the curvature of space-time near a star defines the shortest natural paths, or geodesics—much as the shortest path between any two points on the Earth is not a straight line, which cannot be constructed on that curved surface, but the arc of a great circle route. In Einstein's theory, space-time geodesics define the deflection of light and the orbits of planets.

QUANTUM MECHANICS

The gradual recognition by scientists that radiation has particle-like properties and that matter has wavelike properties provided the impetus for the development of quantum mechanics. Influenced by Newton, most physicists of the 18th century believed that light consisted of particles, which they called corpuscles. From about 1800, evidence began to accumulate for a wave theory of light. At about this time Thomas Young showed that, if monochromatic light passes through a pair of slits, the two emerging beams interfere, so that a fringe pattern of alternately bright and dark bands appears on a screen. The bands are readily explained by a wave theory of light. According to the theory, a bright band is produced when the crests (and troughs) of the waves from the two slits arrive together at the screen; a dark band is produced when the crest of one wave arrives at the same time as the trough of the other, and the effects of the two light beams cancel. Beginning in 1815, a series of experiments by Augustin-Jean Fresnel of France and others showed that, when a parallel beam of light passes through a single slit, the emerging beam is no longer parallel but starts to diverge; this phenomenon is known as diffraction. Given the wavelength of the light and the geometry of the apparatus (i.e., the separation and widths of the slits and the distance from the slits to the screen), one can use the wave theory to calculate the expected pattern in each case; the theory agrees precisely with the experimental data.

PLANCK'S RADIATION LAW

By the end of the 19th century, physicists almost universally accepted the wave theory of light. However, though the ideas of classical physics explain interference and diffraction phenomena relating to the propagation of light, they do not account for the absorption and emission of light. All bodies radiate electromagnetic energy as heat; in fact, a body emits radiation at all wavelengths. The energy radiated at different wavelengths is a maximum at a wavelength that depends on the temperature of the body; the hotter the body, the shorter the wavelength for maximum radiation. Attempts to calculate the energy distribution for the radiation from a blackbody using classical ideas were unsuccessful. (A blackbody is a hypothetical ideal body or surface that absorbs and reemits all radiant energy falling on it.)

In 1900 the German theoretical physicist Max Planck made a bold suggestion. He assumed that the radiation energy is emitted, not continuously, but rather in discrete packets called quanta. The energy E of the quantum is related to the frequency v by $E = hv$. The quantity h, now known as the Planck constant, is a universal constant with the approximate value of 6.626075×10^{-34} joule·second. Planck showed that the calculated energy spectrum then agreed with observation over the entire wavelength range.

EINSTEIN AND THE PHOTOELECTRIC EFFECT

In 1905 Einstein extended Planck's hypothesis to explain the photoelectric effect, which is the emission of electrons by a metal surface when it is irradiated by light or more-energetic photons. The kinetic energy of the emitted electrons depends on the frequency v of the radiation, not on its intensity; for a given metal, there is a threshold frequency v_0 below which no electrons are emitted. Furthermore, emission takes place as soon as the light shines on the surface; there is no detectable delay. Einstein showed that these results can be explained by two assumptions: (1) that light is composed of corpuscles or photons, the energy of which is given by Planck's relationship, and (2) that an atom in the metal can absorb either a whole photon or nothing. Part of the energy of the absorbed photon frees an electron, which requires a fixed energy W, known as the work function of the metal; the rest is converted into the kinetic energy $m_e u^2/2$ of the emitted electron (m_e is the mass of the electron and u is its velocity). Thus, the energy relation is $hv = W + m_e u^2/2$.

If v is less than v_0, where $hv_0 = W$, no electrons are emitted. Not all the experimental results mentioned above were known in 1905, but all Einstein's predictions have been verified since.

BOHR'S THEORY OF THE ATOM

A major contribution to the subject was made by Niels Bohr of Denmark, who applied the quantum hypothesis to atomic spectra in 1913. The spectra of light emitted by gaseous atoms had been studied extensively since the mid-19th century. It was found that radiation from gaseous atoms at low pressure consists of a set of discrete wavelengths. This is quite unlike the radiation from a solid, which is distributed over a continuous range of wavelengths. The set of discrete wavelengths from gaseous atoms is known as a line spectrum because the radiation (light) emitted consists of a series of sharp lines. The wavelengths of the lines are characteristic of the element and may form extremely complex patterns. The simplest spectra are those of atomic hydrogen and the alkali atoms (e.g., lithium, sodium, and potassium). For hydrogen, the wavelengths λ are given by the empirical formula $1/\lambda = R_\infty(1/m^2 - 1/n^2)$, where m and n are positive integers with $n > m$ and R_∞, known as the Rydberg constant, has the value 1.097373177×10^7 per metre. For a given value of m, the lines for varying n form a series. The lines for $m = 1$, the Lyman series, lie in the ultraviolet part of the spectrum; those for $m = 2$, the Balmer series, lie in the visible spectrum; and those for $m = 3$, the Paschen series, lie in the infrared.

Bohr started with a model suggested by the New Zealand-born British physicist Ernest Rutherford. The model was based on the experiments of Hans Geiger and Ernest Marsden, who in 1909 bombarded gold atoms with massive, fast-moving alpha particles; when some of these particles were deflected backward, Rutherford concluded that the atom has a massive, charged nucleus. In Rutherford's model, the atom resembles a miniature solar system with the nucleus acting as the Sun and the electrons as the circulating planets. Bohr made three assumptions. First, he postulated that, in contrast to classical mechanics, where an infinite number of orbits is possible, an electron can be in only one of a discrete set of orbits, which he termed stationary states. Second, he postulated that the only orbits allowed are those for which the angular momentum of the electron is a whole number n times $\hbar$ ($\hbar = h/2\pi$). Third, Bohr assumed that Newton's laws of motion, so successful in calculating the paths of the planets around the Sun, also applied to electrons orbiting the nucleus. The force on the electron (the analogue of the gravitational force between the Sun and a planet) is the electrostatic attraction between the positively charged nucleus and the negatively charged electron. With these simple assumptions, he showed that the energy of the orbit has the form $E_n = -E_o/n^2$, where E_o is a constant that may be expressed by a combination of the known constants e, m_e, and $\hbar$. While in a stationary state, the atom does not give off energy as light; however, when an electron makes a transition from a state with energy E_n to one with lower energy E_m, a quantum of energy is radiated with frequency

v, given by the equation $hv = E_n - E_m$. Inserting the expression for E_n into this equation and using the relation $\lambda v = c$, where c is the speed of light, Bohr derived the formula for the wavelengths of the lines in the hydrogen spectrum, with the correct value of the Rydberg constant.

Bohr's theory was a brilliant step forward. Its two most important features have survived in present-day quantum mechanics. They are (1) the existence of stationary, nonradiating states and (2) the relationship of radiation frequency to the energy difference between the initial and final states in a transition. Prior to Bohr, physicists had thought that the radiation frequency would be the same as the electron's frequency of rotation in an orbit.

SCATTERING OF X-RAYS

Soon scientists were faced with the fact that another form of radiation, X-rays, also exhibits both wave and particle properties. Max von Laue of Germany had shown in 1912 that crystals can be used as three-dimensional diffraction gratings for X-rays; his technique constituted the fundamental evidence for the wavelike nature of X-rays. The atoms of a crystal, which are arranged in a regular lattice, scatter the X-rays. For certain directions of scattering, all the crests of the X-rays coincide. (The scattered X-rays are said to be in phase and to give constructive interference.) For these directions, the scattered X-ray beam is very intense. Clearly, this phenomenon demonstrates wave behaviour. In fact, given the interatomic distances in the crystal and the directions of constructive interference, the wavelength of the waves can be calculated.

In 1922 the American physicist Arthur Holly Compton showed that X-rays scatter from electrons as if they are particles. Compton performed a series of experiments on the scattering of monochromatic, high-energy X-rays by graphite. He found that part of the scattered radiation had the same wavelength λ_0 as the incident X-rays but that there was an additional component with a longer wavelength λ. To interpret his results, Compton regarded the X-ray photon as a particle that collides and bounces off an electron in the graphite target as though the photon and the electron were a pair of (dissimilar) billiard balls. Application of the laws of conservation of energy and momentum to the collision leads to a specific relation between the amount of energy transferred to the electron and the angle of scattering. For X-rays scattered through an angle θ, the wavelengths λ and λ_0 are related by the equation $\lambda - \lambda_0 = h(1 - \cos \theta)/m_e c$. The experimental correctness of Compton's formula is direct evidence for the corpuscular behaviour of radiation.

BROGLIE'S WAVE HYPOTHESIS

Faced with evidence that electromagnetic radiation has both particle and wave characteristics, Louis-Victor de Broglie of France suggested a great unifying hypothesis in 1924. Broglie proposed that matter has wave, as well as particle, properties. He suggested that material particles can behave as waves and that their wavelength λ is related to the linear momentum p of the particle by $\lambda = h/p$.

In 1927 Clinton Davisson and Lester Germer of the United States confirmed Broglie's hypothesis for electrons. Using a crystal of nickel, they diffracted a beam of monoenergetic electrons and showed that the wavelength of the waves is related to the momentum of the electrons by the Broglie equation. Since Davisson and Germer's investigation, similar experiments have been performed with atoms, molecules, neutrons, protons, and many other particles. All behave like waves with the same wavelength-momentum relationship.

STRING THEORY

String theory attempts to merge quantum mechanics with Einstein's general theory of relativity. The name *string theory* comes from the modeling of subatomic particles as tiny one-dimensional "stringlike" entities rather than the more conventional approach in which they are modeled as zero-dimensional point particles. The theory envisions that a string undergoing a particular mode of vibration corresponds to a particle with definite properties such as mass and charge.

Gabriele Veneziano, a young theorist working at the European Organization for Nuclear Research (CERN), contributed a key breakthrough in 1968 with his realization that a 200-year-old formula, the Euler beta function, was capable of explaining much of the data on the strong force then being collected at various particle accelerators around the world. A few years later, three physicists—Leonard Susskind of Stanford University, Holger Nielsen of the Niels Bohr Institute, and Yoichiro Nambu of the University of Chicago—significantly amplified Veneziano's insight by showing that the mathematics underlying his proposal described the vibrational motion of minuscule filaments of energy that resemble tiny strands of string.

In 1974 John Schwarz of the California Institute of Technology and Joel Scherk of the École Normale Supérieure and, independently, Tamiaki Yoneya of Hokkaido University came to a radical conclusion. They suggested that one of the supposedly failed predictions of string theory—the existence of a particular massless particle that no experiment studying the strong force had ever encountered—was actually evidence of the very unification Einstein had anticipated.

The announcement was universally ignored. String theory had already failed in its first incarnation as a description of the strong force, and many felt it was unlikely that it would now prevail as the solution to an even more difficult problem. This view was bolstered by string theory's suffering from its own theoretical problems. For one, some of its equations showed signs of being inconsistent; for another, the mathematics of the theory demanded the universe have not just the three spatial dimensions of common experience but six others (for a total of nine spatial dimensions, or a total of ten space-time dimensions).

Because of these obstacles, the number of physicists working on the theory had dropped to two—Schwarz and Michael Green, of Queen Mary College, London—by the mid-1980s. In 1984, however, they proved that the equations of string theory were consistent after all. According to the theory, the strings are so small that they appear to be points—as particles had long been thought to be—but in reality they have length (about 10^{-33} cm); the mass and charge of a particle is determined by how a string vibrates. For example, string theory posits that an electron is a string undergoing one particular vibrational pattern; a quark is imagined as a string undergoing a different vibrational pattern. Crucially, among the vibrational patterns, physicists argued, would also be the particles found by experiment to communicate nature's forces.

In 1995 Edward Witten of the Institute for Advanced Study revealed a number of new features of string theory. Most dramatically, more exact equations showed that string theory has not six but seven extra spatial dimensions; these more exact equations also revealed membranelike objects of various dimensions, collectively called branes. Finally, new techniques established that various versions of string theory developed over the preceding decades were essentially all the same. Theorists call this unification of formerly distinct string theories by a new name, M-theory.

Experiments have been planned at CERN to search for evidence of supersymmetry, a mathematical property discovered within string theory that requires every known particle species to have a partner particle species, called superpartners. (This property accounts for string theory often being referred to as superstring theory.) Even if these experiments are inconclusive, the physics of string theory may have left faint cosmological signatures on the earliest moments of the universe. It would be a fitting conclusion to Einstein's quest for unification if a theory of the smallest microscopic component of matter were confirmed through observations of the largest astronomical realms of the cosmos.

THE EXPANDING UNIVERSE: THE BIG BANG THEORY

Some of the most spectacular advances in modern astronomy have come from research on the large-scale structure and development of the universe. This research goes back to William Herschel's observations of nebulas at the end of the 18th century. Some astronomers considered them to be "island universes"—huge stellar systems outside of and comparable to the Milky Way Galaxy, to which the solar system belongs. Others, following Herschel's own speculations, thought of them simply as gaseous clouds— relatively small patches of diffuse matter within the Milky Way Galaxy, which might be in the process of developing into stars and planetary systems, as described in Pierre-Simon, marquis de Laplace's nebular hypothesis.

In 1912 Vesto Melvin Slipher began at the Lowell Observatory in Arizona an extensive program to measure the velocities of nebulas, using the Doppler shift of their spectral lines. (Doppler shift is the observed change in wavelength of the radiation from a source that results from the relative motion of the latter along the line of sight.) By 1925 he had studied about 40 nebulas, most of which were found to be moving away from the Earth according to the red shift (displacement toward longer wavelengths) of their spectra.

Although the nebulas were apparently so far away that their distances could not be measured directly by the stellar parallax method, an indirect approach was developed on the basis of a discovery made in 1908 by Henrietta Swan Leavitt at the Harvard College Observatory. Leavitt studied the magnitudes (apparent brightnesses) of a large number of variable stars, including the type known as Cepheid variables. Some of them were close enough to have measurable parallaxes so that their distances and thus their intrinsic brightnesses could be determined. She found a correlation between brightness and period of variation. Assuming that the same correlation holds for all stars of this kind, their observed magnitudes and periods could be used to estimate their distances.

In 1923 the American astronomer Edwin P. Hubble identified a Cepheid variable in the so-called Andromeda Nebula. Using Leavitt's period–brightness correlation, Hubble estimated its distance to be approximately 900,000 light-years. Since this was much greater than the size of the Milky Way system, it appeared that the Andromeda Nebula must be another galaxy (island universe) outside of our own.

In 1929 Hubble combined Slipher's measurements of the velocities of nebulas with further estimates of their distances and found that on the average such objects are moving away from the Earth with a velocity proportional to their distance. Hubble's velocity–distance relation suggested that the universe of galactic nebulas is expanding, starting from an initial state about 2 billion years ago in which all matter was contained in a fairly small volume. Revisions of the distance scale in the 1950s and later increased the "Hubble age" of the universe to more than 10 billion years.

Calculations by Aleksandr A. Friedmann in the Soviet Union, Willem de Sitter in the Netherlands, and Georges Lemaître in Belgium, based on Einstein's general theory of relativity, showed that the expanding universe could be explained in terms of the evolution of space itself. According to Einstein's theory, space is described by the non-Euclidean geometry proposed in 1854 by the German mathematician G.F. Bernhard Riemann. Its departure from Euclidean space is measured by a "curvature" that depends on the density of matter. The universe may be finite, though unbounded, like the surface of a sphere. Thus the expansion of the universe refers not merely to the motion of extragalactic stellar systems within space but also to the expansion of the space itself.

The beginning of the expanding universe was linked to the formation of the chemical elements in a theory developed in the 1940s by the physicist George Gamow, a former student of Friedmann who had emigrated to the United States. Gamow proposed that the universe began in a state of extremely high temperature and density and exploded outward—the so-called big bang. Matter was originally in the form of neutrons, which quickly decayed into protons and electrons; these then combined to form hydrogen and heavier elements.

Gamow's students Ralph Alpher and Robert Herman estimated in 1948 that the radiation left over from the big bang should by now have cooled down to a temperature just a few degrees above absolute zero (0 K, or -459° F). In 1965, as part of an effort to build sensitive microwave-receiving stations for satellite communication, the predicted cosmic background radiation was discovered by Arno A. Penzias and Robert W. Wilson of the Bell Telephone Laboratories. Their finding provided unexpected evidence for the idea that the universe was in a state of very high temperature and density sometime between 10 billion and 20 billion years ago.

THE EVOLUTION OF STARS AND THE FORMATION OF CHEMICAL ELEMENTS

The idea that stars are formed by the condensation of gaseous clouds was part of the 19th-century nebular hypothesis. The gravitational energy released by this condensation could be transformed into heat, but calculations by Hermann von Helmholtz and Lord Kelvin indicated that this process would provide energy to keep the Sun shining for only about 20 million years. Evidence from radiometric dating, starting with the work of the British physicist Ernest Rutherford in 1905, showed that the Earth is probably several billion years old. Astrophysicists were perplexed: what source of energy has kept the Sun shining for such a long time?

In 1925 Cecilia Payne, a graduate student from Britain at Harvard College Observatory, analyzed the spectra of stars using statistical atomic theories that related them to temperature, density, and composition. She found that hydrogen and helium are the most abundant elements in stars, though this conclusion was not generally accepted until it was confirmed four years later by the noted American astronomer Henry Norris Russell. By this time William Prout's hypothesis that all the elements are compounds of hydrogen had been revived by physicists in a somewhat more elaborate form. The deviation of atomic weights from exact integer values (expressed as multiples of hydrogen) could be explained partly by the fact that some elements are mixtures of isotopes with different atomic weights and partly by Einstein's relation between mass and energy (taking account of the binding energy of the forces that hold together the atomic nucleus).

In 1938 the German-born physicist Hans Bethe proposed the first satisfactory theory of stellar energy generation based on the fusion of protons to form helium and heavier elements. He showed that once elements as heavy as carbon had been formed, a cycle of nuclear reactions could produce even heavier elements. Fusion of hydrogen into heavier elements would also provide enough energy to account for the Sun's energy generation over a period of billions of years.

According to the theory of stellar evolution developed by the Indian-born American astrophysicist Subrahmanyan Chandrasekhar and others, a star will become unstable after it has converted most of its hydrogen to helium and may go through stages of rapid expansion and contraction. If the star is much more massive than the Sun, it will explode violently, giving rise to a supernova. The explosion will synthesize heavier elements and spread them throughout the surrounding interstellar medium, where they provide the raw material for the formation of new stars and eventually of planets and living organisms.

After a supernova explosion, the remaining core of the star may collapse further under its own gravitational attraction to form a dense star composed mainly of neutrons. This so-called neutron star, predicted theoretically in the 1930s by the astronomers Walter Baade and Fritz Zwicky, is apparently the same as the pulsar (a source of rapid, very regular pulses of radio waves), discovered in 1967 by Jocelyn Bell of the British radio astronomy group under Antony Hewish at Cambridge University.

More massive stars may undergo a further stage of evolution beyond the neutron star: they may collapse to a black hole, in which the gravitational force is so strong that even light cannot escape. The black hole as a singularity in an idealized space-time universe was predicted from the general relativity theory by the German astronomer Karl Schwarzschild in 1916. Its role in stellar evolution was later described by the American physicists J. Robert Oppenheimer and John Wheeler. During the 1980s, possible black holes were thought to have been located in X-ray sources and at the centre of certain galaxies.

SOLAR-SYSTEM ASTRONOMY

This area of investigation, which lay relatively dormant through the first half of the 20th century, was revived in the 1960s under the stimulus of the Soviet and American space programs. Before the first manned lunar landing in 1969, there were three competing hypotheses about the origin of the Moon: (1) formation in its present orbit simultaneously with the Earth, as described in the nebular hypothesis; (2) formation elsewhere and subsequent capture by the Earth; and (3) ejection from the Earth by fission (popularly known theory that the Moon emanated from what is now the Pacific Ocean Basin). Following the analysis of lunar samples and theoretical criticism of these hypotheses, lunar scientists came to the conclusion that none of them was satisfactory. Photographs of the surface of Mercury taken by the U.S. Mariner 10 spacecraft in 1974, however, showed that it is heavily cratered like the Moon's surface. This finding suggested that the Earth was also probably subject to heavy bombardment soon after its formation. In line with this, a theory proposed by the American astronomers William K. Hartmann and A.G.W. Cameron has become the most popular. According to their theory, the Earth was struck by a Mars-sized object, and the force of the impact vaporized the outer parts of both bodies. The vapour thus

GEORGE GAMOW

(b. March 4, 1904, Odessa, Russian Empire—d. Aug. 19, 1968, Boulder, Colo., U.S.)

George Gamow was a Russian-born U.S. nuclear physicist and cosmologist who developed the big bang model. After studying at Leningrad University with Aleksandr Friedmann (1888–1925), he subsequently developed his quantum theory of radioactivity, the first successful explanation of the behaviour of radioactive elements. His "liquid drop" model of atomic nuclei served as the basis for modern theories of nuclear fission and fusion. After immigrating to the United States in 1934, he collaborated with Edward Teller in researching beta decay (1936) and developing a theory of the internal structures of red giant stars (1942). In the 1950s he became interested in biochemistry, proposing theories of genetic code structure that were later found to be true. Throughout his career he also wrote popular works on such difficult subjects as relativity and cosmology.

produced remained in orbit around the Earth and eventually condensed to form the Moon.

PLATE TECTONICS

The earliest references to the similarity between the outlines of the continents flanking the Atlantic Ocean were made in 1620 by the English philosopher Francis Bacon, in his book *Novum Organum*, and by French naturalist Georges-Louis Leclerc, comte de Buffon, a century later. By the 19th century, the first hypotheses explaining this phenomenon began to emerge. In 1858 French geographer Antonio Snider-Pellegrini proposed that identical fossil plants in North American and European coal deposits could be explained if the two continents had formerly been connected. In the late 19th century, the Austrian geologist Eduard Suess proposed that large ancient continents had been composed of several of the present-day smaller ones, and portions of a single enormous southern continent—designated Gondwanaland, or Gondwana—foundered to become the Atlantic and Indian oceans. In 1908, American geologist Frank B. Taylor postulated that the arcuate mountain belts of Asia and Europe resulted from the equatorward creep of the continents.

ALFRED WEGENER AND THE CONCEPT OF CONTINENTAL DRIFT

In 1912 German meteorologist Alfred Wegener presented the concept of continental drift. Wegener considered the existence of a single supercontinent from about 350 to 245 million years ago, during the late Paleozoic Era, and named it Pangea, meaning "all lands." He unveiled the concept in a lecture in 1912, followed in 1915 by his major published work, *Die Entstehung der Kontinente und Ozeane (The Origin of Continents and Oceans)*.

ISOSTASY

Wegener pointed out that the concept of isostasy rendered large sunken continental blocks, as envisaged by Suess, geophysically impossible. He concluded that, if the continents had been once joined together, their fragments would have drifted away from one another. Wegener's supporting evidence included the continuity of fold belts across oceans, the presence of identical rocks and fossils on widely separated continents, and the paleobiogeographic and paleoclimatological record that indicated otherwise unaccountable shifts in Earth's major climate belts. He contended that if continents could move up and down in the mantle as a result of buoyancy changes, they should be able to move horizontally as well.

DRIVING FORCES

The main obstacle to the acceptance of Wegener's hypothesis was the driving forces he proposed. Despite the opposition of noted British geophysicist Sir Harold Jeffreys, his proposition was attentively received by many European geologists, and in England, Arthur Holmes pointed out that the lack of a driving force was insufficient grounds for rejecting the entire concept. In 1929, Holmes proposed an alternative mechanism—convection of the mantle—which remains today a serious candidate for the force driving the plates.

EVIDENCE SUPPORTING THE HYPOTHESIS

The strikingly similar Paleozoic sedimentary sequences that appear in India and on all southern continents support the continental drift hypothesis. This diagnostic sequence consists of glacial deposits called tillites, followed by sandstones and finally coal measures, typical of warm, moist climates. Placed on a reconstruction of Gondwana, however, the tillites mark two ice ages that occurred during the drift of this continent across the South Pole. About this time, Gondwana collided with Laurentia (the precursor to North America), which was one of the major collisional events that produced Pangea.

Both ice ages resulted in glacial deposits in the southern Sahara during the Silurian Period (more than 400 million years ago) and in southern South America, South Africa, India, and Australia from 380 to 250 million years ago, an interval spanning the end of the Devonian, the Carboniferous, and almost all of the Permian. At each location, the tillites were covered by subtropical desert sands, and these in turn by coal measures, indicating that the region had arrived near the paleoequator.

During the 1950s and 1960s, isotopic dating of rocks showed that the crystalline massifs of Precambrian age (from about 4 billion to 542 million years ago) found on opposite sides of the South Atlantic did indeed closely correspond in age and composition, as Wegener had surmised. They originated as a single assemblage of Precambrian continental nuclei later torn apart by the fragmentation of Pangea. Additional evidence for continental drift was provided in 1964 by British geophysicist Sir Edward Bullard. His computer analysis of the Atlantic Ocean's 1,000-metre (3,300-foot) depth contour revealed an impressive fit between the continents and the Paleozoic mountain ranges of eastern North America and northwestern Europe.

PALEOMAGNETISM, POLAR WANDERING, AND CONTINENTAL DRIFT

Ironically, Wegener's vindication came from the field of geophysics, the subject used by Jeffreys to discredit the original concept. In the 19th century, geologists recognized that many rocks preserve the imprint of Earth's magnetic field as it was at the time of their formation. Iron-rich volcanic rocks such as basalt contain minerals that are good recorders of Earth's paleomagnetic field, and some sediments also align their magnetic particles with Earth's field at the time of deposition. Scientists can then pinpoint the mineral's latitude of origin and orientation relative to the magnetic pole.

During the 1950s, paleomagnetic studies, notably those of Stanley K. Runcorn and his coworkers in England, showed that in the late Paleozoic the north magnetic pole seems to have wandered from a Precambrian position near Hawaii to its present location by way of Japan. This phenomenon could be explained either by the wandering of the pole itself or by the drifting of Europe relative to a fixed pole. The distinction between these two hypotheses came from conflicting paleomagnetic data collected from other continents. The hypothesis involving true-wandering poles was discarded because it would imply separate wanderings of many magnetic poles over the same period. However, these different paths could be reconciled by joining the continents in the manner and at the time suggested by Wegener.

GESTATION AND BIRTH OF PLATE TECTONIC THEORY

After World War II, rapid advances were made in the study of the relief, geology, and geophysics of the ocean basins. Owing in large part to the efforts of Bruce C. Heezen and Henry W. Menard of the United States, these features, which constitute more than two-thirds of Earth's surface, became well enough known to permit serious geologic analysis.

DISCOVERY OF OCEAN BASIN FEATURES

One of the most important discoveries was that of the 65,000-kilometre-long (40,000-mile) oceanic ridge system. Their crests tend to be rugged and are often endowed with a rift valley at their summit where fresh lava, high heat flow, and shallow earthquakes of the extensional type are found.

In addition, long, narrow depressions—oceanic trenches—were also discovered that contain the greatest depths of the ocean basins. These features have low heat flow, are often filled with thick sediments, and lie at the upper edge of the Benioff zone of compressive earthquakes. They may border continents, as in the case of western Central and South America, or may occur in mid-ocean, as, for example, in the southwestern Pacific. Offsets of up to several hundred kilometres along oceanic ridges and, more rarely, trenches were also recognized, and these fracture zones—later termed transform faults—were described as transverse features consisting of linear ridges and troughs.

HESS'S SEAFLOOR-SPREADING MODEL

The existence of these three types of large, striking sea-floor features demanded a global rather than local tectonic explanation. The first comprehensive attempt at such an explanation was made by American geologist Harry H. Hess. Drawing on Holmes's model of convective mantle flow, Hess suggested that oceanic ridges were the results of rising and diverging convective mantle flow, whereas trenches and Benioff zones, with their associated island arcs, marked descending limbs. At the ridge crests the outflow of new oceanic crust would be carried away laterally to cool, subside, and finally be destroyed in the nearest trenches. Consequently, the age of the oceanic crust should increase with distance away from the ridge crests, and very old oceanic crust would not be preserved anywhere. This explained why rocks older than 200 million years had never been encountered in the oceans, whereas the continents preserve rocks up to 3.8 billion years old. Hess's model was later dubbed seafloor spreading by the American oceanographer Robert S. Dietz.

Magnetic Anomalies

In 1961, a magnetic survey of the eastern Pacific Ocean floor off the coast of Oregon and California was published by two geophysicists, Arthur D. Raff and Ronald G. Mason. Unlike on the continents, where regional magnetic anomaly patterns tend to be confused and seemingly random, the seafloor possesses a remarkably regular set of magnetic bands of alternately higher and lower values than the average values of Earth's magnetic field. These positive and negative anomalies are strikingly linear and parallel with the oceanic ridge axis and show distinct offsets along fracture zones.

The Reversal of Earth's Magnetic Field

A key piece to resolving this pattern came with the discovery of magnetized samples from a sequence of basalt lavas. These lavas, extruded in rapid succession in a single locality on land, showed that the north and south poles had apparently repeatedly interchanged, and subsequent studies of rock samples around the world displayed the same reversal at the same time, implying that the polarity of Earth's magnetic field periodically reversed. These studies established a sequence of reversals dated by isotopic methods.

In the early 1960s Drummond H. Matthews of the University of Cambridge, his research student Frederick J. Vine, and Canadian geologist Laurence W. Morley, who worked independently of the others, postulated that new basaltic oceanic crust would have a magnetization aligned with the field at the time of its formation. If the magnetic field was normal, as it is today, the magnetization of the crust would be added to that of Earth and produce a positive anomaly. If intrusion had taken place during a period of reverse magnetic polarity, it would subtract from the present field and appear as a negative anomaly. Subsequent to intrusion, each new block created at the spreading centre would split, and the halves would generate the observed bilateral magnetic symmetry.

Given a constant rate of crustal generation, the widths of individual anomalies should correspond to the intervals between magnetic reversals. Extrapolations based on marine magnetic anomalies (confirmed by deep-sea drilling) has extended the magnetic anomaly time scale far into the Cretaceous Period, which spans the interval from about 145 to 65 million years ago.

DETERMINATION OF PLATE THICKNESS

After marine magnetic anomalies were explained, the concept of seafloor spreading became widely accepted. However, the process responsible for continental drift remained enigmatic. Two important concerns remained. The spreading seafloor was generally seen as a process that involved thin slabs of crust. If only oceanic crust was involved in seafloor spreading, the thinness of the slab would not be problematic. However, the Atlantic Ocean had a well-developed oceanic ridge but lacked trenches adequate to dispose of the excess oceanic crust. This implied that the adjacent continents needed to travel with the spreading seafloor, a process that, given the thin but clearly undeformed slab, strained credulity.

Working independently but along very similar lines, Dan P. McKenzie and Robert L. Parker of Britain and W. Jason Morgan of the United States resolved these issues. McKenzie and Parker showed with a geometric analysis that, if the moving slabs of crust were thick enough to be regarded as rigid, their motions on a sphere would lead precisely to those divergent, convergent, and transform boundaries that are indeed observed. Morgan demonstrated that the directions and rates of movement had been recorded by magnetic anomaly patterns and transform faults. He proposed that the plates extended to the base of a rigid lithosphere, which coincided with the top of the weaker asthenosphere.

In 1968, a computer analysis by the French geophysicist Xavier Le Pichon proved that the plates did indeed form an integrated system where the sum of all crust generated at oceanic ridges is balanced by the amount destroyed in subduction zones. That same year, the American geophysicists Bryan Isacks, Jack Oliver, and Lynn R. Sykes showed that the theory, which they enthusiastically labeled the "new global tectonics," was capable of accounting for the larger part of Earth's seismic activity. Almost immediately, others began to consider the ability of the theory to explain mountain building and sea-level changes.

PLATE-DRIVING MECHANISMS AND THE ROLE OF THE MANTLE

By the late 1960s, details of the processes of plate movement and of boundary interactions, along with much of the plate history of the Cenozoic Era (the past 65 million

ALFRED WEGENER
(b. Nov. 1, 1880, Berlin, Ger. —d. Nov. 1930, Greenland)

The German meteorologist and geophysicist Alfred Lothar Wegener formulated the first complete statement of the continental drift hypothesis. After earning a Ph.D. in astronomy (1905), he became interested in paleoclimatology and traveled to Greenland to research polar air circulation. He formulated the first complete statement of the continental drift hypothesis, which he presented in *The Origin of Continents and Oceans* (1915). His theory won some adherents, but by 1930 most geologists had rejected it because of the implausibility of his postulations for the driving force behind the continents' movement. It was resurrected in the 1960s as part of the theory of plate tectonics. Wegener died during his fourth expedition to Greenland.

years), had been worked out. Yet the driving forces that bedeviled Wegener remained enigmatic because there was little information about what happens beneath the plates. Although most agree that plate movement is the result of the convective circulation of Earth's mantle, how this convection propels the plates remains a topic of considerable debate.

GEOLOGIC TIME

The study of geologic time is thought to have begun after early naturalists observed the occurrence of seashells embedded in the hard rocks of high mountains. This event eventually set off a controversy on the origin of fossils that continued through the 17th century. Xenophanes of Colophon (flourished *c.* 560 BCE) was credited by later writers with observing that seashells occur "in the midst of earth and in mountains." He is said to have believed that these relics originated during a catastrophic event that caused the Earth to be mixed with the sea and then to settle, burying organisms in the drying mud. For these views Xenophanes is sometimes called the father of paleontology.

KNOWLEDGE OF LANDFORMS AND OF LAND-SEA RELATIONS

Changes in the landscape and in the position of land and sea related to erosion and deposition by streams were recognized by some early writers. The Greek historian Herodotus (*c.* 484–*c.* 426 BCE) correctly concluded that the northward bulge of Egypt into the Mediterranean is caused by the deposition of mud carried by the Nile. A similar appreciation of the changes wrought by erosion and deposition was also shared by Chinese writers. In the *Jinshu* ("History of the Jin Dynasty"), Du Yu (222–284 CE) predicted that monumental stelae containing a record of his successes would likely change their relative positions, because the high hills will become valleys and the deep valleys will become hills.

Aristotle guessed that changes in the position of land and sea might be cyclical in character, thus reflecting some sort of natural order. If the rivers of a moist region should build deltas at their mouths, he reasoned, seawater would be displaced and the level of the sea would rise to cover some adjacent dry region. The idea of a cyclical inter-change between land and sea was also presented in the *Discourses of the Brothers of Purity*, a classic Arabic work written between 941 and 982 CE by an anonymous group of scholars at Basra (Iraq).

PALEONTOLOGY AND STRATIGRAPHY

During the 17th century the guiding principles of paleon-tology and historical geology began to emerge in the work of a few individuals. Nicolaus Steno, a Danish scientist and theologian, favoured the organic origin of what are now called fossils. In his 1669 paper entitled "De solido intra naturaliter contento dissertationis" ("A Preliminary Discourse Concerning a Solid Body Enclosed by Processes of Nature Within a Solid"), Steno demonstrated that when the hard parts of an organism are covered with sediment, it is they and not the aggregates of sediment that are firm. Consolidation of the sediment into rock may come later, and, if so, the original solid fossil becomes encased in solid rock. He recognized that sediments settle from fluids to form layers of strata that are originally continuous and nearly horizontal. His principle of superposition of strata states that in a sequence of strata, as originally laid down, younger strata rest upon older strata.

In 1667 and 1668 the English physicist Robert Hooke read papers before the Royal Society in which he expressed many of the ideas contained in Steno's works. Hooke argued for the organic nature of fossils and attributed the elevation of beds containing marine fossils to mountainous heights to the work of earthquakes. Streams attacking these elevated tracts wear down the hills, fill depressions with sediment, and thus level out irregularities of the landscape.

WILLIAM SMITH AND FAUNAL SUCCESSION

In 1683 the zoologist Martin Lister proposed to the Royal Society that a new sort of map be drawn showing the areal distribution of the different kinds of British "soiles" (vegetable soils and underlying bedrock). The work was accomplished 132 years later, when William Smith published his *Geologic Map of England and Wales with Part of Scotland* (1815). A self-educated surveyor and engineer, Smith collected fossils and made careful note of the strata that contained them. He discovered that the different stratified formations in England contain distinctive assemblages of fossils. His map showed 20 different rock units, to which Smith applied local names in common use—e.g., London Clay and Purbeck Beds. In 1816 Smith published a companion work, *Strata Identified by Organized Fossils*, in which the organic remains characteristic of each of his rock units were illustrated. His generalization that each formation is "possessed of properties peculiar to itself [and] has the same organized fossils throughout its course" is the first clear statement of the principle of faunal sequence, which is the basis for worldwide correlation of fossiliferous strata into a coherent system. Smith thus demonstrated two kinds of order in nature: order in the spatial arrangement of rock units and order in the succession of ancient forms of life.

Smith's principle of faunal sequence was another way of saying that there are discontinuities in the sequences of fossilized plants and animals. These discontinuities were interpreted in two ways: as indicators of episodic destruction of life or as evidence for the incompleteness of the fossil record. Baron Georges Cuvier of France was one of the more distinguished members of a large group of naturalists who believed that paleontological discontinuities bore witness to sudden and widespread catastrophes. After reconstructing many vertebrate skeletons found in the Cenozoic rocks of northern France, Cuvier discovered that the fossils in all but the youngest deposits belong to species now extinct. Moreover, these extinct species have definite ranges up and down in the stratigraphic column. Cuvier inferred that the successive extinctions were the result of convulsions that caused the strata of the continents to be dislocated and folded and the seas to sweep across the continents and just as suddenly subside.

Charles Lyell and Uniformitarianism

In opposition to the catastrophist school of thought, the British geologist Charles Lyell proposed a uniformitarian interpretation of geologic history in his *Principles of Geology* (3 vols., 1830–33). His system was based on two propositions: the causes of geologic change operating include all the causes that have acted from the earliest time; and these causes have always operated at the same average levels of energy. These two propositions add up to a "steady-state" theory of the Earth. Changes in climate have fluctuated around a mean, reflecting changes in the position of land and sea. He believed that progress through time in the organic world is likewise an illusion, the effect of an imperfect paleontological record.

LOUIS AGASSIZ AND THE ICE AGE

Huge boulders of granite resting upon limestone of the Jura Mountains were subjects of controversy during the 18th and early 19th centuries. Swiss physicist and geologist Horace Bénédict de Saussure described these in 1779 and called them erratics. He concluded that they had been swept to their present positions by torrents of water. Saussure's interpretation was in accord with the tenets of diluvial geologists, who interpreted erratics and sheets of unstratified sediment (till or drift) spread over the northern parts of Europe and North America as the work of the "Deluge."

In 1837 the Swiss zoologist and paleontologist Louis Agassiz delivered a startling address before the Helvetian Society, proposing that, during a geologically recent stage of refrigeration, glacial ice had covered Eurasia from the North Pole to the shores of the Mediterranean and Caspian. Wherever erratics, till, and striated pavements of rock occur, sure evidence of this recent catastrophe exists. After a cool reception, Agassiz began intensive field studies and in 1840 published his *Études sur les glaciers* ("Studies of Glaciers"), demonstrating that Alpine glaciers had been far more extensive in the past.

GEOLOGIC TIME AND THE AGE OF THE EARTH

By mid-century the fossiliferous strata of Europe had been grouped into systems arrayed in chronological order. The

WILLIAM SMITH

(b. March 23, 1769, Churchill, Oxfordshire, Eng.—d. Aug. 28, 1839, Northampton, Northamptonshire)

The founder of the science of stratigraphy was the English engineer and geologist William Smith. The son of a blacksmith, he was largely self-educated. He produced the first geologic map of England and Wales (1815), setting the style for modern geologic maps, and subsequently a series of geologic maps of the English counties. He introduced many techniques still used, including the use of fossils for the dating of layers. Current geologic maps of England differ from his primarily in detail, and many of the colourful names he applied to the strata are also used today.

stratigraphic column, a composite of these systems, was pieced together from exposures in different regions by application of the principles of superposition and faunal sequence. Time elapsed during the formation of a system became known as a period, and the periods were grouped into eras: the Paleozoic (Cambrian through Permian periods), Mesozoic (Triassic, Jurassic, and Cretaceous periods), and Cenozoic (Tertiary and Quaternary periods).

Charles Darwin's *Origin of Species* (1859) offered a theoretical explanation for the empirical principle of faunal sequence. The fossils of the successive systems are different not only because parts of the stratigraphic record are missing but also because most species have lost in their struggles for survival and those that do survive evolve into new forms over time. Darwin borrowed two ideas from Lyell and the uniformitarians: the idea that geologic time is virtually without limit and the idea that a sequence of minute changes integrated over long periods of time produce remarkable changes in natural entities.

The evolutionists and the historical geologists were embarrassed when, beginning in 1864, William Thomson (later Lord Kelvin) attacked the steady-state theory of the Earth and placed numerical strictures on the length of geologic time. The Earth might function as a heat machine, but it could not also be a perpetual motion machine. Assuming that the Earth was originally molten, Thomson calculated that not less than 20 million and not more than 400 million years could have passed since the Earth first became a solid body. Other physicists of note put even narrower limits on the Earth's age ranging down to 15 or 20 million years. All these calculations, however, were based on the common assumption that the Earth's substance is inert and hence incapable of generating new heat. Shortly before the end of the century this assumption was negated by the discovery of radioactive elements that disintegrate spontaneously and release heat to the Earth in the process.

Chapter 3:
THE ARTS

The theories and ideas that proved to be turning points in the arts form a much more diverse collection than those of previous chapters. The visual arts were transformed by notions of linear perspective, abstraction, Impressionism, and Expressionism. Modernism, an interdisciplinary idea, is probably best recognized for the fruits it bore in arts such as literature and architecture. Other transformative ideas include the concept of harmony in music and the idea of montage in the younger art of filmmaking. Vitruvius's theory of architecture is presented, as is a recent environmental development called green architecture. The ancient roots of the modern science of urban planning also are discussed here.

PERSPECTIVE

The method of graphically depicting three-dimensional objects and spatial relationships on a two-dimensional plane or on a plane that is shallower than the original (for example, in flat relief) is called perspective.

Perceptual methods of representing space and volume, which render them as seen at a particular time and from a fixed position and are characteristic of Chinese and most Western painting since the Renaissance, are in contrast to conceptual methods. Pictures drawn by young children and untrained artists, many paintings of cultures such as ancient Egypt and Crete, India, Islam, and pre-Renaissance Europe, as well as the paintings of many modern artists, depict objects and surroundings independently of one another—as they are known to be, rather than as they are seen to be—and from the directions that best present their most characteristic features. Many Egyptian and Cretan paintings and drawings, for example, show the head and legs of a figure in profile, while the eye and torso are shown frontally. This system produces not the illusion of depth but the sense that objects and their surroundings have been compressed within a shallow space behind the picture plane.

In Western art, illusions of perceptual volume and space are generally created by use of the linear perspectival system, based on the observations that objects appear to the eye to shrink and parallel lines and planes to converge to infinitely distant vanishing points as they recede in space from the viewer. Parallel lines in spatial recession will appear to converge on a single vanishing point, called one-point perspective. Perceptual space and volume may be simulated on the picture plane by variations on this basic principle, differing according to the number and location of the vanishing points. Instead of one-point (or central) perspective, the artist may use, for instance, angular (or oblique) perspective, which employs two vanishing points.

Another kind of system—parallel perspective combined with a viewpoint from above—is traditional in Chinese painting. When buildings rather than natural contours are painted and it is necessary to show the parallel horizontal lines of the construction, parallel lines are drawn parallel instead of converging, as in linear perspective. Often foliage is used to crop these lines before they extend far enough to cause a building to appear warped.

The early European artist used a perspective that was an individual interpretation of what he saw rather than a fixed mechanical method. At the beginning of the Italian Renaissance, early in the 15th century, the mathematical

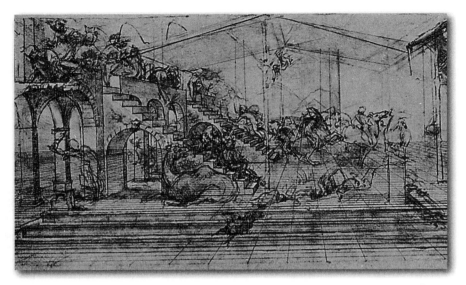

Linear perspective study for The Adoration of the Magi, *silverpoint, pen, and bistre heightened with white on prepared ground by Leonardo da Vinci, c. 1481; in the Uffizi, Florence.* Alinari/Art Resource, New York

laws of perspective were discovered by the architect Filippo Brunelleschi, who worked out some of the basic principles, including the concept of the vanishing point, which had been known to the Greeks and Romans but had been lost. These principles were applied in painting by Masaccio (as in his *Trinity* fresco in Santa Maria Novella, Florence; c. 1427), who within a short period brought about an entirely new approach in painting. A style was soon developed using configurations of architectural exteriors and interiors as the background for religious paintings, which thereby acquired the illusion of great spatial depth. In his seminal *Della pittura* (1436; *On Painting*), Leon Battista Alberti codified, especially for painters, much of the practical work on the subject that had been carried out by earlier artists; he formulated, for example, the idea that "vision makes a triangle, and from this it is clear that a very distant quantity seems no larger than a point."

Linear perspective dominated Western painting until the end of the 19th century, when Paul Cézanne flattened the conventional Renaissance picture space. The Cubists and other 20th-century painters abandoned the depiction of three-dimensional space altogether and hence had no need for linear perspective. Nevertheless, linear perspective continues to play an important part in presentations of ideas for works by architects, engineers, landscape architects, and industrial designers, furnishing an opportunity to view the finished product before it is begun. Differing in principle from linear perspective and used by both Chinese and European painters, aerial perspective is a method of creating the illusion of depth by a modulation of colour and tone.

FILIPPO BRUNELLESCHI
(b. 1377, Florence [Italy]—d. April 15, 1446, Florence)

The Florentine architect and engineer Filippo Brunelleschi was one of the pioneers of early Renaissance architecture in Italy. He was trained as a goldsmith, acquired great skill as a sculptor, and invented machines and mechanical devices. He studied mathematics and hydraulics as well as time and motion and is said to have built clocks.

Entering a competition for bronze reliefs in the baptistery of Florence, Brunelleschi created what is considered his finest work of sculpture, *The Sacrifice of Isaac* (1401–03). This panel displays great narrative movement and drama, but he lost the competition to Lorenzo Ghiberti. Possibly because of his disappointment at losing, Brunelleschi turned to architecture. He rediscovered the principles of linear perspective that had been known to the Greeks and Romans but that had been lost over the centuries. Brunelleschi demonstrated his findings with two painted panels (now lost) of Florentine street scenes. One of his first major architectural projects, the Ospedali degli Innocenti (Foundling Hospital) in Florence, marked the introduction of his new Renaissance architectural style. He designed the lower facade (completed 1427) and other parts of the structure, but later changes have blurred the building's architectural clarity.

Brunelleschi did not design many buildings, and some were unfinished at his death. In the 1420s, when his art reached its full maturity, he saw his first major structure completed: the old sacristy of San Lorenzo, commissioned by Giovanni de' Medici. The building's features demonstrate the various influences that Brunelleschi incorporated into his work, among them both classical and Tuscan. Brunelleschi also drew plans for the basilica of San Lorenzo. Work was begun in 1421, halted in 1428, and begun again in 1441, continuing into the 1460s. His other notable works include a chapel next to Santa Croce, commissioned by the Pazzi family about 1429; Santa Maria degli Angeli, begun in 1434; and Santo Spirito, designed either in 1428 or 1434. All of these have undergone alterations from Brunelleschi's plans, but each shows aspects of his genius, especially in his proportions and sculptural space-molding elements.

It was Brunelleschi's work on the cathedral of Florence that made him famous. The dome, measuring 130 feet (40 meters) in diameter, had challenged other architects, some of whom claimed that it could not be built. In a structural engineering feat, Brunelleschi designed two shells bound together by ribs and tension chains, further reinforced by the use of herringbone brickwork. The dome was completed in 1436 and became a model for Michelangelo's later dome for St. Peter's in Rome.

ABSTRACT ART

Abstract art, also called nonobjective or nonrepresentational art, is a form of painting, sculpture, or graphic art in which the portrayal of things from the visible world plays no part. All art consists largely of elements that can be called abstract—elements of form, colour, line, tone, and texture. Before the 20th century these abstract elements were employed by artists to describe, illustrate, or reproduce the world of nature and of human civilization—and exposition dominated expressive function.

Abstract art has its origins in the 19th century. The period characterized by so vast a body of elaborately representational art produced for the sake of illustrating anecdote also produced a number of painters who examined the mechanism of light and visual perception. The period of Romanticism had put forward ideas about art that denied classicism's emphasis on imitation and idealization and had instead stressed the role of imagination and of the unconscious as the essential creative factors. Gradually many painters of this period began to accept the new freedom and the new responsibilities implied in the coalescence of these attitudes. Maurice Denis's statement of 1890, "It should be remembered that a picture—before being a war-horse, a nude, or an anecdote of some sort—is essentially a flat surface covered with colours assembled in a certain order," summarizes the feeling among the Symbolist and Postimpressionist artists of his time.

All the major movements of the first two decades of the 20th century, including Fauvism, Expressionism, Cubism, and Futurism, in some way emphasized the gap between art and natural appearances.

There is, however, a deep distinction between abstracting from appearances, even if to the point of unrecognizability, and making works of art out of forms not drawn from the visible world. During the four or five years preceding World War I, such artists as Robert Delaunay, Wassily Kandinsky, Kazimir Malevich, and Vladimir Tatlin turned to fundamentally abstract art. (Kandinsky is generally regarded as having been the first modern artist to paint purely abstract pictures containing no recognizable objects, in 1910–11.) The majority of even the progressive artists regarded the abandonment of every degree of representation with disfavour, however. During World War I the emergence of the de Stijl group in the Netherlands and of the Dada group in Zürich further widened the spectrum of abstract art.

Abstract art did not flourish between World Wars I and II. Beset by totalitarian politics and by art movements

Abstract painting by Willem de Kooning, 1949. G. Dagli Orto/DeAgostini Picture Library

placing renewed emphasis on imagery, such as Surrealism and socially critical Realism, it received little notice. But after World War II an energetic American school of abstract painting called Abstract Expressionism emerged and had wide influence. Since the 1950s abstract art has been an accepted and widely practiced approach within European and American painting and sculpture. Abstract art has puzzled and indeed confused many people, but for

MAURICE DENIS
(b. Nov. 25, 1870, Granville, France—d. Nov. 13, 1943, Paris)

The French painter Maurice Denis was one of the leading artists and theoreticians of the Symbolist movement.

Denis studied at the Académie Julian (1888) under Jules Lefebvre and at the École des Beaux-Arts. Reacting against the naturalistic tendencies of Impressionism, Denis fell under the influence of the work of Paul Gauguin, whose style was also much admired by Denis's fellow students Paul Sérusier, Édouard Vuillard, Pierre Bonnard, and Ker Xavier Roussel. With these friends, Denis joined in the Symbolist movement and its later offshoot, the group of painters collectively called the Nabis. The quasi-mystical attitude of the Nabis was perfectly suited to Denis's highly religious nature.

Later, however, after visiting Italy, Denis became greatly influenced by the works of the great Italian fresco painters of the 14th and 15th centuries and began to place emphasis on subject matter, traditional perspective, and modeling, as in *Homage à Cézanne* (1901). Denis's monumental mural decorations are to be seen in many French churches as well as on the ceiling of the Champs Élysées Theatre in Paris. In 1919 he, along with Georges Devallières, founded the Studios of Sacred Art. His later work was one of the chief forces in the revival of religious art in France.

those who have accepted its nonreferential language there is no doubt as to its value and achievements.

IMPRESSIONISM

The major movement known as Impressionism (French: Impressionnisme) developed chiefly in France during the late 19th and early 20th centuries. Impressionist paintings were produced between about 1867 and 1886 by a group of artists who shared a set of related approaches and techniques. The most conspicuous characteristic of Impressionism was an attempt to accurately and objectively record visual reality in terms of transient effects of light and colour. The principal Impressionist painters were Claude Monet, Pierre Auguste Renoir, Camille Pissarro, Alfred Sisley, Berthe Morisot, Armand Guillaumin, and Frédéric Bazille, who worked together, influenced each other, and exhibited together independently. Edgar Degas and Paul Cézanne also painted in an Impressionist style for a time in the early 1870s. The established painter Édouard Manet, whose work in the 1860s greatly influenced Monet and others of the group, himself adopted the Impressionist approach about 1873.

These artists became dissatisfied early in their careers with academic teaching's emphasis on depicting a historical or mythological subject matter with literary or anecdotal overtones. They also rejected the conventional imaginative or idealizing treatments of academic painting. By the late 1860s, Manet's art reflected a new aesthetic—which was to be a guiding force in Impressionist work—in which the importance of the traditional subject matter was downgraded and attention was shifted to the artist's manipulation of colour, tone, and texture as ends in themselves. In Manet's painting the subject became a vehicle for the artful composition of areas of flat colour, and perspectival depth was minimized so that the viewer would look at the surface patterns and relationships of the picture rather than into the illusory three-dimensional space it created. About the same time, Monet was influenced by the innovative painters Eugene Boudin and J.R. Jongkind, who depicted fleeting effects of sea and sky by means of highly coloured and texturally varied methods of paint application. The Impressionists also adopted Boudin's practice of painting entirely out-of-doors while looking at the actual scene, instead of finishing up his painting from sketches in the studio, as was the conventional practice.

In the late 1860s Monet, Pissarro, Renoir, and others began painting landscapes and river scenes in which they tried to dispassionately record the colours and forms of objects as they appeared in natural light at a given time. These artists abandoned the traditional landscape palette of muted greens, browns, and grays and instead painted in a lighter, sunnier, more brilliant key. They began by painting the play of light upon water and the reflected colours of its ripples, trying to reproduce the manifold and animated effects of sunlight and shadow and of direct and reflected light that they observed. In their efforts to reproduce immediate visual impressions as registered on the retina, they abandoned the use of grays and blacks in shadows as inaccurate and used complementary colours instead. More importantly, they learned to build up objects out of discrete flecks and dabs of pure harmonizing or contrasting colour, thus evoking the broken-hued brilliance and the variations of hue produced by sunlight and its reflections. Forms in their pictures lost their clear outlines and became dematerialized, shimmering and vibrating in a re-creation of actual outdoor conditions. And finally, traditional formal compositions were abandoned in favour of a more casual and less contrived

CLAUDE MONET

(b. Nov. 14, 1840, Paris, France—d. Dec. 5, 1926, Giverny)

The French landscape painter Claude Monet was the initiator, leader, and unswerving advocate of the Impressionist style. He spent his early years in Le Havre, where his first teacher, Eugène Boudin, taught him to paint in the open air (plein air). Moving to Paris, he formed lifelong friendships with other young painters, including Pierre-Auguste Renoir, Alfred Sisley, and Paul Cézanne. Beginning in the mid 1860s, Monet pursued a new style; rather than trying to reproduce faithfully the scene before him in detail, he recorded on the spot the impression that relaxed, momentary vision might receive. In 1874 he helped organize an independent exhibition, apart from the official Salon, of work he and his friends produced in this style. Throughout the 1870s, Monet and the other Impressionists explored this style and exhibited together. Even when the original group had dissolved, Monet continued with the same fervour to scrutinize nature. In his mature works Monet developed his method of producing a series of several studies of the same motif (e.g., haystacks, 1891, and Rouen Cathedral, 1894), changing canvases as the light or his interest shifted. In 1893, in the garden at his home in Giverny, Monet created the water-lily pond that inspired his most famous works, the lyrical *Nymphéas* ("Water Lilies") paintings. Wildly popular retrospective exhibitions of his work toured the world during the last decades of the 20th century and established his unparalleled public appeal, sustaining his reputation as one of the most significant and popular figures in the modern Western painting tradition.

disposition of objects within the picture frame. The Impressionists extended their new techniques to depict landscapes, trees, houses, and even urban street scenes and railroad stations.

In 1874 the group held its first show, independent of the official Salon of the French Academy, which had consistently rejected most of their works. Monet's painting *Impression: Sunrise* (1872) earned them the initially derisive name "Impressionists" from the journalist Louis Leroy writing in the satirical magazine *Le Charivari* in 1874. The artists themselves soon adopted the name as descriptive of their intention to accurately convey visual "impressions." They held seven subsequent shows, the last in 1886. During that time they continued to develop their own personal and individual styles. All, however, affirmed in their work the principles of freedom of technique, a personal rather than a conventional approach to subject matter, and the truthful reproduction of nature.

By the mid-1880s the Impressionist group had begun to dissolve as each painter increasingly pursued his own aesthetic interests and principles. In its short existence, however, it had accomplished a revolution in the history of art, providing a technical starting point for the Postimpressionist artists Paul Cézanne, Edgar Degas, Paul Gauguin, Vincent van Gogh, and Georges Seurat and freeing all subsequent Western painting from traditional techniques and approaches to subject matter.

EXPRESSIONISM

An artistic style in direct contrast with Impressionism, known as Expressionism, seeks to capture not objective reality but rather the artist's subjective emotions and responses aroused by objects and events. The artist accomplishes this aim through distortion, exaggeration, primitivism, and fantasy and through the vivid, jarring, violent, or dynamic application of formal elements. In a broader sense Expressionism is one of the main currents of art in the later 19th and the 20th centuries, and its qualities of highly subjective, personal, spontaneous self-expression are typical of a wide range of modern artists and art movements. Expressionism can also be seen as a permanent tendency in Germanic and Nordic art from at least the European Middle Ages, particularly in times of social change or spiritual crisis, and in this sense it forms the converse of the rationalist and classicizing tendencies of Italy and later of France.

THE VISUAL ARTS

More specifically, Expressionism as a distinct style or movement refers to a number of German artists, as well as Austrian, French, and Russian ones, who became active in the years before World War I and remained so throughout much of the interwar period.

The roots of the German Expressionist school lay in the works of Vincent van Gogh, Edvard Munch, and James Ensor, each of whom in the period 1885–1900 evolved a highly personal painting style. These artists used the expressive possibilities of colour and line to explore dramatic and emotion-laden themes, to convey the qualities of fear, horror, and the grotesque, or simply to celebrate nature with hallucinatory intensity. They broke away from the literal representation of nature in order to express more subjective outlooks or states of mind.

The second and principal wave of Expressionism began about 1905, when a group of German artists led by Ernst Ludwig Kirchner formed a loose association called Die

Starry Night, *oil on canvas by Vincent van Gogh, 1888; in the Musée d'Orsay, Paris.* Time Life Pictures/Getty Images

Brücke. The group included Erich Heckel, Karl Schmidt-Rottluff, and Fritz Bleyl. These painters were in revolt against what they saw as the superficial naturalism of academic Impressionism. They wanted to reinfuse German art with a spiritual vigour they felt it lacked, and they sought to do this through an elemental, primitive, highly personal and spontaneous expression. Die Brücke's original members were soon joined by Emil Nolde, Max Pechstein, and Otto Müller. The Expressionists were influenced by their predecessors of the 1890s and were also interested in African wood carvings and the works of such northern European medieval and Renaissance artists as Albrecht Dürer, Matthias Grünewald, and Albrecht Altdorfer. They were also aware of Neo-Impressionism, Fauvism, and other recent movements.

Dance Around the Golden Calf, *oil painting by Emil Nolde, 1910; in the Bayerische Staatsgemaldesammlungen, Munich.* Courtesy of the Nolde-Foundation; photograph, Bayerische Staatsgemaldesammlungen, Munich

The German Expressionists soon developed a style notable for its harshness, boldness, and visual intensity. They used jagged, distorted lines; crude, rapid brushwork; and jarring colours to depict urban street scenes and other contemporary subjects in crowded, agitated compositions notable for their instability and their emotionally charged atmosphere. Many of their works express frustration, anxiety, disgust, discontent, violence, and generally a sort of frenetic intensity of feeling in response to the ugliness, the crude banality, and the possibilities and contradictions that they discerned in modern life. Woodcuts, with their thick jagged lines and harsh tonal contrasts, were one of the favourite media of the German Expressionists.

Indian and Woman, *oil on canvas by Max Pechstein, 1910; in the Saint Louis Art Museum, St. Louis, Missouri.* The Saint Louis Art Museum, bequest of Morton D. May

The works of Die Brücke artists stimulated Expressionism in other parts of Europe. Oskar Kokoschka and Egon Schiele of Austria adopted their tortured brushwork and angular lines, and Georges Rouault and Chaim Soutine in France each developed painting styles marked by intense emotional expression and the violent distortion of figural subject matter. The painter Max Beckmann, the graphic artist Käthe Kollwitz, and the sculptors Ernst Barlach and Wilhelm Lehmbruck, all of Germany, also worked in Expressionist modes. The artists belonging to the group known as Der Blaue Reiter are sometimes regarded as Expressionists, although their art is generally lyrical and abstract, less overtly emotional, more harmonious, and more concerned with formal and pictorial problems than that of Die Brücke artists.

Prone Young Woman with Black Stocking, *gouache, watercolour, and pencil on paper by Egon Schiele, 1913.* In a private collection

LITERATURE AND DRAMA

The tendencies and characteristics of Expressionism in the visual arts also extended to literature and other forms. Literary Expressionism was chiefly a reaction against materialism, complacent bourgeois prosperity, rapid mechanization and urbanization, and the domination of the family within pre-World War I European society. It was the dominant literary movement in Germany during and immediately after World War I.

In forging a drama of social protest, Expressionist writers aimed to convey their ideas through a new style. Their concern was with general truths rather than with particular situations, hence they explored in their plays the predicaments of representative symbolic types rather than of fully developed individualized characters. Emphasis was laid not on the outer world, which is merely sketched in and barely defined in place or time, but on the internal, on an individual's mental state; hence the imitation of life is replaced in Expressionist drama by the ecstatic evocation of states of mind. The leading character in an Expressionist play often pours out his or her woes in long monologues couched in a concentrated, elliptical, almost telegrammatic language that explores youth's spiritual malaise, its revolt against the older generation, and the various political or revolutionary remedies that present themselves. The leading character's inner development is explored through a series of loosely linked tableaux, or "stations," during which he revolts against traditional values and seeks a higher spiritual vision of life.

August Strindberg and Frank Wedekind were notable forerunners of Expressionist drama, but the first full-fledged Expressionist play was Reinhard Johannes Sorge's *Der Bettler* ("The Beggar"), which was written in 1912 but not performed until 1917. The other principal playwrights of the movement were Georg Kaiser, Ernst Toller, Paul Kornfeld, Fritz von Unruh, Walter Hasenclever, and Reinhard Goering, all of Germany.

Expressionist poetry, which arose at the same time as its dramatic counterpart, was similarly nonreferential and sought an ecstatic, hymnlike lyricism that would have considerable associative power. This condensed, stripped-down poetry, utilizing strings of nouns and a few adjectives and infinitive verbs, eliminated narrative and description to get at the essence of feeling. The principal Expressionist poets were Georg Heym, Ernst Stadler, August Stramm, Gottfried Benn, Georg Trakl, and Else Lasker-Schüler of Germany and the Czech poet Franz Werfel. The dominant theme of Expressionist verse was horror over urban life and apocalyptic visions of the collapse of civilization. Some poets were pessimistic and contented themselves with satirizing bourgeois values, while others were more concerned with political and social reform and expressed the hope for a coming revolution. Outside Germany, playwrights who used Expressionist dramatic techniques included the American authors Eugene O'Neill and Elmer Rice.

OTHER ARTS

Strongly influenced by Expressionist stagecraft, the earliest Expressionist films set out to convey through decor the subjective mental state of the protagonist. The most famous of these films is Robert Wiene's *The Cabinet of Dr. Caligari* (1919), in which a madman relates his understanding of how he came to be in the asylum. The misshapen streets and buildings of the set are projections of his own crazy universe, and the other characters have been abstracted through makeup and dress into visual symbols.

Still from Robert Wiene's classic Expressionist film The Cabinet of Dr. Caligari *(1919)*. From a private collection

The film's morbid evocation of horror, menace, and anxiety and the dramatic, shadowy lighting and bizarre sets became a stylistic model for Expressionist films by several major German directors. Paul Wegener's second version of *The Golem* (1920), F.W. Murnau's *Nosferatu* (1922), and Fritz Lang's *Metropolis* (1927), among other films, present pessimistic visions of social collapse or explore the ominous duality of human nature and its capacity for monstrous personal evil.

While some classify the composer Arnold Schoenberg as an Expressionist because of his contribution to the Blaue Reiter almanac, musical Expressionism seems to have found its most natural outlet in opera. Among early examples of such Expressionist works are Paul Hindemith's operatic settings of Kokoschka's proto-Expressionist drama, *Mörder, Hoffnung der Frauen* (1919), and August Stramm's *Sancta Susanna* (1922). Most outstanding of the Expressionist operas, however, are two by Alban Berg: *Wozzeck,* performed in 1925, and *Lulu,* which was not performed in its entirety until 1979.

The decline of Expressionism was hastened by the vagueness of its longing for a better world, by its use of highly poetic language, and in general the intensely personal and inaccessible nature of its mode of presentation. The partial reestablishment of stability in Germany after 1924 and the growth of more overtly political styles of social realism hastened the movement's decline in the late 1920s. Expressionism was definitively killed by the advent of the Nazis to power in 1933. They branded the work of almost all Expressionists as degenerate and forbade them

OSKAR KOKOSCHKA
(b. March 1, 1886, Pöchlarn, Austria—d. Feb. 22, 1980, Villeneuve, Switz.)

The Austrian painter and writer Oskar Kokoschka was one of the leading exponents of Expressionism. After 1912 his portraits came to be painted with increasingly broader strokes of more varied colour and heavier outlines. While recovering from a wound received in World War I, he wrote, produced, and staged three plays; his *Orpheus and Eurydice* (1918) became an opera by Ernst Krenek (1926). The landscapes he produced during 10 years of teaching and travel mark the second peak of his career. Shortly before World War II he fled to London, where his paintings became increasingly political and antifascist. He continued his political art after moving to Switzerland in 1953.

to exhibit or publish and eventually even to work. Many Expressionists went into exile in the United States and other countries.

CUBISM

One of the most influential visual arts styles of the 20th century was created principally by the artists Pablo Picasso and Georges Braque in Paris between 1907 and 1914. Cubism emphasized the flat, two-dimensional surface of the picture plane, rejecting the traditional techniques of perspective, foreshortening, modeling, and chiaroscuro, and refuting time-honoured theories that art should imitate nature. Cubist painters were not bound to copying form, texture, colour, and space; instead, they presented a new reality in paintings that depicted radically fragmented objects.

ORIGINS OF THE STYLE

The volumetric landscapes of Paul Cézanne, whose paintings reflected his belief that everything in nature was modeled after the sphere, the cone, and the cylinder, were one of the chief inspirations for Cubism. Cézanne managed to give his landscapes the exciting and radically new quality of simultaneously representing deep space and flat design. Even so, the work that stands at the forefront of Cubism, that presaged the new style, was Picasso's *Les Demoiselles d'Avignon* (1907).

THE FIRST PHASE

Picasso's painting had been produced under the combined influence of African art and Cézanne's *Great Bathers*.

Enigmatic and paradigm-shifting, the picture presents the forms of five female nudes in fractured, angular shapes. As in Cézanne's work, perspective is rendered through colour, with the warm reddish-browns advancing and the cool blues receding. Those who saw it were astonished and perplexed, not only by the arbitrary disruption in the right-hand part of the picture of the continuity that had always united an image but also by its defiant unloveliness, which made it plain that the traditional beauties of art, the appeal of the subject, and the credibility of its imitation were now, at any rate to Picasso, finally irrelevant. Picasso himself was not sure what to think of the picture; it was not reproduced for 15 years or publicly exhibited for 30. Nevertheless, the effect on his associates was profound.

Henri Matisse and Braque, who, unlike Picasso, had been experimenting with Fauvism, immediately started painting female nudes of similar stridency. Subsequently, however, Matisse turned back toward relatively traditional forms and the flooding colour that chiefly concerned him. Braque, on the other hand, became more and more closely associated with Picasso. When the critic Louis Vauxcelles derided Braque's 1908 work *Houses at L'Estaque* as being composed of cubes, Cubism was born. In the first phase, lasting into 1909, the focus of the Cubists was the accentuation and the disruption of planes. In the next two years Braque went to paint at Cézanne's old sites, and the inspiration of Cézanne's style at this stage is indubitable.

THE SECOND PHASE: ANALYTICAL CUBISM

The movement's development from 1910 to 1912 is often referred to as Analytical Cubism. During this period, the irrelevance of the subject, in any integral form, became evident. It was no longer necessary to travel in search of a motif; any still life would do as well. The essence of the picture was in the treatment. If Analytical Cubism analyzed anything, it was the nature of the treatment. The great Cubist pictures were meditations on the intrinsic character of the detached Cézannesque facets and contours, out of which the almost-illegible images were built. Indeed, the objects were not so much depicted as denoted by linear signs, a spiral for the scrolled head of a violin or the trademark from a label for a bottle, which were superimposed on the shifting, half-contradictory flux of shapes. The element of paradox is essential; even when it approaches monumental grandeur, Cubism has a quality that eludes solemn exposition. Subtle and elegant geometric puns build up into massive demonstrations of pictorial structure, demonstrations that its complex parallels and conjunctions build nothing so firmly and so memorably as the picture itself. This proof that figurative art creates an independent reality is the central proposition of modern art, and it has had a profound effect not only on painting and sculpture, but also on the intellectual climate of the age.

Also during this period, the work of Picasso and Braque became so similar that their paintings are almost indistinguishable. Paintings by both artists show the breaking down, or analysis, of form. Picasso and Braque favoured right-angle and straight-line construction, though occasionally some areas of their paintings appear sculptural, as in Picasso's *Girl with a Mandolin* (1910). They simplified their colour schemes to a nearly monochromatic scale (hues of tan, brown, gray, cream, green, or blue were preferred) in order not to distract the viewer from the artist's primary interest—the structure of form itself. The monochromatic colour scheme was suited to the presentation of complex, multiple views of the object, which was reduced to overlapping opaque and transparent planes.

THE THIRD PHASE: SYNTHETIC CUBISM

The experimental investigation of what reality meant in artistic terms then took a daring turn that was unparalleled since pictorial illusion had been isolated five centuries earlier. The Cubists proceeded to embody real material from the actual world within the picture. They included first stenciled lettering, then pasted paper, and later solid objects; the reality of art as they saw it absorbed them all. This assemblage of material, called collage, led in 1912 to the third phase of the movement, Synthetic Cubism, which continued until 1914. The textured and

GEORGES BRAQUE
(b. May 13, 1882, Argenteuil, France—d. Aug. 31, 1963, Paris)

The revolutionary French painter Georges Braque, together with Pablo Picasso, was one of the most influential figures of the 20th century. He studied painting in Le Havre, then in Paris at a private academy and briefly at the École des Beaux-Arts. Though his earliest works were influenced by Impressionism, his first important paintings (1905–07) were in the style of Fauvism pioneered by André Derain and Henri Matisse; in 1907 he exhibited and sold six of these paintings at the Salon des Indépendants. Abandoning Fauvism in 1907, he worked with Picasso to invent Cubism. He painted mostly still lifes featuring geometric shapes and low-key colour harmonies. In 1912 he introduced the collage, or *papier collé* (pasted-paper picture), by attaching three pieces of wallpaper to the drawing *Fruit Dish and Glass*. By the 1920s he was a prosperous, well-established modern master. In 1923 and 1925 he designed stage sets for Serge Diaghilev's Ballets Russes. In 1961 he became the first living artist to have his works exhibited in the Louvre.

patterned planes were composed into forms more like pictorial objects in themselves than recognizable figurations. In the later work of Picasso and Braque, it is again possible to construe their pictorial code as referring plainly to the objective world. The message of Cubism remained the same: meaning had been shown to reside in the structure of the style, the basic geometry implied in the Postimpressionist handling of life. The message spread rapidly.

The first theoretical work on the movement, *On Cubism*, by the French painters Albert Gleizes and Jean Metzinger, was published in 1912. They argued that geometric and mathematical principles of general validity could be deduced from the style. An exhibition in the same year represented all Cubism's adherents except the two creators. The exhibition was called the Section d'Or ("Golden Section"), after a mathematical division of a line into two sections with a certain proportion to each other. Among the exhibitors were the Spaniard Juan Gris and the Frenchman Fernand Léger, who in their subsequent work were both concerned with combining the basic scheme of Synthetic Cubism with the renewed sense of a coherent subject.

MODERNISM

Modernism in the arts is a movement that made a radical break with the past and the concurrent search for new forms of expression. Modernism fostered a period of experimentation in the arts from the late 19th to the mid-20th century, particularly in the years following World War I.

In an era characterized by industrialization, rapid social change, and advances in science and the social sciences (e.g., Freudian theory), Modernists felt a growing alienation incompatible with Victorian morality, optimism, and convention. New ideas in psychology, philosophy, and political theory kindled a search for new modes of expression.

MODERNISM IN LITERATURE

The Modernist impulse is fueled in various literatures by industrialization and urbanization and by the search for an authentic response to a much-changed world. Although prewar works by Henry James, Joseph Conrad, and other writers are considered Modernist, Modernism as a literary movement is typically associated with the period after World War I. The enormity of the war had undermined humankind's faith in the foundations of Western society and culture, and postwar Modernist literature reflected a sense of disillusionment and fragmentation. A primary theme of T.S. Eliot's long poem *The Waste Land* (1922), a seminal Modernist work, is the search for redemption and renewal in a sterile and spiritually empty landscape. With its fragmentary images and obscure allusions, the poem is typical of Modernism in requiring the reader to take an active role in interpreting the text.

The publication of the Irish writer James Joyce's *Ulysses* in 1922 was a landmark event in the development of Modernist literature. Dense, lengthy, and controversial, the novel details the events of one day in the life of three Dubliners through a technique known as stream of consciousness, which commonly ignores orderly sentence structure and incorporates fragments of thought in an attempt to capture the flow of characters' mental processes. Portions of the book were considered obscene, and *Ulysses* was banned for many years in English-speaking countries.

Other European and American Modernist authors whose works rejected chronological and narrative continuity include Virginia Woolf, Marcel Proust, Gertrude Stein, and William Faulkner.

EZRA POUND

(b. Oct. 30, 1885, Hailey, Idaho, U.S.—d. Nov. 1, 1972, Venice, Italy)

U.S. poet and critic Ezra Pound was a supremely discerning and energetic entrepreneur of the arts who did more than any other single figure to advance a "modern" movement in English and American literature. Pound attended Hamilton College and the University of Pennsylvania, where he studied various languages. In 1908 he sailed for Europe, where he would spend most of his life. He soon became a leader of Imagism and a dominant influence in Anglo-American verse, helping promote writers such as William Butler Yeats, James Joyce, Hilda Doolittle (H.D.), Ernest Hemingway, Robert Frost, D.H. Lawrence, and T.S. Eliot, whose *The Waste Land* he brilliantly edited. He became a quintessential Modernist. After World War I he published two of his most important poems, *Homage to Sextus Propertius* (1919) and *Hugh Selwyn Mauberley* (1920). He also began publishing *The Cantos*, an epic sequence of poems, which would remain his major poetic occupation throughout his life. With the onset of the Great Depression, he increasingly pursued his interest in history and economics, became obsessed with monetary reform, and declared his admiration for Benito Mussolini. In World War II he made pro-fascist radio broadcasts; detained by U.S. forces for treason in 1945, he was initially held at Pisa; *The Pisan Cantos* (1948), written there, are notably moving. He was subsequently held in an American mental hospital until 1958, when he returned to Italy. *The Cantos* (1970) collects his 117 completed cantos.

The term Modernism is also used to refer to literary movements other than the European and American movement of the early to mid-20th century. In Latin American literature, Modernismo arose in the late 19th century in the works of Manuel Gutiérrez Nájera and José Martí. The movement, which continued into the early 20th century, reached its peak in the poetry of Rubén Darío.

MODERNISM IN OTHER ARTS AND ARCHITECTURE

Composers, including Arnold Schoenberg, Igor Stravinsky, and Anton Webern, sought new solutions within new forms and used as-yet-untried approaches to tonality. In dance a rebellion against both balletic and interpretive traditions had its roots in the work of Émile Jaques-Delcroze, Rudolf Laban, and Loie Fuller. Each of them examined a specific aspect of dance—such as the elements of the human form in motion or the impact of theatrical context—and helped bring about the era of modern dance. In the visual arts the roots of Modernism are often traced back to painter Édouard Manet, who, beginning in the 1860s, broke away from inherited notions of perspective, modeling, and subject matter. The avant-garde movements that followed—including Impressionism, Postimpressionism, Cubism, Futurism, Expressionism, Constructivism, de Stijl, and Abstract Expressionism—are generally defined as Modernist.

Over the span of these movements, artists increasingly focused on the intrinsic qualities of their media—e.g., line, form, and colour—and moved away from inherited notions of art. By the beginning of the 20th century, architects also had increasingly abandoned past styles and conventions in favour of a form of architecture based on essential functional concerns. They were helped by advances in building technologies such as the steel frame and the curtain wall. In the period after World War I these tendencies became codified as the International style, which utilized simple geometric shapes and unadorned facades and which abandoned any use of historical reference; the steel-and-glass buildings of Ludwig Mies van der Rohe and Le Corbusier embodied this style. In the mid-to-late 20th century this style manifested itself in clean-lined, unadorned glass skyscrapers and mass housing projects.

HARMONY

When used in reference to music, harmony is the sound of two or more notes heard simultaneously. Usually it refers to the extensively developed system of chords and the rules that allow or forbid relations between chords that characterize Western music.

Musical sound may be regarded as having both horizontal and vertical components. The horizontal aspects are those that proceed during time such as melody, counterpoint (or the interweaving of simultaneous melodies), and rhythm. The vertical aspect comprises the sum total of what is happening at any given moment: the result either of notes that sound against each other in counterpoint, or, as in the case of a melody and accompaniment, of the underpinning of chords that the composer gives the principal notes of the melody. In this analogy, harmony is primarily a vertical phenomenon. It also has a horizontal aspect, however, since the composer not only creates a harmonic sound at any given moment but also joins these sounds in a succession of harmonies that gives the music its distinctive personality.

Melody and rhythm can exist without harmony. By far the greatest part of the world's music is nonharmonic.

Many highly sophisticated musical styles, such as those of India and China, consist basically of unharmonized melodic lines and their rhythmic organization. In only a few instances of folk and primitive music are simple chords specifically cultivated. Harmony in the Western sense is a comparatively recent invention having a rather limited geographic spread. It arose less than a millennium ago in the music of western Europe and is embraced today only in those musical cultures that trace their origins to that area.

The concept of harmony and harmonic relationships is not an arbitrary creation. It is based on certain relationships among musical tones that the human ear accepts almost reflexively and that are also expressible through elementary scientific investigation. These relationships were first demonstrated by the Greek philosopher Pythagoras in the 6th century BCE. In one of his most famous experiments, a stretched string was divided by simple arithmetical ratios (1:2, 2:3, 3:4, . . .) and plucked. By this means he demonstrated that the intervals, or distances between tones, that the string sounded before and after it was divided are the most fundamental intervals the ear perceives. These intervals, which occur in the music of nearly all cultures, either in melody or in harmony, are the octave, the fifth, and the fourth. (An octave, as from C to the C above it, encompasses eight white notes on a piano keyboard, or a comparable mixture of white and black notes. A fifth, as from C to G, encompasses five white notes; a fourth, as from C to F, four white notes.) In Pythagoras's experiment, for example, a string sounding C when cut in half sounds C, or the note an octave above it. In other words, a string divided in the ratio 1:2 yields the octave (c) of its fundamental note (C). Likewise the ratio 2:3 (or two-thirds of its length) yields the fifth, and the ratio 3:4, the fourth.

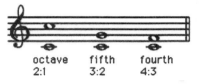

These notes—the fundamental and the notes a fourth, fifth, and octave above it—form the primary musical intervals, the cornerstones on which Western harmony is built.

THE ROOTS OF HARMONY

The organized system of Western harmony as practiced from *c.* 1650 to *c.* 1900 evolved from earlier musical practices: from the polyphony—music in several voices, or parts—of the late Middle Ages and the Renaissance and, ultimately, from the strictly melodic music of the Middle Ages that gave rise to polyphony. The organization of medieval music, in turn, derives from the medieval theorists' fragmented knowledge of ancient Greek music.

Although the music of ancient Greece consisted entirely of melodies sung in unison or, in the case of voices of unequal range, at the octave, the term *harmony* occurs frequently in the writings on music at the time. Leading theorists such as Aristoxenus (flourished 4th century BCE) provide a clear picture of a musical style consisting of a wide choice of "harmonies," and Plato and Aristotle discuss the ethical and moral value of one "harmony" over another.

In Greek music a "harmony" was the succession of tones within an octave—in modern usage, a scale. The Greek system embraced seven "harmonies," or scale types, distinguished from one another by their particular order of succession of tones and semitones (i.e., whole steps and half steps). These "harmonies" were later erroneously called modes, a broader term involving the characteristic contours of a melody, as well as the scale it used.

HARMONY BEFORE THE COMMON PRACTICE PERIOD

By the 9th century the practice arose in many churches of performing portions of plainchant melodies with an added, harmonizing voice—possibly as a means of greater emphasis, or of reinforcing the sound to carry through the larger churches that were being built at the time. This harmonizing technique, called organum, is the first true example of harmony. The first instances were extremely simple, consisting of adding a voice that exactly paralleled the original melody at the interval of a fourth or fifth (parallel organum).

Sit glo - ri - a Do - mi - ni in sae - cu - la

From the booklet edited by Gerald Abraham
accompanying *The History of Music in Sound*
(booklet published by Oxford University Press);
examples reprinted with permission of the publisher

Within a short time the new technique was explored in far greater diversity. Added harmonic lines took on melodic independence, often moving in opposite, or contrary, motion to the given melody. This style was called free organum. In such cases it was impossible to maintain at all times the accepted harmonies of fourth, fifth, and octave. These intervals were considered consonances— i.e., intervals that because of their clear sonority, implied repose, or resolution of tension. In free organum they were used at the principal points of articulation: the beginnings and ends of phrases and at key words in the text. In between occurred other intervals that were relatively dissonant; i.e., they implied less repose and more tension. In the following example of free organum, dissonances are marked by asterisks.

Re - gi   re - gum   glo - ri - o - so

From the booklet edited by Gerald Abraham
accompanying *The History of Music in Sound*
(booklet published by Oxford University Press);
examples reprinted with permission of the publisher

Free organum is an early example of harmonic motion from repose to tension to repose, basic to Western harmony. The emphasis on consonances at the end of compositions set the final points of arrival in strong relief and reinforced the idea of the cadence, or the finality of the keynote of a mode (on which pieces normally ended).

THE RISE OF THE INTERVALS OF THE THIRD AND THE SIXTH

Until the late 14th century the attitude toward consonance, especially among continental composers, adhered largely to the Pythagorean ideal, which accepted as consonances only intervals expressible in the simplest numerical ratios—fourths, fifths, and octaves. But in England the interval of the third (as from C to E) had been in common use for some time, although it is not expressible as such a simple ratio. A kind of English organum known as gymel, in which the voices move parallel to each other at the interval of a third, existed in the late 12th century; and in the famous *Sumer is icumen in* canon of the 13th century, a remarkably elaborate piece for the time, the harmonic style is almost entirely centred on thirds. The sixth (as from E to C), an interval closely related to the third, was also common in English music. These two intervals sounded much sweeter than did the hollow-sounding fourths, fifths, and octaves.

By the early 15th century, in part because of the visits of the illustrious English composer John Dunstable to the courts of northern France, the third and sixth became accepted in European music as consonant intervals (prior to this time they were considered mildly dissonant). The result was an enrichment of the harmony in musical compositions.

This was a time, too, of a developing awareness of tonality, the concept of developing a composition with a definite keynote used as a point of departure at the beginning and as a point of arrival at the final cadence.

At this time there also began the tendency by composers to think of harmony as a "vertical" phenomenon, to regard the sound of notes heard simultaneously as a definite entity. Although the basic style of composition was primarily linear—i.e., concerned with counterpoint—the chords that emerged from the coincidences of notes in contrapuntal lines took on a personality of their own. One phenomenon that bears out this development is faux-bourdon (French: "false bass"), or, in England, faburden. The following example illustrates English faburden of about 1300.

From the booklet edited by Gerald Abraham
accompanying *The History of Music in Sound*
(booklet published by Oxford University Press);
examples reprinted with permission of the publisher

This was a musical style in which three voices move parallel to each other; the middle voice consisted of a succession of notes in parallel organum a fourth below the top voice; the lowest voice paralleled the sequence a third below the middle voice, producing a chord such as G–B–E, known as a $^6/_3$, or first inversion, chord. This was originally an English development adopted in the 15th century by continental composers seeking to enrich their harmonies. It combined the continental fondness for "pure" intervals such as the fourth (here, B–E) with the English taste for parallel thirds (here, G–B) and sixths (here, G–E).

The Weakening of the Modes

A final phenomenon in early 15th-century harmonic practice clearly foreshadowed the end of the ancient modal system in favour of the major and minor modes of the later common practice period. The old modes were used by composers of the time, and they persisted to some extent until the end of the 16th century. But their purity became undermined by a growing tendency to introduce additional notes outside the mode. This was achieved by writing either a flat or sharp sign into the manuscript, or by leaving the performer to understand that he was expected to improvise accordingly. The effect of this musica ficta (Latin: "invented music"), as the technique of introducing nonmodal notes was called, was to break down the distinction between modes. A mode owes its distinctive character to its specific pattern of whole and half steps. Introducing sharps and flats upsets the mode's normal pattern by placing half steps at unusual points. In many cases the resulting change made one mode resemble another. For example, adding an F# to the medieval Mixolydian mode (from G to G on the white keys of the piano) made that mode's intervals identical with those of the Ionian mode (from C to C on the white keys), which in turn is identical with the modern major scale.

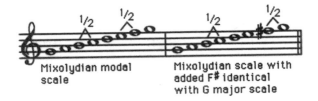

Mixolydian modal scale

Mixolydian scale with added F# identical with G major scale

Likewise, adding a B♭ to the Dorian mode (from D to D) made its intervals equivalent to those of the Aeolian (A to A) mode, which is identical with one form of the modern minor scale. As this practice became increasingly prevalent, the major and minor modes gradually became predominant over the medieval church modes. The process is especially observable in the music of the late Renaissance.

NEW USES OF DISSONANCE

At the same time there emerged a more sophisticated attitude toward dissonance, favouring its use for expressive purposes. By the time of the Flemish Josquin des Prez, the leading composer of the Renaissance, contrapuntal music had assumed a more resonant texture through the use of four-, five-, and six-part writing instead of the older three-part scoring. The increased number of voices led to further enrichment of the harmony. A typical Josquin device using harmony for expressive purposes was the suspension, a type of dissonant harmony that resolved to a consonance. Suspensions arose from the chords occurring in contrapuntal music. In a suspension one note of a chord is sustained while the other voices change to a new chord. In the new chord the sustained, or "suspended," note is dissonant. One or two beats later the suspended voice changes pitch so that it resolves into, or becomes consonant with, the chord of the remaining voices. The following illustration from Jean d'Okeghem's *Missa prolationum* shows a suspension at the cadence.

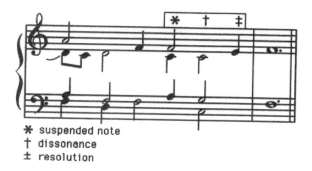

✳ suspended note
† dissonance
± resolution

The suspension, which became a standard musical device, creates tension because the expected harmony is delayed until the suspended voice resolves. Its use as the next to last chord of a cadence, or stopping point, was favoured by composers as a way to enhance, through dissonance resolving to consonance, the sense of completeness of the final chord. The use of suspensions indicates a growing awareness of chords as entities, rather than coincidences, that have expressive potential and of the concept that harmony moves through individual chords toward a goal. This concept was developed in the harmony of the common practice period.

At the end of the 16th century there was an upheaval in musical style. Contrapuntal writing was frequently abandoned, and composers sought out a style that placed greater emphasis on an expressive melodic line accompanied, or supported, by harmonies. This style, called monody, brought about no marked changes in the harmonic language (the particular chords used), although such composers as the Italian Claudio Monteverdi did experiment with a heightened use of dissonance toward expressive ends. The major change at this time was in the conception of harmony. The bass line became the generating force upon which harmonies were built. It was often written out with figures below it to represent the harmonies to be built upon it. From this single line—plus figures, known variously as figured bass, basso continuo, or thorough bass—the accompanying instrumentalists were expected to improvise, or "realize," a full harmonic underpinning for the melody of the topmost voice or voices. In the example below, from the continuo madrigal *Amarilli* by Giulio Caccini, the second line shows the harmonies supplied by the keyboard player.

W.J. Starr and G.F. Devine, *Music Scores Omnibus*, © 1964
figured bass from "Amarilli" by Giulio Caccini, reproduced by
permission of Prentice-Hall, Inc., Englewood Cliffs, N.J.

There was, thus, a polarization between the melodic and bass lines, with everything in the middle regarded as harmonic filling-in. This contrasts markedly with the older concept, in which all voices were regarded as of equal importance, with the harmony resulting from the inter-weaving of all parts.

CLASSICAL WESTERN HARMONY

The approach to harmony according to which chords are purposely built up from their bass note marked the beginning of the common practice period of Western harmony. The transition began around 1600 and was nearly complete by 1650. Certain new concepts became important. These had their roots in the harmonic practices of the late Middle Ages and Renaissance and in the medieval modal system. They include the concepts of key, of functional harmony, and of modulation.

A key is a group of related notes belonging to either a major or minor scale, plus the chords that are formed from those notes, and the hierarchy of relationships among those chords. In a key the tonic, or keynote, such as C in the key of C—and thus the chord built on the keynote—is a focal point toward which all chords and notes in the key gravitate. This is a further development of the idea of a harmonic goal that appeared in the music of the late Renaissance and that ultimately developed from the medieval idea that modes have characteristic final notes.

In the new system keys further assumed relationships to one another. The larger organizational system embracing keys, key relationships, chord relationships, and harmonic goals was called tonality, or the major-minor system of tonality, because the keys were built on major and minor scales. In the tonal system, given chords assumed specific functions in moving toward or away from harmonic goals, and the system assigning goals to all chords was called functional harmony. The main goal was the keynote, or tonic, of the principal, or tonic, key. Modulation, or change of key, became an important factor in composition because it allowed the composer to exploit the listener's ability to sense the relations between keys.

The approach to harmony that emerged about 1650 (the bass-note approach) was soon formalized in one of the most important musical treatises of the common practice period, *Traité de l'harmonie* (1722), by the French composer Jean-Philippe Rameau. The crux of Rameau's theory is the argument that all harmony is based on the "root" or fundamental note of a chord; for example, D. Other notes are placed a third (as D–F or D–F#) and a fifth (as D–A) above the root. A chord formed in this way is a triad (as D–F–A or D–F#–A), the basic chord type of the common practice period. The third and fifth above the triad can be placed within the same octave as the root (close position) or can be spread out over several octaves (open position) in compound intervals such as an octave plus a third or two octaves plus a fifth. A triad can exist in its basic, or root position, with the root as the lowest, or bass, note (as D–F#–A). It can also exist in inversions or rearrangements of its notes placing the third or fifth in the bass, as F#–A–D (first inversion) and A–D–F# (second inversion).

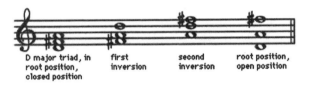

D major triad, in root position, closed position first inversion second inversion root position, open position

Theorists after Rameau observed that inverted chords are less stable than chords in root position; at the end of a composition, for example, they do not have sufficient finality. Although Rameau's monumental work contains certain elements that later practices tended to disprove, his writing remains the basis for the study of common-practice harmony.

JEAN-PHILIPPE RAMEAU
(baptized Sept. 25, 1683, Dijon, France—d. Sept. 12, 1764, Paris)

The French Baroque composer and music theorist Jean-Philippe Rameau is best known today for his harpsichord music, operas, and works in other theatrical genres. In his lifetime, however, he was also a noted music theorist. The son of an organist, he himself held organist posts until age 49. His *Treatise on Harmony* (1722) established him as a major music theorist. In it he asserted that harmony is the basis of music, and that chords, which had been understood principally as collections of intervals above a bass, should instead be seen as representing inversions of more fundamental harmonic entities. From 1733 he wrote a series of highly successful operas, including *Hippolyte et Aricie* (1733) and *The Gallant Indies* (1735), assuring his place as the most important French opera composer since Jean-Baptiste Lully. In the *querelles des bouffons* ("war of the buffoons," 1752–53), a famous artistic controversy about the relative merits of French and Italian opera, Rameau's music exemplified the French style. He also won renown for his many keyboard pieces, mostly composed for harpsichord.

MONTAGE

Perhaps the most essential characteristic of the motion picture is montage, from the French *monter*, "to assemble." *Montage* refers to the editing of the film, the cutting and piecing together of exposed film in a manner that best conveys the intent of the work. Montage is what distinguishes motion pictures from the performing arts, which exist only within a performance. The motion picture, by contrast, uses the performances as the raw material, which is built up as a novel or an essay or a painting, studiously put together piece by piece, with an allowance for trial and error, second thoughts, and, if necessary, reshooting. The order in which the segments of film are presented can have drastically different dramatic effects.

Several major contributions to the theory of montage were made by Soviet directors. After the Russian Revolution of 1917, Soviet films were encouraged for their propaganda value, but film stocks were scarce. Soviet directors carefully studied the films of D. W. Griffith and other masters to make the most effective use of their own meagre resources. One of these early Russian directors, Lev Kuleshov, conducted an experiment involving identical shots of an actor's expressionless face. He inserted it in a film before a shot of a bowl of soup, again before a shot of a child playing, and still again before one of a dead old woman. An unsuspecting audience, which was asked to evaluate the actor's performance, praised his ability to express, respectively, hunger, tenderness, and grief.

Sergey Eisenstein, who excelled both as a director and as a teacher, based much of his theory of film on montage, which he compared to the compounding of characters in Japanese writing. The character for "dog" added to the character for "mouth," he noted, results not merely in "dog's mouth" but in the new concept of "bark"; similarly, film montage results in more than the sum of its parts. Still another great Russian director, Vsevolod I. Pudovkin, also stressed the importance of the carryover in the spectator's mind. Only if an object is presented as part of a synthesis, he said, is it endowed with filmic life.

Three types of montage may be distinguished—narrative, graphic, and ideational. In narrative montage the multifarious images and scenes involve a single subject followed from point to point. In a fiction film, a character or location is explored from multiple angles while the audience builds a comprehensive image of the situation being explored or explained. Graphic montage occurs when shots are juxtaposed not on the basis of their subject matter but because of their physical appearance. Some avant-garde works depend on the spectator's ability to match the graphic relations of assorted images, such as the people, objects, and the shapes of numerical and alphabetical figures in Fernand Léger's *Le Ballet mécanique* (1924) or the torpedoes, swimming seals, and blimps in Bruce Conner's *A Movie* (1958). In graphic montage, cutting usually occurs during shots of movement rather than ones of static action. This cutting on motion facilitates the smooth replacement of one image by the next. In ideational montage, two separate images are related to a third thing, an idea that they help to produce and by which they are governed. In *Stachka* (1924; *Strike*), for example, the director Eisenstein, to whom the theory of ideational montage is credited, effectively conveys the idea of slaughter by intercutting a shot of cattle being butchered with shots of workers being cut down by cavalry.

These three types of montage seldom appear in their pure form. Most ideational montage proceeds on the basis of the graphic similarity of its components, as does narrative montage when relying on graphic cutting to cover its movement. Similarly, the graphic matches between torpedoes, seals, and blimps in *A Movie* ultimately construct an idea of movement toward explosion and destruction. Besides the complications brought about by the intermixing of these types, the addition of the sound track multiplies the possibilities and effects of montage. Eisenstein and Pudovkin referred to such possibilities as "vertical" montage, opposing it to the "horizontal" unrolling of shot after shot. Because sound

SERGEY EISENSTEIN

(b. Jan. 23, 1898, Riga, Latvia—d. Feb. 11, 1948, Moscow, U.S.S.R.)

Sergey Eisenstein was a Russian film director and theorist whose works rank among the classics of film—notably *Potemkin* (1925), *Alexander Nevsky* (1938), and *Ivan the Terrible* (released in two parts, 1944 and 1958). In his concept of film montage, images, perhaps independent of the "main" action, are presented for maximum psychological impact. Eisenstein began his career at a workers' theatre in Moscow in 1920, designing costumes and scenery. After studying stage direction with Vsevolod Meyerhold, he turned to filmmaking. In *Strike* (1924) he introduced his influential concept of film montage, adding startling and often discordant images to the main action to create the maximum psychological impact. He further developed the style in *The Battleship Potemkin* (1925), a commissioned propaganda film that is one of the most influential films of all time. Among his other films are *October* (1928; *Ten Days That Shook the World*) and *The General Line* (1929). He spent a frustrating period in Hollywood and Mexico (1930–33) before he returned to the Soviet Union and made two later classics.

permits the establishment of relations between what is seen and heard at each moment, the film image can no longer be said to be a self-contained unit; it interacts with the sound that accompanies it. Sound relations (including dialogue, music, and ambient noise or effects) may be built in constant rapport with the image track or may create a parallel organization and design that subtends what is seen. In all, montage appears to be the most extraordinary factor differentiating the motion picture from the other arts, and it is the one often singled out as the basis of the medium. Nevertheless, many films, including those of Mizoguchi Kenji of Japan, Roberto Rossellini of Italy, and Jancsó Miklós of Hungary, rely not on montage but on the medium's unique qualities of luminosity, movement, and realism to convey their power and beauty.

THEORY OF ARCHITECTURE

The term *theory of architecture* was originally simply the accepted translation of the Latin term *ratiocinatio* as used by Vitruvius, a Roman architect-engineer of the 1st century CE, to differentiate intellectual from practical knowledge in architectural education; but it has come to signify the total basis for judging the merits of buildings or building projects. Such reasoned judgments are an essential part of the architectural creative process. A building can be designed only by a continuous creative, intellectual dialectic between imagination and reason in the mind of each creator.

Many interpretations have been given to the term *architectural theory* by those who have written or spoken on the topic in the past. Before 1750 every comprehensive treatise or published lecture course on architecture could appropriately be described as a textbook on architectural theory. But, after the changes associated with the Industrial Revolution, the amount of architectural knowledge that could be acquired only by academic study increased to the point where a complete synthesis became virtually impossible in a single volume.

The historical evolution of architectural theory is assessable mainly from manuscripts and published treatises, from critical essays and commentaries, and from the surviving buildings of every epoch. It is thus in no way a type of historical study that can reflect accurately the spirit of each age and in this respect is similar to the history of philosophy itself. Some architectural treatises were intended to publicize novel concepts rather than to state widely accepted ideals. The most idiosyncratic theories could (and often did) exert a wide and sometimes beneficial influence; but the value of these influences is not necessarily related to the extent of this acceptance.

The analysis of surviving buildings provides guidance that requires great caution, since, apart from the impossibility of determining whether or not any particular group of buildings (intact or in ruins) constitutes a reliable sample of the era, any such analyses will usually depend on preliminary evaluations of merit and will be useless unless the extent to which the function, the structure, and the detailing envisaged by the original builders can be correctly re-established. Many erudite studies of antique theories are misleading because they rest on the assumption that the original character and appearance of fragmentary ancient Greek and Hellenistic architectural environments can be adequately deduced from verbal or graphic "reconstructions." Even when buildings constructed before 1500 remain intact, the many textbooks dealing with antique and medieval theories of architecture seldom make qualitative distinctions and generally imply that all surviving antique and medieval buildings were good, if not absolutely perfect.

Nevertheless, the study of the history of architectural philosophy, like that of the history of general philosophy, not only teaches what past generations thought but can help the individual decide how he himself should act and judge. For those desirous of establishing a viable theory of architecture for their own era, it is generally agreed that great stimulus can be found in studying historical evidence and in speculating on the ideals and achievements of those who created this evidence.

DISTINCTION BETWEEN THE HISTORY AND THEORY OF ARCHITECTURE

The distinction between the history and theory of architecture did not emerge until the mid-18th century; indeed, the establishment of two separate academic disciplines was not even nominal until 1818, when separate professorships with these titles were established at the École des Beaux-Arts in Paris. Even then, however, the distinction was seldom scrupulously maintained by either specialist. It is impossible to discuss meaningfully the buildings of the immediate past without discussing the ideals of those who built them, just as it is impossible to discuss the ideals of bygone architects without reference to the structures they designed. Nevertheless, since any two disciplines that are inseparably complementary can at the same time be logically distinguishable, it may be asserted that this particular distinction first became manifest in *Les Ruines des plus beaux monuments de la Grèce* ("The Ruins of the Most Beautiful Monuments of Greece"), written in 1758 by a French architecture student, Julien-David LeRoy. Faced with the problem of discussing Athenian buildings constructed in the time of Vitruvius, he decided to discuss them twice, by treating them separately under two different headings. Before this date, "history" was of architectural importance only as a means of justifying, by reference to classical mythology, the use of certain otherwise irrational elements, such as caryatids. Even Jacques-François Blondel, who in 1750 was probably the first architectural teacher to devote a separate section of his lecture courses to "history," envisaged the subject mainly as an account of the literary references to architecture found in antique manuscripts — an attitude already developed by the 15th-century Renaissance architect Leon Battista Alberti.

The modern concept of architectural history was in fact simply part of a larger trend stimulated by the leading writers of the French Enlightenment, an 18th-century intellectual movement that developed from interrelated conceptions of reason, nature, and man. As a result of discussing constitutional law in terms of its evolution, every branch of knowledge (especially the natural and social sciences) was eventually seen as a historical sequence. In the philosophy of architecture, as in all other kinds of philosophy, the introduction of the historical method not only facilitated the teaching of these subjects but also militated against the elaboration of theoretical speculation. Just as those charged with the responsibility of lecturing on ethics found it very much easier to lecture on the history of ethics, rather than to discuss how a person should or should not act in specific contemporary circumstances, so those who lectured on architectural theory found it easier to recite detailed accounts of what had been done in the past, rather than to recommend practical methods of dealing with current problems.

Moreover, the system of the Paris École des Beaux-Arts (which provided virtually the only organized system of architectural education at the beginning of the 19th century) was radically different from that of the prerevolutionary Académie Royale d'Architecture. Quatremère de Quincy, an Italophile archaeologist who had been trained as a sculptor, united the school of architecture with that of painting and sculpture to form a single organization, so that, although architectural students were ultimately given their own professor of theory, the whole theoretical background of their studies was assimilated to the other two fine arts by lecture courses and textbooks such as Hippolyte Taine's *Philosophie de l'art*, Charles Blanc's *Grammaire des arts du dessin*, and Eugène Guillaume's *Essais sur la théorie du dessin*.

Similarly, whereas before 1750 the uniformity of doctrine (the basic premises of which were ostensibly unchanged since the Renaissance) allowed the professor of architecture to discuss antique and 16th-century buildings as examples of architectural theory and to ignore medieval buildings completely, the mid-19th-century controversy between "medievalists" and "classicists" (the "Battle of the Styles") and the ensuing faith in Eclecticism turned the studies of architectural history into courses on archaeology.

Thus, the attitudes of those scholars who, during the 19th and early 20th centuries, wished to expound a theory of architecture that was neither a philosophy of art nor a history of architecture tended to become highly personal, if not idiosyncratic. By 1950 most theoretical writings concentrated almost exclusively on visual aspects of architecture, thereby identifying the theory of architecture with what, before 1750, would have been regarded as simply that aspect that Vitruvius called *venustas* (i.e., "beauty"). This approach did not necessarily invalidate the conclusions reached; but many valuable ideas then put forward as theories of architecture were only partial theories, in which it was taken for granted that theoretical concepts concerning construction and planning were dealt with in other texts.

DISTINCTION BETWEEN THE THEORY OF ARCHITECTURE AND THE THEORY OF ART

Before embarking on any discussion as to the nature of the philosophy of architecture, it is essential to distinguish between two mutually exclusive theories that affect the whole course of any such speculation. The first theory regards the philosophy of architecture as the application of a general philosophy of art to a particular type of art. The second, on the contrary, regards the philosophy of architecture as a separate study that, though it may well have many characteristics common to the theories of other arts, is generically distinct.

The first notion (i.e., that there exists a generic theory of art of which the theory of architecture is a specific extension) has been widely held since the mid-16th century, when the artist and writer Giorgio Vasari published his *Le vite de' più eccellenti pittori, scultori ed architettori italiani . . .* (*The Lives of the Most Eminent Italian Painters, Sculptors and Architects . . .*). He asserted that painting, sculpture, and architecture are all of common ancestry in that all depend on the ability to draw. This idea became particularly prevalent among English-speaking theorists, since the word design is used to translate both *disegno* ("a drawing") and *concetto* ("a mental plan"). But its main influence on Western thought was due to Italophile Frenchmen, after Louis XIV had been induced to establish in Rome a French Academy modelled on Italian art academies.

As a result of the widespread influence of French culture in the 17th and 18th centuries, the concept of the *beaux arts* (literally "beautiful arts" but usually translated into English as "fine arts") was accepted by Anglo-Saxon theorists as denoting a philosophical entity, to the point where it was generally forgotten that in France itself the architectural profession remained totally aloof from the Académie Royale de Peinture et de Sculpture until they were forced to amalgamate after the French Revolution.

This theory of fine art might not have been so widely adopted but for the development of aesthetics, elaborated after 1750. Thus, when academies of fine art were being established successively in Denmark, Russia, and England on the model of the French Academy in Rome, German philosophers were gradually asserting (1) that it was possible to elaborate a theory of beauty without reference to function (*Zweck*); (2) that any theory of beauty should be applicable to all sensory perceptions, whether visual or auditory; and (3) that the notion of beauty was only one aspect of a much larger concept of life-enhancing sensory stimuli.

The alternative theory (i.e., that a philosophy of architecture is unique and can therefore be evolved only by specific reference to the art of building) will be dealt with below with reference to the traditional triad usually cited in the formula coined by the English theorist Sir Henry Wotton in his book *The Elements of Architecture*, namely "commodity, firmness, and delight."

Generally speaking, writers on aesthetics have been noticeably reluctant to use architectural examples in support of speculations as to the nature of their general theories; but references to buildings have been used in most "philosophies of art" ever since the German philosophers Immanuel Kant and Georg Wilhelm Friedrich Hegel first popularized the philosophical discipline. Kant, in his *Kritik der Urteilskraft* (1790; *Critique of Judgment*), distinguished between what he termed free beauty (*pulchritudo vaga*) and dependent beauty (*pulchritudo adhaerens*). He classified architecture as dependent beauty, saying that in a thing that is possible only by means of design (*Absicht*) — a building or even an animal — the regularity consisting in symmetry must express the unity of the intuition that accompanies the concept of purpose (*Zweck*), and this regularity belongs to cognition. Nevertheless, he claimed that a flower should be classified as free beauty (where the judgment of taste is "pure") "because hardly anyone but a botanist knows what sort of thing a flower ought to be; and even he, though recognizing in the flower the reproductive organ of the plant, pays no regard to this natural purpose if he is passing judgment on the flower by taste." What Kant's reaction would have been to a modern plastic imitation flower is impossible to guess; but it will readily be perceived (1) why those who, in the 19th century, accepted the notion that beauty in architecture is *pulchritudo adhaerens* felt such antipathy toward "shams," (2) how the distinction between "pure art" and "functional art" (*Zweckkunst*) became confused, and (3) why there arose a tendency to pursue definitions of "pure beauty" or "pure art" without specifically referring to the function and structure of any particular class of beautiful or artistic objects, such as buildings.

This latter tendency was reinforced when the French philosopher Victor Cousin, writing in 1835, classified the history of philosophy under three distinct headings: the true, the beautiful, and the good. The ensuing acceptance of the idea that beauty was to be studied independently of truth and goodness produced a tendency not merely to regard beauty as something added to a building (rather than conceptually inseparable from the truth and goodness of its structure and function) but to regard beauty as limited to visual and emotional qualities.

In the first half of the 20th century, philosophers grew less dogmatic about aesthetics. But its influence on theories of architecture became stronger because of the popular view that sculpture was essentially nonrepresentational. Thus, although the assertion that "aesthetically, architecture is the creation of sculpture big enough to walk about inside" is meaningful in the 20th century, it would have seemed nonsensical to any architectural theorist living before 1900, when sculpture was invariably thought of either as representational or as a carved refinement of load-bearing wood or stone.

Functionalism

The notion of functional art, most actively promoted by German writers and termed by them *Zweckkunst*, is most appropriately related to architectural theory under three headings, namely (1) the idea that no building is beautiful unless it properly fulfills its function, (2) the idea that if a building fulfills its function it is ipso facto beautiful, and (3) the idea that, since form relates to function, all artifacts, including buildings, are a species of industrial, or applied, art (known in German as *Kunstgewerbe*).

The first proposition will be dealt with later under the heading *utilitas*. The second proposition, though widely popularized through the publication of the French architect Jean-Nicholas-Louis Durand's lectures delivered during the economic depression of the beginning of the 19th century, has had little influence except during similar periods of economic depression. The third proposition has, however, had a wide influence, since, unlike the second proposition, it is closely akin to (rather than antagonistic toward) the theory of aesthetics, in that it regards all the visual arts as generically related.

This last theory seems to have been popularized, if not originated, by Gottfried Semper, an architect from Dresden who, after finding political asylum in England (where he then helped to organize the Great Exhibition of 1851), published a book in German on arts and crafts that seems to have been influential not only in Germany but also in areas of the United States heavily populated by German-speaking immigrants, such as Chicago. Later, in 20th-century Germany, the Bauhaus (officially Hochschule für Gestaltung; "Academy for Form Giving") was ostensibly intended to train students in separate creative disciplines, but its didactic method was based on the assumption—implied by the general introductory courses—that, if one could design anything, one could design everything. In the explanatory words of its founder, the architect Walter Gropius, "The approach to any kind of design—a chair, a building, a whole town or a regional plan—should be essentially identical."

THE ART OF BUILDING

The notion that architecture is the art of building was implied by Alberti in the first published treatise on the theory of architecture, *De re aedificatoria* (1485; Eng. trans., *Ten Books on Architecture*); for, although he was a layman writing for other lay scholars, he rejected, by his title, the idea that architecture was simply applied mathematics, as had been claimed by Vitruvius. The specific denotation of architecture as "the art of building," however, seems to be a French tradition, deriving perhaps from the medieval status of master masons, as understood by the 16th-century architect Philibert Delorme. This definition occurs in most French treatises published before 1750; and, although the humanistic and antiquarian aspects of fine building were rarely questioned after the Renaissance, the distinction between "architecture" and "building" never had any appreciable significance before Renaissance ideas succumbed to the combined assault of "aesthetics" and the Gothic Revival movement.

Before the 18th century it was generally accepted that the theory of architecture was concerned mainly with important private or civic buildings such as palaces, mansions, churches, and monasteries. Buildings such as these required the superior skill that only book learning could provide, and so relatively little attention was given, in theoretical writings, to simple and straightforward buildings that could be competently built in accordance with local traditions by unlettered craftsmen. But, with the expansion of the architectural profession, with the perversion of the idea that social prestige was symbolized by ornamentation, with the wider distribution of wealth, and with the growing urge toward individualism in an increasingly egalitarian society, the real distinction between these two kinds of buildings was obscured, and in its place was substituted an antithesis. Henceforth, "building" was associated with the notion of cheapness, whereas "architecture" was associated with what John Ruskin would have called "sacrifice" (but which his antagonists would have called conspicuous waste). A distinction was made between the respective attitudes of "art architects" and practical-minded civil engineers. This distinction persisted because of the different methods of training candidates for the two professions. Whereas a fledgling engineering student is seldom asked to design a whole structure (such as a bridge), architectural students begin by designing whole structures and proceed with structures of increasing size and complexity, either graphically or by means of small-scale models.

It was doubtless the difference in educational methods that prompted Le Corbusier to state:

The engineer, inspired by the law of economy and led by mathematical calculation, puts us in accord with the laws of the universe. He achieves harmony. The architect, by his arrangement of forms, achieves an order which is a pure creation of his spirit . . . it is then that we experience beauty.

Yet some 80 years previously the English critic James Fergusson had felt obliged to qualify, with a comparable distinction, his enthusiasm for the new architecture of the Crystal Palace, by observing that "it has not a sufficient amount of decoration about its parts to take it entirely out of the category of first-class engineering and to make it entirely an object of fine art." The distinction between architecture and "mere building" was stated by Nikolaus Pevsner in the opening paragraph of his *Outline of European Architecture* (1942): "a bicycle shed is a building; Lincoln Cathedral is a piece of architecture . . . the term *architecture* applies only to buildings designed with a view to aesthetic appeal." Whatever the justification for such assertions, it must nevertheless be recognized that neither of these authors suggests that aesthetic appeal or art are synonyms for superfluity. Although adjustment in proportions or refinement of profiles may increase the thickness of short-span structural members beyond the structural analytical minima, this does not necessarily imply any radical decrease in real economy but simply indicates a concept of economy that takes into account the assembly and amenity of spatial enclosures and admits that there is value in environmental harmony. It is thus as misleading to imply (as Fergusson implied) that architecture is civil engineering plus ornament as it is to imply (as Le Corbusier did) that the status of the two professions is to be distinguished by the relative superiority of beauty over harmony.

It is important to insist that the theory of architecture is concerned primarily with the attainment of certain environmental ideals rather than with their cost; for these two problems are philosophically distinct, as is clear if one considers such a concept as, for example, that of standardization. The financial saving made by standardizing rolled-steel sections or by casting concrete in reusable formwork is so obvious that it requires no elaboration with respect to Vitruvius's demand for *oeconomia*. But such standardization also fulfills Vitruvius's concurrent demand for order, arrangement, eurythmy, symmetry, and propriety.

The Place Vendôme in Paris is adorned with over 100 identical pilasters and half columns, all carved with the same Corinthian capitals under the supervision of a member of the Académie Royale de Peinture et de Sculpture. Whether or not the resultant uniformity was or still is both pleasing and desirable is certainly open to discussion; but it will be perceived that any argument about architectural standardization must primarily be a question of value, rather than of cost, and it is with values that architectural theory has always been predominantly concerned.

"COMMODITY, FIRMNESS, AND DELIGHT": THE ULTIMATE SYNTHESIS

It has been generally assumed that a complete theory of architecture is always concerned essentially in some way or another with these three interrelated terms, which, in Vitruvius's Latin text, are given as *firmitas*, *utilitas*, and *venustas* (i.e., structural stability, appropriate spatial accommodation, and attractive appearance). Nevertheless, a number of influential theorists after 1750 sought to make modifications to this traditional triad (1) by giving its components a radically different equilibrium (such as the primacy given by the 18th-century French architect Étienne-Louis Boullée to the effects of geometric forms in light or the claim made by J.N.L. Durand that the fulfillment of function was the sole essence of architectural beauty), (2) by adding ethical values (such as Ruskin's "sacrifice" and "obedience"), or (3) by introducing new scientific concepts (such as Siegfried Giedion's "space-time").

Furthermore, it has been argued that the traditional concept of *firmitas*, *utilitas*, and *venustas* ceased to have any real value after 1800, when engineers began creating structures that seemed so ostentatiously to defy the stonemasons' laws of gravity, when scientific studies were creating more and more doubts as to the economical, sociological, psychological, acoustical, thermal, or optical determinants of appropriate spatial accommodation and when beauty was "altogether in the eye of the beholder."

Clearly, one must be wary of attributing too much importance to the sequence, since a slight variation occurs in the writings of even the most traditional theorists.

Vitruvius gives these terms in the sequence *firmitas, utilitas, venustas*, whereas both Alberti and, following him, the 16th-century Venetian architect and theorist Andrea Palladio reverse the order of the first two. Thus, Sir Henry Wotton's sequence (which is normally used in English-language texts) does not, as so often stated, derive directly from the Latin text of Vitruvius but from the Italian text of Palladio's *I quattro libri dell' architettura* (i.e., *comodità, perpetuità, bellezza*). But it does seem worth noting that *venustas* generally comes last, implying that *firmitas* and *utilitas* are to be regarded as essential logical prerequisites of architectural beauty.

On the other hand, the practical advantages, in academic treatises, of giving priority to *venustas* are evident. Jacques-François Blondel, in his nine-volume *Cours d'architecture* (1771–77) used this sequence because he observed that considerations of "decoration" are almost entirely within the domain of the theory of architecture, whereas neither distribution (*utilitas*) nor construction (*firmitas*) can be explained properly without practical experience. The growing emphasis on aesthetics, combined with developments in psychology and the influence of art-historical methods, added weight to this argument, while the corresponding independence of scientific techniques of structural and spatial analysis led many teachers of architecture to consider *utilitas* and *firmitas* as totally separate academic disciplines. Important exceptions can be found to this generalization. At the end of the 19th century, Julien Guadet, in reaction against the creation of a chair of aesthetics at the Paris École des Beaux-Arts, considered it his duty, as professor of architectural theory, to devote his lectures to the study of architectural planning, and this method, which achieved prestige as a result of his keen mind and wide historical knowledge, was pursued by many later scholars. But Guadet's approach became unfashionable, and since the 1960s the predominant methods of teaching architectural theory have ranged from a return to the synthesis of structural, spatial, and formal values espoused by Robert Venturi to the exploration of the architectural implications of general theories of linguistics advanced by Christian Norberg-Schulz.

VENUSTAS

This Latin term for "beauty" (literally, the salient qualities possessed by the goddess Venus) clearly implied a visual quality in architecture that would arouse the emotion of love; but it is of interest to note that one of the crucial aspects of this problem was already anticipated by Alberti in the 15th century, as is made clear by his substitution of the word *amoenitas* ("pleasure") for Vitruvius's more anthropomorphic term *venustas*. Alberti not only avoids the erotic implications of the term *venustas* but, by subdividing *amoenitas* into *pulchritudo* and *ornamentum*, gives far more precise indications as to the type of visual satisfaction that architecture should provide. *Pulchritudo*, he asserts, is derived from harmonious proportions that are comparable to those that exist in music and are the essence of the pleasure created by architecture. *Ornamentum*, he claims, is only an "auxiliary brightness," the quality and extent of which will depend essentially on what is appropriate and seemly. Both *pulchritudo* and *ornamentum* were thus related to function and environment in that, ideally, they were governed by a sense of decorum; and, since the etymological roots of both "decoration" and "decorum" are the same, it will be understood why, before 1750, the term decoration had in both English and French a far less superficial architectural implication than it often does today.

After the German philosopher and educator Alexander Gottlieb Baumgarten had introduced the neologism aesthetics in about 1750, the visual merits of all artifacts tended to be assessed more subjectively than objectively; and, in the criticism of all those sensory stimuli that, for want of a better term, critics somewhat indiscriminately lumped together as the fine arts, the visual criteria were extended to include not only beauty but also sublimity, picturesqueness, and even ugliness. Now it is clear that, once ugliness is equated with beauty, both terms (being contradictory) become virtually meaningless. But ugliness, after the mid-19th century, was not only one of the most important themes of many popular dramas and novels; ugliness was also often considered the most appropriate architectural expression for all sorts of virtues — especially those of manliness, sincerity, and so on.

Before 1750, architects had expressed these qualities more subtly (e.g., by slight modifications of proportions or by unobtrusive ornament). In later years, when the value of proportion and ornament became highly controversial, architectural theorists tended to avoid committing themselves to any criteria that might be subsumed under the heading *venustas*. In the last resort, however, some concept of beauty must be essential to any theory of architecture; and, whether one considers Le Corbusier's buildings beautiful or not, his most stabilizing contribution toward the theory of modern architecture was undoubtedly his constant reiteration of this term and his insistence on the traditional view that beauty in architecture is essentially based on harmonious proportions, mathematically conceived.

In the 20th century the main obstacle to an acceptance of Alberti's notions of *pulchritudo* and *ornamentum* resulted from the influence of nonrepresentational sculpture after 1918, whereby ornament was no longer conceived as an enrichment of proportioned structure but as an integral, all-pervading part of each building's totality. This ideal of the fusion between good proportions and "auxiliary brightness" was expressed by Walter Gropius in *The New Architecture and the Bauhaus* when in 1935 he wrote:

> *Our ultimate goal, therefore, was the composite but inseparable work of art, the great building, in which the old dividing-line between monumental and decorative elements would have disappeared for ever.*

The idea was accepted in most schools of architecture by the mid-20th century; but one may question whether it fully justified the expectations of its protagonists, once it had been exemplified and proliferated in so many urban environments. It is by no means certain that Gropius's concept of the fundamental interdependence of architectural proportion and architectural ornament was irrevocably established by the Bauhaus theorists or that future architectural theorists need only concentrate on such minor modifications to the concept as may be required by sociological and technological developments.

UTILITAS

The notion that a building is defective unless the spaces provided are adequate and appropriate for their intended usage would seem obvious. Yet the statement itself has been a source of controversy since the 1960s. The main reasons for the controversy are: first, whereas there are seldom exact statistical means of computing spatial adequacy or appropriateness, there are many building types or building elements for which one cannot even establish the optimum forms and dimensions with any confidence that they will be generally accepted. Second, edifices are frequently used for purposes other than those for which they were originally planned. Furthermore, there is some doubt as to whether "form follows function" or "function

follows form," since, although, in general, it can reasonably be assumed that an architect's task is to construct
specific spaces for the fulfillment of predetermined functions, there is plenty of historical evidence to suggest that
many important social institutions have resulted from
spaces already built. No better example could be found
than the evolution of parliamentary systems. The British
system, based on the concept of legislatures in which the
sovereign's government and the sovereign's opposition
confront each other, originated in the fact that the earliest
parliaments met in the medieval palace chapel. The French
system, created concurrently with the Greek and Roman
revivals, was based on the concept of legislatures addressed
by orators, and its environment was that of an antique
theatre. In the former system the seating was designed in
accordance with the liturgical requirements of a Christian
church; in the latter, with the evolution of Greek drama.
Neither had anything to do with preconceived notions
regarding the most effective environment for parliamentary debate, yet both have had divergent influences on
constitutional procedures, thereby deeply affecting the
whole theory of government.

Third, the exact significance of what is meant by "adequate appropriate spaces" becomes far more complex in
buildings requiring a large number of interrelated spaces
than it is in single-cell buildings. The emotional effect of
transitions from spacious to constricted volumes and vice
versa transcends in architectural importance the statistical evaluation of floor areas; a fact which explains the
attractiveness of theories that have tacitly adopted places
of worship as spatial paradigms and bolstered their arguments by historical reference to temples and churches.
This bias is perceptible not only in the most influential
theories enunciated before 1900 (when the prototypes
were either primeval, antique, or medieval) but also in the

most influential ideas promulgated by such great architectural leaders of the 20th century as Frank Lloyd Wright and Ludwig Mies van der Rohe.

The idealization of monumental single-cell spaces is sometimes justified, but the difficulty of evolving theories of planning by the use of historical prototypes should be emphasized. It is in this branch of architectural theory that the influences of historicism have been most insidious, precisely because they are less obvious here than in systems of construction, of proportions, and of ornamentation. Such influences persist mainly because of art-historical indifference to the essential distinction between building types, since such distinction conflicts with the chronological sequence of particular architects' stylistic evolution; but it is for this reason that Julien Guadet's greatest contribution to the theory of architecture may well have been his decision to evolve a history of architecture in which all buildings were classified solely in accordance with their function.

FIRMITAS

Two plausible reasons can be given for according logical primacy in the Vitruvian triad to *firmitas*. The first is the notion that architecture is essentially the "art of building." The second is that, since the uses or functions of a building tend to change, the structures serving such functions may be considered as taking logical precedence over them. This idea was expressed with characteristic lapidary vigour by the 20th-century French architect Auguste Perret when he asserted that

> *architecture is the art of organizing space; but it is by construction that it expresses itself . . . Functions, customs, and building regulations and fashions impose conditions which are only transitory.*

Some later architectural theorists have become so concerned with the rapid obsolescence of modern buildings that they have envisaged edifices that express the temporary nature of these transitory qualities and are therefore built in such a way as to enable the structures themselves to be discarded completely after a few years. On the other hand (since the economic feasibility of this technique is questionable), there are still many architects who believe in the inevitability of permanent buildings and who therefore hold views more compatible with this belief.

From the time of the Renaissance to the mid-18th century—as also before the decline of the ancient Roman Empire on which the culture of this era was modelled—little concern seems to have been given to the idea that there was any virtue in manifesting the actual structural system of a building. Alberti recommended a distinctive articulation of the skeleton frame in conformity with the antique concept of trabeation, or the post-and-lintel system (and hence the independence of the "infilling" elements, such as arches or solid walling); but the more commonly accepted notion seems to have been that, provided a trabeated system was expressed externally, the relationship of this visual expression to the actual system of construction was relatively unimportant. Theoretical pronouncements on this matter depended of course on the architectural traditions of each country. In Italy (where the traditional technique of building had, even during the Middle Ages, assumed that structure was independent of appearance and where it was common to complete a building in brick before adding its marble facades) the idea that there could be any theoretical dilemma regarding the unison between these two elements was virtually inconceivable. Palladio and his generation seem to have generally accepted the idea that, in regions where masonry was scarce, the use of stuccoed, painted, or veneered brickwork, with plastered timber beams, was architecturally as "genuine" as the use of stone, provided it was all of one colour. But in the Île-de-France region around Paris, on the contrary, the medieval traditions of French masonry construction, combined with the abundance of good freestone, caused theorists from the Renaissance to the time of the French Revolution to favour a less tenuous relationship between the external appearance of a building and the system by which it was constructed. Nevertheless, it is probably fair to say that in all European countries before the end of the 18th century, as well as in their American colonies, the only problem concerned with *firmitas* (other than technical problems) was the problem of the relationship between "real and apparent stability"; and, when theorists pronounced on this problem, it was usually to assert that a building should not only be structurally stable but should also appear to be so.

A violent assault upon this point of view was launched by the Gothic Revivalists, who in the mid-19th century contended that the breathtaking counterpoise of a cathedral's flying buttresses was far more dramatically expressive of *firmitas* than the ponderous massiveness of its sturdy western towers. It was in this era that the term *daring* (which Ruskin had frequently used with reference to the paintings of the English Romantic artist Joseph Mallord William Turner) became popular as a laudatory epithet, thereby indicating an ideal of structural expression that was to be increasingly exploited when steel and reinforced concrete permitted higher buildings with fewer and more slender supports.

But the most controversial issue concerning *firmitas* in the 19th century—which also arose through the influence of the Gothic Revival movement—concerned the extent to which a building should manifest its structural system and the materials used. The attraction of this particular interpretation of the concept of truthful architecture was probably due to the popularity of new attitudes toward experimental science and to the disrepute into which mythology had been cast by the philosophers of the Enlightenment. Presumably, truth was no less prized in the 17th or 18th centuries than in the 19th century (though shams may have been less rife), while hypocrisy was regarded with as much contempt. Moreover, although the 19th century was a period of growing realism in literature, it was also a period of growing expressiveness in painting and music. Whatever the reason for this change of attitude, the 19th century saw a general acceptance of the notion that buildings were "true" only insofar as their structural form and appearance corresponded to the structural systems and materials employed, and this dogma was developed by means of many elaborate biological and mechanical analogies.

This particular doctrine had a highly beneficial influence on architectural evolution during the 20th century, since it helped to demonstrate why the radical changes in building technology rendered earlier concepts of architectural form (based on load-bearing masonry construction) theoretically untenable. For, while it may readily be admitted that a building can express many other things besides its function and structure, failure to express the latter in some manner, however remote, must always lead to arbitrariness. This would not only be harmful to the evolution of architectural form but would inevitably result in a somewhat cynical concept of building as "pure form"— a concept that only those who regard architecture as nothing more than large-scale packaging or abstract sculpture could accept.

VITRUVIUS
(fl. 1st century BCE)

The Roman architect and engineer Marcus Vitruvius Pollio was the author of the celebrated treatise *De architectura* (*On Architecture*), a handbook for Roman architects.

Little is known of Vitruvius's life, except what can be gathered from his writings, which are somewhat obscure on the subject. Although he nowhere identifies the emperor to whom his work is dedicated, it is likely that the first Augustus is meant and that the treatise was conceived after 27 BCE. Since Vitruvius describes himself as an old man, it may be inferred that he was also active during the time of Julius Caesar. Vitruvius himself tells of a basilica he built at Fanum (now Fano).

De architectura was based on his own experience, as well as on theoretical works by famous Greek architects such as Hermogenes. The treatise covers almost every aspect of architecture, but it is limited, since it is based primarily on Greek models, from which Roman architecture was soon decisively to depart in order to serve the new needs of proclaiming a world empire. *De architectura* is divided into 10 books dealing with city planning and architecture in general; building materials; temple construction and the use of the Greek orders; public buildings (theatres, baths); private buildings; floors and stucco decoration; hydraulics; clocks, mensuration, and astronomy; and civil and military engines. Vitruvius's outlook is essentially Hellenistic. His wish was to preserve the classical tradition in the design of temples and public buildings, and his prefaces to the separate books of his treatise contain many pessimistic remarks about the contemporary architecture. Most of what Pliny says in his *Natural History* about Roman construction methods and wall painting was taken from Vitruvius, though unacknowledged. Vitruvius's expressed desire that his name be honoured by posterity was realized. Throughout the antique revival of the Renaissance, the classical phase of the Baroque, and in the Neoclassical period, his work was the chief authority on ancient classical architecture.

The text of *De architectura* with an English translation is published in the Loeb Classical Library in two volumes.

GREEN ARCHITECTURE

A philosophy of architecture that advocates sustainable energy sources, the conservation of energy, the reuse and safety of building materials, and the siting of a building with consideration of its impact on the environment is commonly called green architecture.

In the early 21st century the building of shelter (in all its forms) consumed more than half of the world's resources — translating into 16 percent of the Earth's freshwater resources, 30–40 percent of all energy supplies, and 50 percent by weight of all the raw materials withdrawn from Earth's surface. Architecture was also responsible for 40–50 percent of waste deposits in landfills and 20–30 percent of greenhouse gas emissions.

Many architects after the post-World War II building boom were content to erect emblematic civic and corporate icons that celebrated profligate consumption and omnivorous globalization. At the turn of the 21st century, however, a building's environmental integrity—as seen in the way it was designed and how it operated—became an important factor in how it was evaluated.

THE RISE OF ECO-AWARENESS

In the United States, environmental advocacy, as an organized social force, gained its first serious momentum as part of the youth movement of the 1960s. In rebellion against the perceived evils of high-rise congestion and suburban sprawl, some of the earliest and most dedicated eco-activists moved to rural communes, where they lived in tentlike structures and geodesic domes. In a certain sense, this initial wave of green architecture was based on admiration of the early Native American lifestyle and its minimal impact on the land. At the same time, by isolating themselves from the greater community, these youthful environmentalists were ignoring one of ecology's most important principles: that interdependent elements work in harmony for the benefit of the whole.

Influential pioneers who supported a more integrative mission during the 1960s and early 1970s included the American architectural critic and social philosopher Lewis Mumford, the Scottish-born American landscape architect Ian McHarg, and the British scientist James Lovelock. They led the way in defining green design, and they contributed significantly to the popularization of environmental principles. For example, in 1973 Mumford proposed a straightforward environmental philosophy:

> *The solution of the energy crisis would seem simple: transform solar energy via plants and produce enough food power and manpower in forms that would eliminate the wastes and perversions of power demanded by our high-energy technology. In short, plant, eat, and work!*

McHarg, who founded the department of landscape architecture at the University of Pennsylvania, laid the

Inhabitants of Colorado's Drop City, an early experiment in eco-sensitive communal living, going about their daily work in 1967. The geodesic dome structures were inexpensive and sturdy. Carl Iwasaki—Time & Life Pictures/Getty Images

ground rules for green architecture in his seminal book *Design with Nature* (1969). Envisioning the role of human beings as stewards of the environment, he advocated an organizational strategy, called "cluster development," that would concentrate living centres and leave as much natural environment as possible to flourish on its own terms. In this regard McHarg was a visionary who perceived Earth as a self-contained and dangerously threatened entity.

This "whole Earth" concept also became the basis of Lovelock's Gaia hypothesis. Named after the Greek Earth goddess, his hypothesis defined the entire planet as a single unified organism, continuously maintaining itself for survival. He described this organism as

> *a complex entity involving the Earth's biosphere, atmosphere, oceans, and soil; the totality constituting a feedback or cybernetic system which seeks an optimal physical and chemical environment for life on this planet.*

During the 1970s the Norwegian environmental philosopher Arne Naess proposed a theory of "deep ecology" (or "ecosophy"), asserting that every living creature in nature is equally important to Earth's precisely balanced system. Working in exact opposition to this philosophy, the politics and economics of that decade accelerated the development of green awareness. The lack of business regulation in the United States meant unlimited consumption of fossil fuels. Meanwhile, the 1973 OPEC oil crisis brought the cost of energy into sharp focus and was a painful reminder of worldwide dependence on a very small number of petroleum-producing countries. This crisis, in turn, brought into relief the need for diversified sources of energy and spurred corporate and government investment in solar, wind, water, and geothermal sources of power.

Green Design Takes Root

By the mid-1980s and continuing through the 1990s, the number of environmental advocacy societies radically expanded; groups such as Greenpeace, Environmental Action, the Sierra Club, Friends of the Earth, and the Nature Conservancy all experienced burgeoning memberships. For architects and builders a significant milestone was the formulation in 1994 of Leadership in Energy and Environmental Design (LEED) standards, established and administered by the U.S. Green Building Council. These standards provided measurable criteria for the design and construction of environmentally responsible buildings. The basic qualifications are as follows:

Sustainable site development involves, whenever possible, the reuse of existing buildings and the preservation of the surrounding environment. The incorporation of earth shelters, roof gardens, and extensive planting throughout and around buildings is encouraged.

Water is conserved by a variety of means including the cleaning and recycling of gray (previously used) water and the installation of building-by-building catchments for rainwater. Water usage and supplies are monitored.

Energy efficiency can be increased in a variety of ways, for example, by orienting buildings to take full advantage of seasonal changes in the sun's position and by the use of diversified and regionally appropriate energy sources, which may—depending on geographic location—include solar, wind, geothermal, biomass, water, or natural gas.

The most desirable materials are those that are recycled or renewable and those that require the least energy to manufacture. They ideally are locally sourced and free from harmful chemicals. They are made of nonpolluting raw ingredients and are durable and recyclable.

Indoor environmental quality addresses the issues that influence how the individual feels in a space and involves such features as the sense of control over personal space, ventilation, temperature control, and the use of materials that do not emit toxic gases.

The 1980s and early 1990s brought a new surge of interest in the environmental movement and the rise to prominence of a group of more socially responsive and philosophically oriented green architects. The American architect Malcolm Wells opposed the legacy of architectural ostentation and aggressive assaults on the land in favour of the gentle impact of underground and earth-sheltered buildings—exemplified by his Brewster, Mass., house of 1980. The low impact, in both energy use and visual effect, of a structure that is surrounded by earth creates an almost invisible architecture and a green ideal. As Wells explained, this kind of underground building is "sunny, dry, and pleasant" and "offers huge fuel savings and a silent, green alternative to the asphalt society."

The American physicist Amory Lovins and his wife, Hunter Lovins, founded the Rocky Mountain Institute in 1982 as a research centre for the study and promotion of the "whole system" approach favoured by McHarg and Lovelock. Years before the LEED standards were published, the institute, which was housed in a building that was both energy-efficient and aesthetically appealing, formulated the fundamental principle of authentic green architecture: to use the largest possible proportion of regional resources and materials. In contrast to the conventional, inefficient practice of drawing materials and energy from distant, centralized sources, the Lovins team followed the "soft energy path" for architecture—i.e., they drew from alternative energy sources.

The Center for Maximum Potential Building Systems (Max Pot; founded in 1975 in Austin, Texas, by the American architect Pliny Fisk III) in the late 1980s joined with others to support an experimental agricultural community called Blueprint Farm, in Laredo, Texas. Its broader mission— with applications to any geographic location—was to study the correlations between living conditions, botanical life,

the growing of food, and the economic-ecological impera-
tives of construction. This facility was built as an integrative
prototype, recognizing that nature thrives on diversity. Fisk
concluded that single-enterprise and one-crop territories
are environmentally dysfunctional—meaning, for example,
that all of a crop's predators converge, natural defenses are
overwhelmed, and chemical spraying to eliminate insects
and weeds becomes mandatory. In every respect, Blueprint
Farm stood for diversified and unpredictable community
development. The crops were varied, and the buildings were
constructed of steel gathered from abandoned oil rigs and
combined with such enhancements as earth berms, sod
roofs, and straw bales. Photovoltaic panels, evaporative
cooling, and wind power were incorporated in this utopian
demonstration of the symbiotic relationships between
farming and green community standards.

The American architect William McDonough rose to
green design fame in 1985 with his Environmental Defense
Fund Building in New York City. That structure was one of
the first civic icons for energy conservation resulting from
the architect's close scrutiny of all of its interior products,
construction technology, and air-handling systems. Since
then, McDonough's firm established valuable planning
strategies and built numerous other green buildings—most
significantly, the Herman Miller factory and offices (Holland,
Mich., 1995), the corporate offices of Gap, Inc. (San Bruno,
Calif., 1997), and Oberlin College's Adam Joseph Lewis
Center for Environmental Studies (Oberlin, Ohio, 2001).

McDonough's main contribution to the evolution of
sustainable design was his commitment to what he has
called "ecologically intelligent design," a process that
involves the cooperation of the architect, corporate leaders, and scientists. This design principle takes into account
the "biography" of every aspect of manufacture, use, and
disposal: the choice of raw ingredients, transport of

materials to the factory, fabrication process, durability of goods produced, usability of products, and recycling potential. McDonough's latest version of the principle— referred to as "cradle-to-cradle" design—is modeled after nature's own waste-free economy and makes a strong case for the goal of reprocessing, in which every element that is used in or that results from the manufacturing process has its own built-in recycling value.

THE PRINCIPLES OF BUILDING GREEN

The advances in research and in building techniques achieved by the above-mentioned green design luminaries have been compiled into a reliable database of environmental construction methods and sustainable materials—some of which have been in use for thousands of years yet remain the basis for contemporary advances in environmental technology. For private residences of the 21st century, the essential green design principles are as follows:

> **Alternative energy sources.** Whenever feasible, build homes and communities that supply their own power; such buildings may operate entirely off the regional power grid, or they may be able to feed excess energy back onto the grid. Wind and solar power are the usual alternatives. The quality of solar collectors and photovoltaic panels continues to improve with the advance of technology; practical considerations for choosing one supplier over another include price, durability, availability, delivery method, technology, and warranty support.
>
> **Energy conservation.** Weatherize buildings for maximum protection against the loss of warm

or cool air. Major chemical companies have developed responsibly manufactured, dependable, moisture-resistant insulating materials that do not cause indoor humidity problems. Laminated glass was also radically improved at the end of the 20th century; some windows provide the same insulation value as traditional stone, masonry, and wood construction. In regions that experience extreme heat, straw-bale or mud-brick construction—used since ancient times—is a good way to save money and energy.

Reuse of materials. Use recycled building materials. Although such products were scarce in the early 1990s, since the early 21st century they have been readily available from a burgeoning number of companies that specialize in salvaging materials from demolition sites.

Careful siting. Consider using underground or earth-sheltered architecture, which can be ideal for domestic living. Starting at a depth of about 1.5 metres (5 feet) below the surface, the temperature is a constant 52 °F (11 °C)—which makes the earth itself a dependable source of climate control.

Individual, corporate, and governmental efforts to comply with or enforce LEED standards include recycling at household and community levels, constructing smaller and more efficient buildings, and encouraging off-the-grid energy supplies. Such efforts alone cannot preserve the global ecosystem, however. On the most basic level, the ultimate success of any globally sanctioned environmental movement depends as much on its social, psychological, and aesthetic appeal as on its use of advanced technologies.

The environmental movement in the 21st century can succeed only to the extent that its proponents achieve a broad-based philosophical accord and provide the same kind of persuasive catalyst for change that the Industrial Revolution offered in the 19th century. This means shaping a truly global (as well as optimistic and persuasive) philosophy of the environment. Much depends on the building arts and integrative thinking. Architects will have to abandon 20th-century specialization and reliance on technology and, with builders and clients, help support grassroots, community-oriented, and globally unifying objectives. In the words of Earth Day founder Gaylord Nelson,

> *The ultimate test of man's conscience may be his willingness to sacrifice something today for future generations whose words of thanks will not be heard.*

THE CHALLENGES TO ARCHITECTURE

If architecture is to become truly green, then a revolution of form and content—including radical changes in the entire look of architecture—is essential. This can only happen if those involved in the building arts create a fundamentally new language that is more contextually integrative, socially responsive, functionally ethical, and visually germane.

The potentialities of environmental science and technology must be creatively examined. Already there exists a rich reservoir of ideas from science and nature—cybernetics, virtual reality, biochemistry, hydrology, geology, and cosmology, to mention a few. Furthermore, just as the Industrial Revolution once generated change in many fields in the 19th century, so too the information revolution, with its model of integrated systems, serves as a conceptual model in the 21st century for a new approach to architecture and design in the broader environment.

As community governments begin to legislate state-of-the-art green standards, they must encourage appropriate artistic responses to such regional attributes as surrounding topography, indigenous vegetation, cultural history, and territorial idiosyncrasy. For instance, communities might encourage innovative fusions of architecture with land-scape—where trees and plants become as much a part of architectural design as construction materials—so that buildings and their adjacent landscapes essentially merge. In such thinking, buildings are not interpreted as isolated objects, and the traditional barriers between inside and outside and between structure and site are challenged.

Likewise, green architecture in the 21st century has similar obligations to the psychological and physical needs of its inhabitants. Buildings are most successful when they respond to multiple senses—meaning that truly green design engages touch, smell, and hearing as well as sight in the design of buildings and public spaces.

Continuing advances in environmental technology have significantly strengthened the goals of sustainable architecture and city planning over the last decade. Yet many people consider the environmental crisis beyond their comprehension and control. Though technological solutions are necessary, they represent only one facet of the whole. Indeed, the transfer of responsibility to engineers and scientists threatens the social and psychological commitment needed for philosophical unity.

Increasing numbers of people seek new symbiotic relationships between their shelter and the broader ecology. This growing motivation is one of the most promising signs in the development of a consensus philosophy of the environment. As the environmental movement gains momentum, it underlines the anthropologist Margaret Mead's observation:

Never doubt that a small group of thoughtful, committed citizens can change the world. Indeed, it is the only thing that ever has.

RENZO PIANO AND THE CALIFORNIA ACADEMY OF SCIENCES

The Italian architect Renzo Piano is one of the best known contemporary architects to build a major museum practicing green architecture. He has received numerous awards and prizes, including the Japan Art Association's Praemium Imperiale prize for architecture (1995), the Pritzker Architecture Prize (1998), and the American Institute of Architects Gold Medal (2008).

Piano was born on Sept. 14, 1937, in Genoa, Italy, into a family of builders. After graduating from the Polytechnic in Milan in 1964, he worked with a variety of architects, including his father, until he established a partnership with the British architect Richard Rogers from 1970 to 1977. Their high-tech design for the Centre Georges Pompidou in Paris (1971–77), made to look like an "urban machine," immediately gained the attention of the international architectural community. Colourful airducts and elevators positioned on the building's exoskeleton created a vivid aesthetic impression, and the structure's playfulness challenged staid, institutional ideas of what a museum should be. From a functional standpoint, the position of service elements such as elevators on the exterior allowed an open, flexible plan in the building's interior. While many complained that it did not fit the context of the historic neighbourhood, the Pompidou nonetheless helped bring about the revitalization of the area when it became an internationally renowned landmark.

Piano's interest in technology and modern solutions to architectural problems was evident in all his designs, although he often took greater account of the structure's context. His design for the Menil Collection museum (1982–86; with Richard Fitzgerald) in Houston, Texas, utilized ferroconcrete leaves in the roof, which served as both a heat source and a form of protection against ultraviolet light. At the same time, the building's low scale and continuous veranda are in keeping with the mostly residential structures nearby. In his San Nicola Soccer Stadium (1987–90) in Bari, Italy, Piano used reinforced concrete petals supported by elegant pillars. The beauty and grace of the design reflect architectural traditions of the region; at the same time, by keeping the fans of opposing teams separate and creating an open plan that made all areas visible, the design discouraged the riots and violence that sometimes attended soccer events. His other important commissions include the Kansai International Airport Terminal (1988–94) in Ōsaka, Japan, the Auditorium Parco della Musica (1994–2002) in Rome, and the Beyeler Foundation Museum (1992–97) in Basel, Switz.

One of his most celebrated 21st-century projects, notable for its green architecture, was a new building for the California Academy of Sciences (completed 2008) in San Francisco's Golden Gate Park. The building has a number of noteworthy features, especially its "Living Roof." Not only does its shape complement the cityscape with its several hillocks, but the specially designed structure holds native California plants. These not only do the work that all plants do in converting carbon dioxide into oxygen, but they aid in cooling the building naturally during daylight hours. Piano's roof design additionally enables the capture and repurposing of rainwater.

URBAN PLANNING

The design and regulation of the uses of space that focus on the physical form, economic functions, and social impacts of the urban environment and on the location of different activities within it is the purpose of urban planning. Because urban planning draws upon engineering, architectural, and social and political concerns, it is variously a technical profession, an endeavour involving political will and public participation, and an academic discipline. Urban planning concerns itself with both the development of open land ("greenfields sites") and the revitalization of existing parts of the city, thereby involving goal setting, data collection and analysis, forecasting, design, strategic thinking, and public consultation. Increasingly, the technology of geographic information systems (GIS) has been used to map the existing urban system and to project the consequences of changes. In the late 20th century the term *sustainable development* came to represent an ideal outcome in the sum of all planning goals. As advocated by the United Nations-sponsored World Commission on Environment and Development in *Our Common Future* (1987), *sustainability* refers to "development that meets the needs of the present without compromising the ability of future generations to meet their own needs." While there is widespread consensus on this general goal, most major planning decisions involve trade-offs between subsidiary objectives and thus frequently involve conflict.

The modern origins of urban planning lie in a social movement for urban reform that arose in the latter part of the 19th century as a reaction against the disorder of the industrial city. Many visionaries of the period sought an ideal city, yet practical considerations of adequate sanitation, movement of goods and people, and provision of amenities also drove the desire for planning. Contemporary planners seek to balance the conflicting demands of social equity, economic growth, environmental sensitivity, and aesthetic appeal. The result of the planning process may be a formal master plan for an entire city or metropolitan area, a neighbourhood plan, a project plan, or a set of policy alternatives. Successful implementation of a plan usually requires entrepreneurship and political astuteness on the part of planners and their sponsors, despite efforts to insulate planning from politics. While based in government, planning increasingly involves private-sector participation in "public-private partnerships."

Urban planning emerged as a scholarly discipline in the 1900s. In Great Britain the first academic planning program began at the University of Liverpool in 1909, and the first North American program was established at Harvard University in 1924. It is primarily taught at the postgraduate level, and its curriculum varies widely from one university to another. Some programs maintain the traditional emphasis on physical design and land use; others, especially those that grant doctoral degrees, are oriented toward the social sciences. The discipline's theoretical core, being somewhat amorphous, is better defined by the issues it addresses than by any dominant paradigm or prescriptive approach. Representative issues especially concern the recognition of a public interest and how it should be determined, the physical and social character of the ideal city, the possibility of achieving change in accordance with consciously determined goals, the extent to which consensus on goals is attainable through communication, the role of citizens versus public officials and private investors in shaping the city, and, on a methodological level, the appropriateness of quantitative analysis and the "rational model" of decision making. Most degree programs in urban planning consist principally of applied courses on topics ranging from environmental policy to transportation planning to housing and community economic development.

The Development of Urban Planning

Far from being a modern idea, urban planning is an ancient idea. Evidence of planning has been unearthed in the ruins of cities in China, India, Egypt, Asia Minor, the Mediterranean world, and South and Central America.

Early History

Early examples of efforts toward planned urban development include orderly street systems that are rectilinear and sometimes radial; division of a city into specialized functional quarters; development of commanding central sites for palaces, temples, and civic buildings; and advanced systems of fortification, water supply, and drainage. Most of the evidence is in smaller cities that were built in comparatively short periods as colonies. Often the central cities of ancient states grew to substantial size before they achieved governments capable of imposing controls.

For several centuries during the Middle Ages, there was little building of cities in Europe. Eventually towns grew up as centres of church or feudal authority, of marketing or trade. As the urban population grew, the constriction caused by walls and fortifications led to overcrowding, the blocking out of air and light, and very poor sanitation. Certain quarters of the cities, either by custom or fiat, were restricted to different nationalities, classes, or trades, as still occurs in many contemporary cities of the developing world.

The physical form of medieval and Renaissance towns and cities followed the pattern of the village, spreading along a street or a crossroads in circular patterns or in irregular shapes, though rectangular patterns tended to characterize some of the newer towns. Most streets were little more than footpaths—more a medium for communication than for transportation—and even in major European cities paving was not widely introduced before the 12th century (1184 in Paris, 1235 in Florence, and 1300 in Lübeck). As the population of the city grew, walls were often expanded, but few cities at the time exceeded a mile in length. Sometimes sites were changed, as in Lübeck, and many new cities emerged with increasing population—frequently about one day's walk apart. Towns ranged in population from several hundred to perhaps 40,000 (as in London in the late 14th century, although London's population had been as high as 80,000 before the arrival of the Black Death). Paris and Venice were exceptions, reaching 100,000.

Conscious attempts to plan cities reemerged in Europe during the Renaissance. Although these efforts partly aimed at improving circulation and providing military defense, their prime objective was often the glorification of a ruler or a state. From the 16th century to the end of the 18th, many cities were laid out and built with monumental splendour. The result may have pleased and inspired the citizens, but it rarely contributed to their health, to the comfort of their homes, or to efficiency in manufacturing, distribution, and marketing.

The New World absorbed the planning concepts of European absolutism to only a limited degree. Pierre L'Enfant's grandiose plan for Washington, D.C. (1791), exemplified this transference, as did later City Beautiful projects, which aimed for grandeur in the siting of public buildings but exhibited less concern for the efficiency of residential, commercial, and industrial development. More influential on the layout of U.S. cities, however, was the rigid grid plan of Philadelphia, designed by William Penn (1682). This plan traveled west with the pioneers, since it was the simplest method of dividing surveyed territory. Although it took no cognizance of topography, it facilitated the development of land markets by establishing standard-sized lots that could be easily bought and sold—even sight unseen.

In much of the world, city plans were based on the concept of a centrally located public space. The plans differed, however, in their prescriptions for residential development. In the United States the New England town grew around a central commons; initially a pasture, it provided a focus of community life and a site for a meetinghouse, tavern, smithy, and shops and was later reproduced in the central squares of cities and towns throughout the country. Also from the New England town came the tradition of the freestanding single-family house that became the norm for most metropolitan areas. The central plaza, place, or square provided a focal point for European city plans as well. In contrast to American residential development, though, European domestic architecture was dominated by the attached house, while elsewhere in the world the marketplace or bazaar rather than an open space acted as the cynosure of cities. Courtyard-style domiciles characterized the Mediterranean region, while compounds of small houses fenced off from the street formed many African and Asian settlements.

THE ERA OF INDUSTRIALIZATION

In both Europe and the United States, the surge of industry during the mid- and late 19th century was accompanied by rapid population growth, unfettered business enterprise, great speculative profits, and public failures in managing the unwanted physical consequences of development.

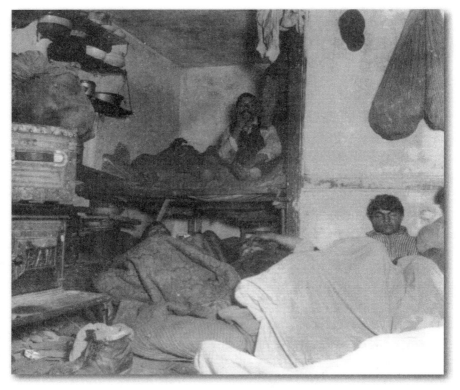

Shelter for immigrants in a New York City tenement, photograph by Jacob Riis, 1888. Library of Congress, Washington, D.C. (digital file no. 3a18572)

Giant sprawling cities developed during this era, exhibiting the luxuries of wealth and the meanness of poverty in sharp juxtaposition. Eventually the corruption and exploitation of the era gave rise to the Progressive movement, of which city planning formed a part. The slums, congestion, disorder, ugliness, and threat of disease provoked a reaction in which sanitation improvement was the first demand. Significant betterment of public health resulted from engineering improvements in water supply and sewerage, which were essential to the further growth of urban populations. Later in the century the first housing reform measures were enacted. The early regulatory laws (such as Great Britain's Public Health Act of 1848 and the New York State Tenement House Act of 1879) set minimal standards for housing construction. Implementation, however, occurred only slowly, as governments did not provide funding for upgrading existing dwellings, nor did the minimal rent-paying ability of slum dwellers offer incentives for landlords to improve their buildings. Nevertheless, housing improvement occurred as new structures were erected, and new legislation continued to raise standards, often in response to the exposés of investigators and activists such as Jacob Riis in the United States and Charles Booth in England.

Also during the Progressive era, which extended through the early 20th century, efforts to improve the urban environment emerged from recognition of the need for recreation. Parks were developed to provide visual relief and places for healthful play or relaxation. Later, playgrounds were carved out in congested areas, and facilities for games and sports were established not only for children but also for adults, whose workdays gradually shortened. Supporters of the parks movement believed that the opportunity for outdoor recreation would have a civilizing effect on the working classes, who were otherwise consigned to overcrowded housing and unhealthful workplaces. New York's Central Park, envisioned in the 1850s and designed by architects Calvert Vaux and Frederick Law Olmsted, became a widely imitated model. Among its contributions were the separation of pedestrian and vehicular traffic, the creation of a romantic landscape within the heart of the city, and a demonstration that the creation of parks could greatly enhance real-estate values in their surroundings.

The Mall at Central Park, New York City, in 1902. Library of Congress, Washington D.C. (neg. no. LC-USZ62-121334 DLC)

Concern for the appearance of the city had long been manifest in Europe, in the imperial tradition of court and palace and in the central plazas and great buildings of church and state. In Paris during the Second Empire (1852–70), Georges-Eugène, Baron Haussmann, became the greatest of the planners on a grand scale, advocating straight arterial boulevards, advantageous vistas, and a symmetry of squares and radiating roads. The resulting urban form was widely emulated throughout the rest of continental Europe. Haussmann's efforts went well beyond beautification, however; essentially they broke down the barriers to commerce presented by medieval Paris, modernizing the city so as to enable the efficient transportation of goods as well as the rapid mobilization of military troops. His designs involved the demolition of antiquated tenement structures and their replacement by new apartment houses intended for a wealthier clientele, the construction of transportation corridors and commercial space that broke up residential neighbourhoods, and the displacement of poor people from centrally located areas. Haussmann's methods provided a template by which urban redevelopment programs would operate in Europe and the United States until nearly the end of the 20th century, and they would extend their influence in much of the developing world after that.

As the grandeur of the European vision took root in the United States through the City Beautiful movement, its showpiece became the World's Columbian Exposition of 1893, developed in Chicago according to principles set out by American architect Daniel Burnham. The architectural style of the exposition established an ideal that many cities imitated. Thus, the archetype of the City Beautiful— characterized by grand malls and majestically sited civic buildings in Greco-Roman architecture—was replicated in civic centres and boulevards throughout the country, contrasting with and in protest against the surrounding disorder and ugliness. However, diffusion of the model in the United States was limited by the much more restricted power of the state (in contrast to European counterparts) and by the City Beautiful model's weak potential for enhancing businesses' profitability.

Whereas Haussmann's approach was especially influential on the European continent and in the design of American civic centres, it was the utopian concept of the garden city, first described by British social reformer Ebenezer Howard in his book *Garden Cities of To-Morrow* (1902), that shaped the appearance of residential areas in the United States and Great Britain. Essentially a suburban form, Howard's garden city incorporated low-rise homes on winding streets and culs-de-sac, the separation of commerce from residences, and plentiful open space lush with greenery. Howard called for a "cooperative commonwealth" in which rises in property values would be shared by the community, open land would be communally held, and manufacturing and retail establishments would be clustered within a short distance of residences. Successors abandoned Howard's socialist ideals but held on to the residential design form established in the two new towns built during Howard's lifetime (Letchworth and Welwyn Garden City), ultimately imitating the garden city model of winding roads and ample greenery in the forming of the modern suburban subdivision.

Perhaps the single most influential factor in shaping the physical form of the contemporary city was transportation technology. The evolution of transport modes from foot and horse to mechanized vehicles facilitated tremendous urban territorial expansion. Workers were able to live far from their jobs, and goods could move quickly from point of production to market. However, automobiles and buses rapidly congested the streets in the older parts of cities. By threatening strangulation of traffic, they dramatized the need to establish new kinds of orderly circulation systems. Increasingly, transportation networks became the focus of planning activities, especially as subway systems were constructed in New York, London, and Paris at the beginning of the 20th century. To accommodate increased traffic, municipalities invested heavily in widening and extending roads.

Many city governments established planning departments during the first third of the 20th century. The year 1909 was a milestone in the establishment of urban planning as a modern governmental function: it saw the passage of Britain's first town-planning act and, in the United States, the first national conference on city planning, the publication of Burnham's plan for Chicago, and the appointment of Chicago's Plan Commission (the first recognized planning agency in the United States, however, was created in Hartford, Conn., in 1907). Germany, Sweden, and other

European countries also developed planning administration and law at this time.

The colonial powers transported European concepts of city planning to the cities of the developing world. The result was often a new city planned according to Western principles of beauty and separation of uses, adjacent to unplanned settlements both new and old, subject to all the ills of the medieval European city. New Delhi, India, epitomizes this form of development. Built according to the scheme devised by the British planners Edwin Lutyens and Herbert Baker, it grew up cheek by jowl with the tangled streets of Old Delhi. At the same time, the old city, while less salubrious, offered its inhabitants a sense of community, historical continuity, and a functionality more suited to their way of life. The same pattern repeated itself throughout the British-ruled territories, where African capitals such as Nairobi, Kenya, and Salisbury, Southern Rhodesia (now Harare, Zimbabwe), were similarly designed to accommodate their white colonial rulers. Although the decorative motifs imposed by France in its colonial capitals reflected a somewhat different aesthetic sensibility, French planners likewise implanted broad boulevards and European-style housing in their colonial outposts.

Urban Form

A number of issues in urban planning began to make themselves felt with increasing urgency in the early decades of the 20th century.

Zoning and Subdivision Controls

As Western industrial cities rapidly expanded during the first part of the 20th century, factories encroached upon residential areas, tenements crowded in among small houses, and skyscrapers overshadowed other buildings. To preserve property values and achieve economy and efficiency in the structure and arrangement of the city, policy makers perceived a need to sort out incompatible activities, set some limits upon building size, and protect established areas from despoilment. Master plans prescribed the desired patterns of traffic circulation, bulk and density levels, and necessary public improvements. Zoning regulations, first instituted in the early decades of the 20th century, were the principal means for achieving these goals. They set maximums for building breadth and height and designated acceptable configurations of structures within demarcated areas (zones); most important in terms of their effect on urban development, zoning codes segregated particular uses of urban space. Thus, housing, manufacturing, and retail activities, which formerly intermixed, now took place in different parts of the city. Although zoning protected residents from adjacent noxious uses, it had the less-desirable further effect of forcing long trips to work and increasing routine travel, thereby contributing to traffic congestion and limiting activity in each part of the city to different times of the day. Some zoning codes provoked disputes. Court cases in the United States challenged zoning ordinances that, by requiring large single-residence dwellings on large lots, restricted the construction of affordable homes for low-income households. In some states courts struck down exclusionary zoning, and some remedial legislation was passed.

Parallel to the evolution of zoning in the United States was the development of subdivision controls, which subjected the initial laying out of vacant land to public regulation. These regulations affected the design of new developments and specified that new streets had to conform to the overall city plan. Some subdivision ordinances required property developers to provide the land needed for streets, playgrounds, and school sites and to pay all or most of the cost of building these facilities.

NEW TOWNS

After World War II a number of European countries, especially France, the Netherlands, Germany, and the Soviet Union, undertook the building of new towns (comprehensive new developments outside city centres) as governmental enterprises. Concerned with what they regarded as too much density within urban areas, governments constructed these new towns as a means of capturing the overspill from cities within planned developments rather than allowing haphazard exurban growth. Most of them, except in the Soviet Union, were primarily residential suburbs, although some British towns such as Milton Keynes did succeed in attracting both industry and population within low-rise conurbations. In Sweden the government successfully constructed accessible high-rise residential suburbs with mixed-income occupancy. Tapiola, in metropolitan Helsinki, Finland, was a low-rise ensemble embodying many of Howard's original ideas and incorporating architecture of the highest order. New town development in France, Italy, Spain, and Belgium, however, mostly resulted in large, uninviting high-rise residential projects for the working class on the urban periphery.

American postwar new town development depended largely on private initiative, with Reston, Virginia; Columbia, Maryland; Irvine, California; and Seaside, Florida, serving as some of the better-known examples. Preceding these efforts, however, were a number of small, privately planned suburbs, including Riverside, Illinois, a planned community outside Chicago that was designed by Frederick Law Olmsted in 1868–69, and Radburn, New Jersey, built in 1929 according to plans conceived by

Clarence Stein and Henry Wright. There are a few outstanding examples of planned new cities in such widely scattered places as India (where Le Corbusier designed Chandigarh), the Middle East, and South America.

In Asia the emerging industrial economies of the post-World War II period produced large, densely populated, congested metropolises. Some Asian governments addressed the problems of rapid expansion through massive construction projects that encompassed skyscraper office buildings, shopping malls, luxury apartments and hotels, and new airports. In Shanghai, in the span of little more than a decade, the Chinese government created Pudong New Area—a planned central business district along with factories and residences in Pudong, across the Huangpu River from Shanghai's old downtown core. Many developing countries, however, are still preoccupied with political and economic problems and have made little progress toward establishing an environmental planning function capable of avoiding the insalubrious conditions that characterized Western cities in the 19th century.

THE SCOPE OF PLANNING

Throughout the first half of the 20th century, the influence of planning broadened within Europe as various national and local statutes increasingly guided new development. European governments became directly involved with housing provision for the working class, and decisions concerning the siting of housing construction shaped urban growth. In the United States, local planning in the form of zoning began with the 1916 New York City zoning law, but it was not until the Great Depression of the 1930s that the federal government intervened in matters of housing and land use. During World War II, military mobilization and the need to coordinate defense production caused the development of the most extensive planning frameworks ever seen in the United States and Britain. Although the wartime agencies were demobilized after hostilities ended, they set a precedent for national economic and demographic planning, which, however, was much more extensive in Britain than in the United States.

POSTWAR APPROACHES

During the postwar period European governments mounted massive housing and rebuilding programs within their devastated cities. These programs were guided by the principles of modernist planning promulgated through the Congrès International d'Architecture Moderne (CIAM), based on the ideas of art and architectural historian Siegfried Giedion, Swiss architect Le Corbusier, and the International school rooted in Germany's Bauhaus. High-rise structures separated by green spaces prevailed in the developments built during this period. Their form reflected both the need to produce large-scale, relatively inexpensive projects and the architects' preference for models that exploited new materials and technologies and could be replicated universally. Government involvement in housing development gave the public sector a more direct means of controlling the pattern of urban growth through its investments, rather than relying on regulatory devices as a means of restricting private developers.

Within Britain the Greater London Plan of Leslie Patrick Abercrombie called for surrounding the metropolitan area with an inviolate greenbelt, construction of new towns beyond the greenbelt that would allow for lowering of population densities in the inner city, and the building of circumferential highways to divert traffic from the core. The concept of the sharp separation of city from country prevailed also throughout the rest of Britain and was widely adopted in the Scandinavian countries,

Germany, and the Netherlands as well. In the United States the burgeoning demand for housing stimulated the construction of huge suburban subdivisions. Construction was privately planned and financed, but the federal government encouraged it through tax relief for homeowners and government-guaranteed mortgages. Suburban planning took place at the municipal level in the form of zoning and subdivision approval, public development of sewerage and water systems, and schools. The lack of metropolitan-wide planning jurisdictions resulted in largely unplanned growth and consequent urban sprawl. Within central cities, however, the federal government subsidized land clearance by local urban renewal authorities and the construction of public housing (i.e., publicly owned housing for low-income people). Local government restricted its own reconstruction activities to public facilities such as schools, police stations, and recreation centres. It relied on private investors for the bulk of new construction, simply indicating what would be desirable. Consequently, many cleared sites lay vacant for decades when the private market did not respond.

PLANNING AND GOVERNMENT

The place of the city-planning function in the structure of urban government developed in different ways in different countries. In many countries today, private developers must obtain governmental permission in order to build. In the United States, however, they may build "as of right" if their plans conform to the municipality's zoning code. On the European continent, where municipal administration is strongly centralized, city planning occurs within the sphere of an executive department with substantial authority. In the United Kingdom the local planning authority is the elected local council, while a planning department acts in an executive and advisory capacity.

Developers denied permission to build can appeal the verdict to the central government.

Although the mayor and council have final decision-making power in U.S. cities, an independent planning commission of appointed members usually takes primary responsibility for routine planning functions. Planning activity primarily consists of the approval or disapproval of private development proposals. In larger cities the commission has a staff reporting to it. During the period of a large, federally financed urban renewal program in place from 1949 to 1974, most American cities had powerful semi-independent urban renewal authorities that were responsible for redevelopment planning. Some of these still exist, but in most places they either became subordinate to the mayor or combined with economic development agencies, which are often quasi-autonomous corporations. While they are appointed by the mayor and council, these agencies usually report to an independent board of directors drawn primarily from the business community. Especially as city government became preoccupied with economic development planning, the agencies were authorized to enter into development agreements with private investors.

In some countries, most notably in northern Europe, national governments made city planning part of their overall effort to deal with issues of growth and social welfare. Even in the United States—where the initiative remained with local governments and where metropolitan government never gained a significant foothold—the federal government became involved with local planning issues through the creation and execution of national housing and urban renewal legislation and through the supervisory role of the federal Department of Housing and Urban Development (HUD), established in 1965. As developing countries gained independence from colonial powers in the 1960s and 1970s, planning structures became highly centralized within the new national governments, which typically laid down the framework for city planning.

COMPETING MODELS

Starting in the 20th century, a number of urban planning theories came into prominence and, depending on their popularity and longevity, influenced the appearance and experience of the urban landscape. The primary goal of city planning in the mid-20th century was comprehensiveness. An increasing recognition of the interdependence of various aspects of the city led to the realization that land use, transport, and housing needed to be designed in relation to each other. Developments in other disciplines, particularly management science and operations research, influenced academic planners who sought to elaborate a universal method—also known as "the rational model"—whereby experts would evaluate alternatives in relation to a specified set of goals and then choose the optimum solution. The rational model was briefly hegemonic, but this scientific approach to public-policy making was quickly challenged by critics who argued that the human consequences of planning decisions could not be neatly quantified and added up.

The modernist model, involving wholesale demolition and reconstruction under the direction of planning officials isolated from public opinion, came under fierce attack both intellectually and on the ground. Most important in undermining support for the modernist approach was urbanologist Jane Jacobs. In her book *The Death and Life of Great American Cities* (1961), she sarcastically described redeveloped downtowns and housing projects as comprising the "radiant garden city"—a sly reference to the influence of Le Corbusier's "towers in the park" (from his *cité radieuse* concept) and Ebenezer Howard's antiurban garden city. Jacobs criticized large-scale clearance operations for destroying the complex social fabric of cities and imposing an inhuman orderliness. Rather than seeing high population density as an evil, she regarded it as an important factor in urban vitality. She considered that a lively street life made cities attractive, and she promoted diversity of uses and population groups as a principal value in governing urban development. According to Jacobs, urban diversity contributes to sustainable growth, whereas undifferentiated urban settings tend to depend upon unsustainable exploitation, exhibited in the extreme form by lumber or mining towns that collapse after the valuable resources have been removed. Jacobs was not alone in her criticism. Beginning in the 1960s, urban social movements, at times amounting to insurrection, opposed the displacements caused by large-scale modernist planning. In cities throughout the United States and Europe, efforts at demolishing occupied housing provoked fierce opposition. Within developing countries, governmental attempts to destroy squatter settlements stimulated similar counteroffensives.

By the end of the 20th century, planning orthodoxy in the United States and Europe began to take Jacobs's arguments into account. New emphasis was placed on the rehabilitation of existing buildings, historical preservation, adaptive reuse of obsolete structures, mixed-use development, and the "24-hour city"—i.e., districts where a variety of functions would create around-the-clock activity. Major new projects, while still sometimes involving demolition of occupied housing or commercial structures, increasingly came to be built on vacant or "brownfields" sites such as disused railroad yards, outmoded port facilities, and abandoned factory districts. Within developing countries, however, the modernist concepts of the earlier period still retained a significant hold. Thus, for example, China, in preparation for the Beijing Olympics of 2008, engaged in major displacement of its urban population to construct roads and sports facilities, and it likewise developed new commercial districts by building high-rise structures along the functionalist Corbusian model.

CONTEMPORARY PLANNING

The ways in which planning operated at the beginning of the 21st century did not conform to a single model of either a replicable process or a desirable outcome. Within Europe and the United States, calls for a participatory mode—one that involved residents most likely to be affected by change in the planning process for their locales—came to be honoured in some cities but not in others. The concept of participatory planning has spread to the rest of the world, although it remains limited in its adoption. Generally, the extent to which planning involves public participation reflects the degree of democracy enjoyed in each location. Where government is authoritarian, so is planning. Within a more participatory framework, the role of planner changes from that of expert to that of mediator between different groups, or "stakeholders." This changed role has been endorsed by theorists supporting a concept of "communicative rationality." Critics of this viewpoint, however, argue that the process may suppress innovation or simply promote the wishes of those who have the most power, resulting in outcomes contrary to the public interest. They are also concerned that the response of "not in my backyard" ("NIMBYism") precludes building affordable housing and needed public facilities if neighborhood residents are able to veto any construction that they fear will lower their property values.

In sum, the enormous variety of types of projects on which planners work, the lack of consensus over processes and goals, and the varying approaches taken in different cities and countries have produced great variation within contemporary urban planning. Nevertheless, although the original principle of strict segregation of uses continues to prevail in many places, there is an observable trend toward mixed-use development—particularly of complementary activities such as retail, entertainment, and housing—within urban centres.

Changing Objectives

Although certain goals of planning, such as protection of the environment, remain important, emphases among the various objectives have changed. In particular, economic development planning, especially in old cities that have suffered from the decline of manufacturing, has come to the fore. Planners responsible for economic development behave much like business executives engaged in marketing: they promote their cities to potential investors and evaluate physical development in terms of its attractiveness to capital and its potential to create jobs, rather than by its healthfulness or conformity to a master plan. Such planners work to achieve development agreements with builders and firms that will contribute to local commerce. Especially in the United States and the United Kingdom, planning agencies have concerned themselves with promoting economic development and have become involved in negotiating deals with private developers. In the United Kingdom these can include the trading of planning permission for "planning gain" or other community benefits; in other words, developers may be allowed to build in return for providing funds, facilities, or other benefits to the community. In the United States, where special permission is not required if the building fits into the zoning ordinance, deals usually involve some kind of public subsidy. Typical development agreements involve offering land, tax forgiveness, or regulatory relief to property developers in return for a commitment to invest in an area or to provide amenities. An agreement may also be struck between the city and a private firm in which the firm agrees to move into or remain in an area in return for various concessions. Many such arrangements generate controversy, especially if a municipality exercises the right of eminent domain and takes privately owned land for development projects.

A late 20th-century movement in planning, variously called *new urbanism*, *smart growth*, or *neotraditionalism*, has attracted popular attention through its alternative views of suburban development. Reflecting considerable revulsion against urban sprawl, suburban traffic congestion, and long commuting times, this movement has endorsed new construction that brings home, work, and shopping into proximity, encourages pedestrian traffic, promotes development around mass-transit nodes, and mixes types of housing. Within the United Kingdom, Prince Charles, heir apparent to the British throne, became a strong proponent of neotraditional planning through his sponsorship of Poundbury, a new town of traditional appearance in Dorset. Similar efforts in the United States, where growth on the metropolitan periphery continued unabated, chiefly arose as limited areas of planned development amid ongoing dispersal and sprawl. Although the movement's primary influence has been in new suburban development, it has also been applied to the redevelopment of older areas within the United Kingdom and the United States. Paternoster Square in London, adjacent to Saint Paul's Cathedral, and a number of HOPE VI schemes in the United States (built under a federal program that demolished public housing projects and replaced them with mixed-income developments) have been erected in accordance with neotraditional or new urbanist ideas.

New Pluralism

Universal principles regarding appropriate planning have increasingly broken down as a consequence of several

JANE JACOBS

(b. May 4, 1916, Scranton, Pa., U.S.—d. April 25, 2006, Toronto, Ont., Can.)

American-born Canadian urbanologist Jane Jacobs was noted for her clear and original observations on urban life and its problems.

Born Jane Butzner, she worked at the *Scranton Tribune* after graduating from high school. In 1934 she moved to New York City, where she held several different jobs while writing articles for various newspapers and magazines. In 1944 she met and married architect Robert Hyde Jacobs. Already keenly interested in city neighbourhoods and their vitality, both as a writer and—increasingly—as a community activist, she explored urban design and planning at length with her husband. In 1952 she became an associate editor of *Architectural Forum*, where she worked for a decade.

In 1961 Jacobs published her first full-length book, *The Death and Life of Great American Cities*, a brash and passionate reinterpretation of the multiple needs of modern urban places. The book, translated into several languages, established her as a force to be reckoned with by planners and economists. *The Economy of Cities* (1969) discusses the importance of diversity to a city's prosperity, and it, too, challenged much of the conventional wisdom on urban planning. Opposed to the Vietnam War and worried that her sons would be drafted, Jacobs and her family moved to Canada in 1968; she later became a Canadian citizen. Her other works include *Cities and the Wealth of Nations* (1984) and *The Nature of Economies* (2000). *Dark Age Ahead* (2004) centred on the decline of American culture.

trends. First, intellectual arguments against a "one plan fits all" approach have gained ascendancy. The original consensus on the form of orderly development embodying separation of uses and standardized construction along modernist lines has been replaced by sensitivity to local differences and greater willingness to accept democratic input. Second, it has become widely recognized that, even where the imposition of standards might be desirable, many places lack the resources to attain them. Within the developing world, informal markets and settlements, formerly condemned by planners, now appear to be inevitable and often appropriate in serving the needs of poor communities. Planners in these contexts, influenced by international aid institutions, increasingly endeavour to upgrade squatter settlements and street markets rather than eliminate them in the name of progress. Third, political forces espousing the free market have forced planners to seek market-based solutions to problems such as pollution and the provision of public services. This has led to privatization of formerly publicly owned facilities and utilities and to the trading of rights to develop land and to emit pollutants in place of a purely regulatory approach.

Planning in its origins had an implicit premise that a well-designed, comprehensively planned city would be a socially ameliorative one. In other words, it tended toward environmental determinism. The goals of planning have subsequently become more modest, and the belief that the physical environment can profoundly affect social behaviour has diminished. Nevertheless, planning as practice and discipline relies upon public policy as an instrument for producing a more equitable and attractive environment that, while not radically altering human behaviour, nonetheless contributes to improvements in the quality of life for a great number of people.

*C*hapter 4:
THE SOCIAL
SCIENCES,
PHILOSOPHY,
AND RELIGION

I deas that over the centuries have engaged philosophers and theologians—and most of the general public as well—include notions of one god, sin, the soul, evil, just war, natural law, punishment, human rights, and utopia. These and other philosophical and theological ideas are explored in this chapter, as are turning points in the social sciences such as the concept of mass production and theories of child development.

MASS PRODUCTION

The application of the principles of specialization, division of labour, and standardization of parts to the manufacture of goods is known as mass production. Such manufacturing processes attain high rates of output at low unit cost, with lower costs expected as volume rises. Mass production methods are based on two general principles: (1) the division and specialization of human labour; and (2) the use of tools, machinery, and other equipment, usually automated, in the production of standard, interchangeable parts and products. The use of modern methods of mass production has brought such improvements in the cost, quality, quantity, and variety of goods available that the largest global population in history is now sustained at the highest general standard of living.

THE INDUSTRIAL REVOLUTION
AND EARLY DEVELOPMENTS

The principle of the division of labour and the resulting specialization of skills can be found in many human activities, and there are records of its application to manufacturing in ancient Greece. The first unmistakable examples of manufacturing operations carefully designed to reduce production costs by specialized labour and the use of machines appeared in the 18th century in England. They were signaled by five important inventions in the textile industry: (1) John Kay's flying shuttle in 1733, which permitted the weaving of larger widths of cloth and significantly increased weaving speed; (2) Edmund Cartwright's power loom in 1785, which increased weaving speed still further; (3) James Hargreaves' spinning jenny in 1764; (4) Richard Arkwright's water frame in 1769; and (5) Samuel Crompton's spinning mule in 1779. The last three inventions improved the speed and quality of thread-spinning operations. A sixth invention, the steam engine, perfected by James Watt, was the key to further rapid development. After making major improvements in steam engine design in 1765, Watt continued his development and refinement of the engine until, in 1785, he successfully used one in a cotton mill. Once human, animal, and water power could be replaced with a reliable, low-cost source of motive energy, the Industrial Revolution was clearly established, and the next 200 years would witness invention and innovation the likes of which could never have been imagined.

In 1776 Adam Smith, in his *Wealth of Nations*, observed the benefits of the specialization of labour in the manufacture of pins. Although earlier observers had noted this phenomenon, Smith's writings commanded widespread attention and helped foster an awareness of industrial production and broaden its appeal.

The next major advance was made in 1797 when Eli Whitney, inventor of the cotton gin, proposed the manufacture of flintlocks with completely interchangeable parts, in contrast to the older method under which each gun was the individual product of a highly skilled gunsmith and each part was hand-fitted.

During the same period similar ideas were being tried out in Europe. In England Marc Brunel, a French-born inventor and engineer, established a production line to manufacture blocks (pulleys) for sailing ships, using the principles of division of labour and standardized parts. Brunel's machine tools were designed and built by Henry Maudslay, who has been called the father of the machine tool industry. Maudslay recognized the importance of precision tools that could produce identical parts; he and his student, Joseph Whitworth, also manufactured interchangeable, standardized metal bolts and nuts.

By the middle of the 19th century the general concepts of division of labour, machine-assisted manufacture, and assembly of standardized parts were well established. Large factories were in operation on both sides of the Atlantic, and some industries, such as textiles and steel, were using processes, machinery, and equipment that would be recognizable even in the late 20th century. The growth of manufacturing was accelerated by the rapid expansion of rail, barge, ship, and road transportation. The new transport companies not only enabled factories to obtain raw materials and to ship finished products over increasingly large distances, but they also created a substantial demand for the output of the new industries.

At this point in the Industrial Revolution, the methods and procedures used to organize human labour, to plan and control the flow of work, and to handle the myriad details on the shop floor were largely informal and were based on historical patterns and precedents. One man changed all of that.

PIONEERS OF MASS PRODUCTION METHODS

In 1881, at the Midvale Steel Company in the United States, Frederick W. Taylor began studies of the organization of manufacturing operations that subsequently formed the foundation of modern production planning. After carefully studying the smallest parts of simple tasks, such as the shoveling of dry materials, Taylor was able to design methods and tools that permitted workers to produce significantly more with less physical effort. Later, by making detailed stopwatch measurements of the time required to perform each step of manufacture, Taylor brought a quantitative approach to the organization of production functions.

At the same time, Frank B. Gilbreth and his wife, Lillian M. Gilbreth, U.S. industrial engineers, began their pioneering studies of the movements by which people carry out tasks. Using the then new technology of motion pictures, the Gilbreths analyzed the design of motion patterns and work areas with a view to achieving maximum economy of effort. The "time-and-motion" studies of Taylor and the Gilbreths provided important tools for the design of contemporary manufacturing systems.

In 1916 Henri Fayol, who for many years had managed a large coal mining company in France, began publishing his ideas about the organization and supervision of work, and by 1925 he had enunciated several principles and functions of management. His idea of unity of command, which stated that an employee should receive orders from only one supervisor, helped to clarify the organizational structure of many manufacturing operations.

Manufacturing Pioneers

Much of the credit for bringing these early concepts together in a coherent form, and creating the modern, integrated, mass production operation, belongs to the U.S. industrialist Henry Ford and his colleagues at the Ford Motor Company, where in 1913 a moving-belt conveyor was used in the assembly of flywheel magnetos. With it assembly time was cut from 18 minutes per magneto to five minutes. The approach was then applied to automobile body and motor assembly. The design of these production lines was highly analytical and sought the optimum division of tasks among work stations, optimum line speed, optimum work height, and careful synchronization of simultaneous operations.

The success of Ford's operation led to the adoption of mass production principles by industry in the United States and Europe. The methods made major contributions to the large growth in manufacturing productivity that has characterized the 20th century and produced phenomenal increases in material wealth and improvements in living standards in the industrialized countries.

THE ASSEMBLY LINE

Mass production operations are enhanced by the industrial arrangement of machines, equipment, and workers for continuous flow of workpieces, an arrangement known as an assembly line.

The design for an assembly line is determined by analyzing the steps necessary to manufacture each product component as well as the final product. All movement of material is simplified, with no cross flow, backtracking, or repetitious procedure. Work assignments, numbers of machines, and production rates are programmed so that all operations along the line are compatible.

An automotive assembly line starts with a bare chassis. Components are attached successively as the growing assemblage moves along a conveyor. Parts are matched into subassemblies on feeder lines that intersect the main line to deliver exterior and interior parts, engines, and other assemblies. As the units move by, each worker along the line performs a specific task, and every part and tool is delivered to its point of use in synchronization with the line. A number of different assemblies are on the line simultaneously, but an intricate system of scheduling and control ensures that the appropriate body type and colour, trim, engine, and optional equipment arrive together to make the desired combinations.

Automated assembly lines consist entirely of machines run by machines, with little or no human supervision. In such continuous-process industries as petroleum refining and chemical manufacture and in many modern automobile-engine plants, assembly lines are completely mechanized and consist almost entirely of automatic, self-regulating equipment.

Many products, however, are still assembled by hand because many component parts are not easily handled by machines. Expensive and somewhat inflexible, automatic assembly machines are economical only if they produce a high level of output. However, the development of versatile machinery and the increased use of industrial robots have improved the efficiency of fully automated assembly operations.

THEORIES OF CHILD DEVELOPMENT

The systematic study of children is less than 200 years old, and 90 percent of its research has been published since the mid-1940s. Basic philosophical differences over the fundamental nature of children and their growth have long occupied psychologists. The most important of such controversies concerned the relative importance of genetic endowment and environment, or "nature" and "nurture," in determining development during infancy and childhood. Most researchers now recognize, however, that it is the interaction of inborn biological factors with external factors, rather than the mutually exclusive action or predominance of one or the other force, that guides and influences human development.

The advances in cognition, emotion, and behaviour that normally occur at certain points in the life span require both maturation (i.e., genetically driven biological changes in the central nervous system) and events, experiences, and influences in the physical and social environment. Generally, maturation by itself cannot cause a psychological function to emerge; it does, however, permit such a function to occur and sets limits on its earliest time of appearance.

Three theories of human development have been dominant during the 20th century, each addressing different aspects of psychological growth. In retrospect, these and other theories seem to have been neither logically rigorous nor able to account for both intellectual and emotional growth within the same framework. Research in the field has thus tended to be descriptive, since developmental psychology lacks a tight net of interlocking theoretical propositions that reliably permit satisfying explanations.

Psychoanalytic Theories

Sigmund Freud's psychoanalytic theories were influenced by Charles Darwin's theory of evolution and by the physical concept of energy as applied to the central nervous system. Freud's most basic hypothesis was that each child is born with a source of basic psychological energy called libido. Further, each child's libido becomes successively focused on various parts of the body (in addition to people and objects) in the course of his emotional development. During the first postnatal year, libido is initially focused on the mouth and its activities; nursing enables the infant to derive gratification through a pleasurable reduction of tension in the oral region. Freud called this the oral stage of development. During the second year, the source of excitation is said to shift to the anal area, and the start of toilet training leads the child to invest libido in the anal functions. Freud called this period of development the anal stage. During the period from three through six years, the child's attention is attracted to sensations from the genitals, and Freud called this stage the phallic stage. The half dozen years before puberty are called the latency stage. During the final and so-called genital stage of development, mature gratification is sought in a heterosexual love relationship with another. Freud believed that adult emotional problems result from either deprivation or excessive gratification during the oral, anal, or phallic stages. A child with libido fixated at one of these stages would in adulthood show specific neurotic symptoms, such as anxiety.

Freud devised an influential theory of personality structure. According to him, a wholly unconscious mental structure called the id contains a person's inborn, inherited drives and instinctual forces and is closely identified with his basic psychological energy (libido). During infancy and childhood, the ego, which is the reality-oriented portion of the personality, develops to balance and complement the id. The ego utilizes a variety of conscious and unconscious mental processes to try to satisfy id instincts while also trying to maintain the individual comfortably in relation to the environment. Although id impulses are constantly directed toward obtaining immediate gratification of one's major instinctual drives (sex, affection, aggression, self-preservation), the ego functions to set limits on this process. In Freud's language, as the child grows, the reality principle gradually begins to control the pleasure principle; the child learns that the environment does not always permit immediate gratification. Child development, according to Freud, is thus primarily concerned with the emergence of the functions of the ego, which is responsible for channeling the discharge of fundamental drives and for controlling intellectual and perceptual functions in the process of negotiating realistically with the outside world.

Although Freud made great contributions to psychological theory—particularly in his concept of unconscious urges and motivations—his elegant concepts cannot be verified through scientific experimentation and empirical observation. But his concentration on emotional development in early childhood influenced even those schools of thought that rejected his theories. The belief that personality is affected by both biological and psychosocial forces operating principally within the family, with the major foundations being laid early in life, continues to prove fruitful in research on infant and child development.

Freud's emphasis on biological and psychosexual motives in personality development was modified by the

German-born American psychoanalyst Erik Erikson to include psychosocial and social factors. Erikson viewed emotional development over the life span as a sequence of stages during which there occur important inner conflicts whose successful resolution depends on both the child himself and his environment. These conflicts can be thought of as interactions between instinctual drives and motives on the one hand and social and other external factors on the other. Erikson evolved eight stages of development, the first four of which are (1) infancy: trust versus mistrust, (2) early childhood: autonomy versus shame and doubt, (3) preschool: initiative versus guilt, and (4) school age: industry versus inferiority. Conflicts at any one stage must be resolved if personality problems are to be avoided.

PIAGET'S THEORY

The Swiss psychologist Jean Piaget took the intellectual functioning of adults as the central phenomenon to be explained and wanted to know how an adult acquired the ability to think logically and to draw valid conclusions about the world from evidence. Piaget's theory rests on the fundamental notion that the child develops through stages until he arrives at a stage of thinking that resembles that of an adult. The four stages given by Piaget are (1) the sensorimotor stage from birth to 2 years, (2) the preoperational stage from 2 to 7 years, (3) the concrete-operational stage from 7 to 12 years, and (4) the stage of formal operations that characterizes the adolescent and the adult. One of Piaget's fundamental assumptions is that early intellectual growth arises primarily out of the child's interactions with objects in the environment. For example, Piaget believed that as a two-year-old child repeatedly builds and knocks down a tower of blocks, he is learning that the arrangement of objects in the world can be reversed. According to Piaget, children organize and adapt their experiences with objects into increasingly sophisticated cognitive models that enable them to deal with future situations in more effective ways. The older child, for instance, who has learned the concept of reversibility, will be able to execute an intelligent and logical search for a missing object, retracing his steps, for example, in order to determine where he may have dropped a set of keys. As children pass through successive stages of cognitive development, their knowledge of the world assumes different forms, with each stage building on the models and concepts acquired in the preceding stage. Adolescents in the final developmental stage, that of formal operations, are able to think in a rational and systematic manner about hypothetical problems that are not necessarily in accord with their experience.

LEARNING THEORY

A more distinctively American theoretical view focuses primarily on the child's actions, rather than on his emotions or thinking. This point of view, called learning theory, is concerned with identifying those mechanisms that can be offered to explain differences in behaviour, motives, and values among children. Its major principles stress the effects of reward and punishment (administered by parents, teachers, and peers) on the child's tendency to adopt the behaviour and values of others. Learning theory is thus directed to the overt actions of the child, rather than to inner psychological states or mechanisms.

Learning is any relatively permanent change in behaviour that results from past experience. There are two generally recognized learning processes: classical and instrumental conditioning, both of which use associations, or learned relations between events or stimuli, to create or shape behavioural responses. In classical conditioning, a close temporal relation is maintained between pairs of stimuli in order to create an association between the two. If, for example, an infant hears a tone and one second later receives some sweetened water in his mouth, the infant will make sucking movements to the sweet taste. After a dozen repetitions of this sequence of the tone followed by the sweet water, the infant associates the sounding of the tone with the receipt of the sweetened water and will, on subsequent repetitions, make sucking movements to the tone even though no sugar water is delivered.

Instrumental, or operant, conditioning involves creating a relationship between a response and a stimulus. If the experiment described above is changed so that after the tone is heard, the infant is required to turn his head to the right in order to receive the sweetened water, the infant will learn to turn his head when the tone sounds. The infant learns a relation between the response of turning his head and the subsequent receipt of the sweet taste. This set of relations is referred to as instrumental conditioning because the child must do something in order to receive the reward; the latter, in turn, makes the infant's head-turning response more likely in future occurrences of the situation. Rewards, such as praise and approval from parents, act as positive reinforcers of specific learned behaviours, while punishments decrease the likelihood of repeating such behaviours. Scientists who believe in the importance of these principles use them to explain the changing behaviour of children over the course of development.

JEAN PIAGET
(b. Aug. 9, 1896, Neuchâtel, Switz. — d. Sept. 17, 1980, Geneva)

The Swiss psychologist Jean Piaget was the first to make a systematic study of the acquisition of understanding in children. Trained in zoology and philosophy, Piaget later studied psychology in Zürich (from 1918) with Carl Gustav Jung and Eugen Bleuler, and he was subsequently affiliated with the University of Geneva from 1929 until his death. He developed a theory of "genetic epistemology," a natural timetable for the development of the child's ability to think in which he traced four stages—the sensorimotor (ages 0–2), preoperational or symbolic (2–7), concrete operational (7–12), and formal operational (through adulthood)—each marked by increased cognitive sophistication and ability to use symbols. In 1955 Piaget founded and became director (to 1980) of an international centre for genetic epistemology in Geneva. His numerous books include *The Language and Thought of the Child* (1923), *Judgment and Reasoning in the Child* (1924), *The Origin of Intelligence in Children* (1948), and *The Early Growth of Logic in the Child* (1964). He is regarded as the foremost developmental psychologist of the 20th century.

PSYCHOANALYTIC THEORY

The Austrian neurologist Sigmund Freud did not begin to fully develop his psychoanalytic theory until a decade after his colleague and business partner physician Josef Breuer had first treated a "hysterical" female patient with a "talking cure." The theory started with Freud's development of the technique of free association. In part an extrapolation of the automatic writing promoted by the German Jewish writer Ludwig Börne a century before, in part a result of his own clinical experience with other hysterics, this revolutionary method was announced in the work Freud published jointly with Breuer in 1895, *Studien über Hysterie* (*Studies in Hysteria*). By encouraging the patient to express any random thoughts that came associatively to mind, the technique aimed at uncovering hitherto unarticulated material from the realm of the psyche that Freud, following a long tradition, called the unconscious.

Because of its incompatibility with conscious thoughts or conflicts with other unconscious ones, this material was normally hidden, forgotten, or unavailable to conscious reflection. Difficulty in freely associating—sudden silences, stuttering, or the like—suggested to Freud the importance of the material struggling to be expressed, as well as the power of what he called the patient's defenses against that expression. Such blockages Freud dubbed resistance, which had to be broken down in order to reveal hidden conflicts. Unlike Jean-Martin Charcot and Breuer, Freud came to the conclusion, based on his clinical experience with female hysterics, that the most insistent source of resisted material was sexual in nature. And even more momentously, he linked the etiology of neurotic symptoms to the same struggle between a sexual feeling or urge and the psychic defenses against it. Being able to bring that conflict to consciousness through free association and then probing its implications was thus a crucial step, he reasoned, on the road to relieving the symptom, which was best understood as an unwitting compromise formation between the wish and the defense.

SCREEN MEMORIES

At first, however, Freud was uncertain about the precise status of the sexual component in this dynamic conception of the psyche. His patients seemed to recall actual experiences of early seductions, often incestuous in nature. Freud's initial impulse was to accept these as having happened. But then, as he disclosed in a now famous letter to Wilhelm Fliess of Sept. 2, 1897, he concluded that, rather than being memories of actual events, these shocking recollections were the residues of infantile impulses and desires to be seduced by an adult. What was recalled was not a genuine memory but what he would later call a screen memory, or fantasy, hiding a primitive wish. That is, rather than stressing the corrupting initiative of adults in the etiology of neuroses, Freud concluded that the fantasies and yearnings of the child were at the root of later conflict.

The absolute centrality of his change of heart in the subsequent development of psychoanalysis cannot be doubted. For in attributing sexuality to children, emphasizing the causal power of fantasies, and establishing the importance of repressed desires, Freud laid the groundwork for what many have called the epic journey into his own psyche, which followed soon after the dissolution of his partnership with Breuer.

Freud's work on hysteria had focused on female sexuality and its potential for neurotic expression. To be fully universal, psychoanalysis — a term Freud coined in 1896 — would also have to examine the male psyche in a condition of what might be called normality. It would have to become more than a psychotherapy and develop into a complete theory of the mind. To this end Freud accepted the enormous risk of generalizing from the experience he knew best: his own. Significantly, his self-analysis was both the first and the last in the history of the movement he spawned; all future analysts would have to undergo a training analysis with someone whose own analysis was ultimately traceable to Freud's of his disciples.

Freud's self-exploration was apparently enabled by a disturbing event in his life. In October 1896, Jakob Freud died shortly before his 81st birthday. Emotions were released in his son that he understood as having been long repressed, emotions concerning his earliest familial experiences and feelings. Beginning in earnest in July 1897, Freud attempted to reveal their meaning by drawing on a technique that had been available for millennia: the deciphering of dreams. Freud's contribution to the tradition of dream analysis was path-breaking, for in insisting on them as "the royal road to a knowledge of the unconscious," he provided a remarkably elaborate account of why dreams originate and how they function.

THE INTERPRETATION OF DREAMS

In what many commentators consider his master work, *Die Traumdeutung* (published in 1899, but given the date of the dawning century to emphasize its epochal character; *The Interpretation of Dreams*), he presented his findings. Interspersing evidence from his own dreams with evidence from those recounted in his clinical practice, Freud contended that dreams played a fundamental role in the psychic economy. The mind's energy—which Freud called libido and identified principally, but not exclusively, with the sexual drive—was a fluid and malleable force capable of excessive and disturbing power. Needing to be discharged to ensure pleasure and prevent pain, it sought whatever outlet it might find. If denied the gratification provided by direct motor action, libidinal energy could seek its release through mental channels. Or, in the language of *The Interpretation of Dreams*, a wish can be satisfied by an imaginary wish fulfillment. All dreams, Freud claimed, even nightmares manifesting apparent anxiety, are the fulfillment of such wishes.

More precisely, dreams are the disguised expression of wish fulfillments. Like neurotic symptoms, they are the effects of compromises in the psyche between desires and prohibitions in conflict with their realization. Although sleep can relax the power of the mind's diurnal censorship of forbidden desires, such censorship, nonetheless, persists in part during nocturnal existence. Dreams, therefore, have to be decoded to be understood, and not merely because they are actually forbidden desires experienced in distorted fashion. For dreams undergo further revision in the process of being recounted to the analyst.

The Interpretation of Dreams provides a hermeneutic for the unmasking of the dream's disguise, or dreamwork, as Freud called it. The manifest content of the dream, that which is remembered and reported, must be understood as veiling a latent meaning. Dreams defy logical entailment and narrative coherence, for they intermingle the residues of immediate daily experience with the deepest, often most infantile wishes. Yet they can be ultimately decoded by attending to four basic activities of the dreamwork and reversing their mystifying effect.

The first of these activities, condensation, operates through the fusion of several different elements into one. As such, it exemplifies one of the key operations of psychic life, which Freud called overdetermination. No direct correspondence between a simple manifest content and its multidimensional latent counterpart can be assumed. The second activity of the dreamwork, displacement, refers to the decentring of dream thoughts, so that the most urgent wish is often obliquely or marginally represented on the manifest level. Displacement also means the associative substitution of one signifier in the dream for another, say, the king for one's father. The third activity Freud called representation, by which he meant the transformation of thoughts into images. Decoding a dream thus means translating such visual representations back into intersubjectively available language through free association. The final function of the dreamwork is secondary revision, which provides some order and intelligibility to the dream by supplementing its content with narrative coherence. The process of dream interpretation thus reverses the direction of the dreamwork, moving from the level of the conscious recounting of the dream through the preconscious back beyond censorship into the unconscious itself.

FURTHER THEORETICAL DEVELOPMENT

In 1904 Freud published *Zur Psychopathologie des Alltagslebens* (*The Psychopathology of Everyday Life*), in which he explored such seemingly insignificant errors as slips of the tongue or pen (later colloquially called Freudian slips), misreadings, or forgetting of names. These errors Freud understood to have symptomatic and thus interpretable importance. But unlike dreams they need not betray a repressed infantile wish yet can arise from more immediate hostile, jealous, or egoistic causes.

In 1905 Freud extended the scope of this analysis by examining *Der Witz und seine Beziehung zum Unbewussten* (*Jokes and Their Relation to the Unconscious*). Invoking the idea of "joke-work" as a process comparable to dreamwork, he also acknowledged the double-sided quality of jokes, at once consciously contrived and unconsciously revealing. Seemingly innocent phenomena like puns or jests are as open to interpretation as more obviously tendentious, obscene, or hostile jokes. The explosive response often produced by successful humour, Freud contended, owes its power to the orgasmic release of unconscious impulses, aggressive as well as sexual. But insofar as jokes are more deliberate than dreams or slips, they draw on the rational dimension of the psyche that Freud was to call the ego as much as on what he was to call the id.

In 1905 Freud also published the work that first thrust him into the limelight as the alleged champion of a pansexualist understanding of the mind: *Drei Abhandlungen zur Sexualtheorie* (*Three Contributions to the Sexual Theory*, later translated as *Three Essays on the Theory of Sexuality*), revised and expanded in subsequent editions. The work established Freud, along with Richard von Kraft-Ebing, Havelock Ellis, Albert Moll, and Iwan Bloch, as a pioneer in the serious study of sexology. Here he outlined in greater detail than before his reasons for emphasizing the sexual component in the development of both normal and pathological behaviour. Although not as reductionist as popularly assumed, Freud nonetheless extended the concept of sexuality beyond conventional usage to include a panoply of erotic impulses from the earliest childhood years on. Distinguishing between sexual aims (the act toward which instincts strive) and sexual objects (the person, organ, or physical entity eliciting attraction), he elaborated a repertoire of sexually generated behaviour of astonishing variety. Beginning very early in life, imperiously insistent on its gratification, remarkably plastic in its expression, and open to easy maldevelopment, sexuality, Freud concluded, is the prime mover in a great deal of human behaviour.

SIGMUND FREUD

(b. May 6, 1856, Freiberg, Moravia, Austrian Empire—d. Sept. 23, 1939, London, Eng.)

Austrian neuropsychologist Sigmund Freud founded psychoanalysis and was one of the major intellectual figures of the 20th century. Trained in Vienna as a neurologist, Freud went to Paris in 1885 to study with Jean-Martin Charcot, whose work on hysteria led Freud to conclude that mental disorders might be caused purely by psychological rather than organic factors. Returning to Vienna (1886), Freud collaborated with the physician Josef Breuer (1842–1925) in further studies on hysteria, resulting in the development of some key psychoanalytic concepts and techniques, including free association, the unconscious, resistance (later defense mechanisms), and neurosis. In 1899 he published *The Interpretation of Dreams*, in which he analyzed the complex symbolic processes underlying dream formation: he proposed that dreams are the disguised expression of unconscious wishes. In his controversial *Three Essays on the Theory of Sexuality* (1905), he delineated the complicated stages of psychosexual development (oral, anal, and phallic) and the formation of the Oedipus complex. During World War I, he wrote papers that clarified his understanding of the relations between the unconscious and conscious portions of the mind and the workings of the id, ego, and superego. Freud eventually applied his psychoanalytic insights to such diverse phenomena as jokes and slips of the tongue, ethnographic data, religion and mythology, and modern civilization. Works of note include *Totem and Taboo* (1913), *Beyond the Pleasure Principle* (1920), *The Future of an Illusion* (1927), and *Civilization and Its Discontents* (1930). Freud fled to England when the Nazis annexed Austria in 1938; he died shortly thereafter. Despite the relentless and often compelling challenges mounted against virtually all of his ideas, both in his lifetime and after, Freud has remained one of the most influential figures in contemporary thought.

HUMAN RIGHTS

Human rights are the rights that belong to an individual as a consequence of being human. They refer to a wide continuum of values that are universal in character and in some sense equally claimed for all human beings.

The origins of the concept of human rights are usually agreed to be found in the Greco-Roman natural-law doctrines of stoicism, which held that a universal force pervades all creation and that human conduct should therefore be judged according to the law of nature, and in the *jus gentium* ("law of nations"), in which certain universal rights were extended beyond the rights of Roman citizenship. These concepts taught more of duties than rights, however, and allowed for slavery and serfdom.

It was during the period from the Renaissance until the 17th century that the beliefs and practices of society so changed that the idea of human (or natural) rights could take hold as a general social need and reality. The writings of St. Thomas Aquinas and Hugo Grotius, as well as Magna Carta, the Petition of Rights of 1628, and the English Bill of Rights, all reflected the view that human beings are endowed with certain eternal and inalienable rights.

This modernist conception of natural law as meaning natural rights was elaborated in the 17th and 18th centuries by such writers as René Descartes, Gottfried Leibniz, Benedict de Spinoza, and Francis Bacon. Particularly to be noted are the writings of the English philosopher John Locke, who was perhaps the most important natural-law theorist of modern times, and the Philosophes, including Denis Diderot, Voltaire, Charles-Louis de Secondat Montesquieu, and Jean-Jacques Rousseau.

The struggle against political absolutism in the late 18th and the 19th centuries further advanced the concept of human rights. Thomas Jefferson and the marquis de Lafayette gave eloquence to the plain prose of the previous century, and freedoms were specified in a variety of historic documents such as The Declaration of the Rights of Man and of the Citizen (1789) and the Bill of Rights (1791) of the Constitution of the United States (1787).

The idea that natural law is the foundation for human rights came under attack during the late 18th century by such men as conservatives Edmund Burke and David Hume, as well as by Jeremy Bentham, a founder and leading proponent of utilitarianism. This assault continued into the early 20th century. Such writers as John Stuart Mill, Friedrich Karl von Savigny, Sir Henry Maine, John Austin, and Ludwig Wittgenstein sought other justifications for, and definitions of, those rights. But efforts to assert and protect the rights of humanity continued to multiply in one form or another—the abolition of slavery, labour laws, popular education, trade unionism, universal suffrage—during the 19th and early 20th centuries, and the notion of human rights had achieved universal acceptance, at least in principle, by the second half of the 20th century, following the fall of Nazi Germany.

This general agreement that all human beings are entitled to some basic rights marked the birth of the international and universal recognition of human rights. In the charter establishing the United Nations, all members were pledged to achieve "universal respect for, and observance of, human rights and fundamental freedoms for all without distinction as to race, sex, language, or religion," and the UN has continued to affirm its commitment to human rights, particularly in such documents as the Universal Declaration of Human Rights (1948).

International concern for human rights has also been evident outside of the United Nations. For example, the Conference on Security and Cooperation in Europe, which met in Helsinki in 1973–75, produced the Helsinki Final Act. The European Convention for the Protection of Human Rights and Fundamental Freedoms, which first met in 1950, eventually produced the International Covenant on Civil and Political Rights and the European Social Charter; the Ninth Pan-American Conference of 1948 adopted the American Declaration on the Rights and Duties of Man; and the Organization of African Unity in 1981 adopted the African Charter on Human and Peoples' Rights.

UNIVERSAL DECLARATION OF HUMAN RIGHTS

The document by this name was adopted by the United Nations General Assembly on Dec. 10, 1948 (now celebrated annually as Human Rights Day). Drafted by a committee chaired by former first lady Eleanor Roosevelt, it was adopted without dissent but with eight abstentions. Among its 30 articles are definitions of civil and political rights (including the rights to life, liberty, and a fair trial) as well as definitions of economic, social, and cultural rights (including the right to social security and to participation in the cultural life of one's community), all of which are owed by UN member states to those under their jurisdiction. It has acquired more juridical status than originally intended and has been widely used, even by national courts, as a means of judging compliance with member states' human-rights obligations. The declaration has been the foundation of the work of nongovernmental organizations such as Amnesty International.

There are also a number of private groups involved in human-rights advocacy. One of the best-known international human-rights agencies is Amnesty International (founded in 1961), an organization dedicated to publicizing violations of human rights, especially freedoms of speech and religion and the right of political dissent.

CONSCIENCE

The personal sense of the moral content of one's own conduct, intentions, or character with regard to a feeling of obligation to do right or be good is termed conscience. This sense, usually informed by acculturation and instruction, is thus generally understood to give intuitively authoritative judgments regarding the moral quality of single actions.

Historically, almost every culture has recognized the existence of such a faculty. Ancient Egyptians, for example, were urged not to transgress against the dictates of the heart, for one "must stand in fear of departing from its guidance." In some belief systems, conscience is regarded as the voice of God and therefore a completely reliable guide of conduct: among the Hindus it is considered "the invisible God who dwells within us." Among Western religious groups, the Society of Friends (or Quakers) places particular emphasis on the role of conscience in apprehending and responding through conduct to the "Inner Light" of God.

Outside the context of religion, philosophers, social scientists, and psychologists have sought to understand conscience in both its individual and universal aspects. The view that holds conscience to be an innate, intuitive faculty determining the perception of right and wrong is called intuitionism. The view that holds conscience to be a cumulative and subjective inference from past experience giving direction to future conduct is called empiricism. The behavioral scientist, on the other hand, may view the conscience as a set of learned responses to particular social stimuli. Another explanation of conscience was put forth in the 20th century by Sigmund Freud in his postulation of the superego. According to Freud, the superego is a major element of personality that is formed by the child's incorporation of moral values through parental approval or punishment. The resulting internalized set of prohibitions, condemnations, and inhibitions is that part of the superego known as conscience.

GEORGE FOX

(b. July 1624, Drayton-in-the-Clay, Leicestershire, Eng.—d. Jan. 13, 1691, London)

The English preacher George Fox became the founder of the Society of Friends, or Quakers. The son of a weaver, he left home at age 18 in search of religious experience. Probably beginning as a Puritan, he reacted even more strongly than the Puritans against the tradition of the Church of England and came to regard personal experience as the true source of authority, placing God-given "inward light," or inspiration, above creeds and scripture. He traveled the countryside on foot, preaching to small groups, and he and other preachers established congregations. The Society of Friends arose in the 1650s. The Quakers' denunciation of ministers and public officials and their refusal to pay tithes or take oaths led to persecution, and Fox was imprisoned eight times between 1649 and 1673. He made missionary trips to Ireland, the Caribbean islands, North America, and northern Europe. His *Journal* gives an account of his life and of the rise of Quakerism.

SIN

Sin, or moral evil, is regarded in Judaism and Christianity as the deliberate and purposeful violation of the will of God.

The concept of sin has been present in many cultures throughout history, where it was usually equated with an individual's failure to live up to external standards of conduct or with his violation of taboos, laws, or moral codes. Some ancient societies also had concepts of corporate, or collective, sin—referred to by John Calvin and other Christian theologians as original sin—affecting all human beings and dating from a mythical "fall of man" out of a state of primitive and blissful innocence. In ancient Greek thought, sin was looked upon as, in essence, a failure on the part of a person to achieve his true self-expression and to preserve his due relation to the rest of the universe; it was attributed mainly to ignorance.

In the Old Testament, sin is directly linked to the monotheistic beliefs of the Hebrews. Sinful acts are viewed as a defiance of God's commandments, and sin itself is regarded as an attitude of defiance or hatred of God. The New Testament accepts the Judaic concept of sin but regards humanity's state of collective and individual sinfulness as a condition that Jesus came into the world to heal. Redemption through Christ could enable men to overcome sin and thus to become whole. Both Christianity and Judaism see sin as a deliberate violation of the will of God and as being attributable to human pride, self-centredness, and disobedience. While insisting more strongly than most religions upon the gravity of sin, both in its essence and in its consequences, both Christianity and Judaism have emphatically rejected the Manichaean doctrine that either the created world as a whole or the material part of it is inherently evil. Christianity holds rather that evil is the result of the misuse of their free will by created beings and that the body, with its passions and impulses, is to be neither ignored nor despised but sanctified; in the Bible, the "flesh" that is spoken of disparagingly is not the human body but human nature in rebellion against God.

Theologians divide sin into "actual" and "original." Actual sin is sin in the ordinary sense of the word and consists of evil acts, whether of thought, word, or deed. Original sin (the term can be misleading) is the morally vitiated condition in which one finds oneself at birth as a member of a sinful race. In Genesis 3, this is depicted as an inherited consequence of the first human sin, i.e., that of Adam. Theologians differ as to the interpretation of this narrative, but it is agreed that original sin, however mysterious its origin and nature may be, arises from human beings having come into the world not as isolated individuals but as members of a corporate race inheriting both good and evil features from its past history.

Actual sin is subdivided, on the basis of its gravity, into mortal and venial. This distinction is often difficult to apply but can hardly be avoided. A mortal sin is a deliberate turning away from God; it is a sin in a grave matter that is committed in full knowledge and with the full consent of the sinner's will, and until it is repented it cuts the sinner off from God's sanctifying grace. A venial sin usually involves a less important matter and is committed with less self-awareness of wrongdoing. While a venial sin weakens the sinner's union with God, it is not a deliberate turning from him and so does not wholly block the inflow of sanctifying grace.

Actual sin is also subdivided into material and formal. Formal sin is both wrong in itself and known by the sinner to be wrong; it therefore involves him in personal guilt. Material sin consists of an act that is wrong in itself (because contrary to God's law and human moral nature) but which the sinner does not know to be wrong and for which he is therefore not personally culpable.

JOHN CALVIN

(b. July 10, 1509, Noyon, Picardy, France—d. May 27, 1564,
Geneva, Switz.)

The French Protestant theologian John Calvin (French:
Jean Cauvin) was a major figure of the Reformation. He
studied religion at the University of Paris and law in
Orléans and Bourges. When he returned to Paris in 1531 he
studied the Bible and became part of a movement that
emphasized salvation by grace rather than by works.
Government intolerance prompted him to move to Basel,
Switz., where he wrote the first edition of *Institutes of the
Christian Religion* (1536). Gaining a reputation among
Protestant leaders, he went to Geneva to help establish
Protestantism in that city. He was expelled by city fathers
in 1538 but returned in 1541, when the town council instituted the church order outlined in his *Ecclesiastical
Ordinances*, including enforcement of sexual morality and
abolition of Catholic "superstition." He approved the
arrest and conviction for heresy of Michael Servetus. By
1555 Calvin had succeeded in establishing a theocracy in
Geneva, where he served as pastor and head of the Genevan
Academy and wrote the sermons, biblical commentaries,
and letters that form the basis of Calvinism.

SOUL

In religion and philosophy, the soul is the immaterial
aspect or essence of a human being, that which confers
individuality and humanity, and it is often considered to
be synonymous with the mind or the self. In theology, the
soul is further defined as that part of the individual which

partakes of divinity and often is considered to survive the death of the body.

Many cultures have recognized some incorporeal principle of human life or existence corresponding to the soul, and many have attributed souls to all living things. There is evidence even among prehistoric peoples of a belief in an aspect distinct from the body and residing in it. Despite widespread and longstanding belief in the existence of a soul, however, different religions and philosophers have developed a variety of theories as to its nature, its relationship to the body, and its origin and mortality.

Among ancient peoples, both the Egyptians and the Chinese conceived of a dual soul. The Egyptian *ka* (breath) survived death but remained near the body, while the spiritual *ba* proceeded to the region of the dead. The Chinese distinguished between a lower, sensitive soul, which disappears with death, and a rational principle, the *hun,* which survives the grave and is the object of ancestor worship.

The early Hebrews apparently had a concept of the soul but did not separate it from the body, although later Jewish writers developed the idea of the soul further. Old Testament references to the soul are related to the concept of breath and establish no distinction between the ethereal soul and the corporeal body. Christian concepts of a body-soul dichotomy originated with the ancient Greeks and were introduced into Christian theology at an early date by St. Gregory of Nyssa and by St. Augustine.

Ancient Greek concepts of the soul varied considerably according to the particular era and philosophical school. The Epicureans considered the soul to be made up of atoms like the rest of the body. For the Platonists, the soul was an immaterial and incorporeal substance, akin to the gods yet part of the world of change and becoming.

Aristotle's conception of the soul was obscure, though he did state that it was a form inseparable from the body.

In Christian theology, St. Augustine spoke of the soul as a "rider" on the body, making clear the split between the material and the immaterial, with the soul representing the "true" person. However, although body and soul were separate, it was not possible to conceive of a soul without its body. In the European Middle Ages, St. Thomas Aquinas returned to the Greek philosophers' concept of the soul as a motivating principle of the body, independent but requiring the substance of the body to make an individual.

From the Middle Ages onward, the existence and nature of the soul and its relationship to the body continued to be disputed in Western philosophy. To René Descartes, man was a union of the body and the soul, each a distinct substance acting on the other; the soul was equivalent to the mind. To Benedict de Spinoza, body and soul formed two aspects of a single reality. Immanuel Kant concluded that the soul was not demonstrable through reason, although the mind inevitably must reach the conclusion that the soul exists because such a conclusion was necessary for the development of ethics and religion. To William James at the beginning of the 20th century, the soul as such did not exist at all but was merely a collection of psychic phenomena.

Just as there have been different concepts of the relation of the soul to the body, there have been numerous ideas about when the soul comes into existence and when and if it dies. Ancient Greek beliefs were varied and evolved over time. Pythagoras held that the soul was of divine origin and existed before and after death. Plato and Socrates also accepted the immortality of the soul, while Aristotle considered only part of the soul, the *noûs*, or intellect, to have that quality. Epicurus believed that

AUGUSTINE

(b. Nov. 13, 354, Tagaste, Numidia—d. Aug. 28, 430, Hippo Regius; feast day August 28)

The Christian theologian Augustine (also called Saint Augustine of Hippo) was one of the Latin Fathers of the Church and one of the most significant Christian thinkers. Born in Roman North Africa, he adopted Manichaeism, taught rhetoric in Carthage, and fathered a son. After moving to Milan he converted to Christianity under the influence of Ambrose, who baptized him in 387. He returned to Africa to pursue a contemplative life, and in 396 he became bishop of Hippo (now Annaba, Alg.), a post he held until his death while the city was under siege by a Vandal army. His best-known works include the *Confessions*, an autobiographical meditation on God's grace, and *The City of God*, on the nature of human society and the place of Christianity in history. His theological works *On Christian Doctrine* and *On the Trinity* are also widely read. His sermons and letters show the influence of Neoplatonism and carry on debates with the proponents of Manichaeism, Donatism, and Pelagianism. His views on predestination influenced later theologians, notably John Calvin. He was declared a Doctor of the Church in the early Middle Ages.

both body and soul ended at death. The early Christian philosophers adopted the Greek concept of the soul's immortality and thought of the soul as being created by God and infused into the body at conception.

In the Hindu religion, each atman ("breath," or "soul") is considered to have been created at the beginning of time and imprisoned in an earthly body at birth. At the death of the body, the atman passes into a new body, its position in the Chain of Being determined by karma, or the cumulative consequences of actions. The cycle of death and rebirth (samsara) is eternal according to some Hindus but others say it persists only until the soul has attained karmic perfection, thus merging with the Absolute. Buddhism negates the concept of atman, asserting that any sense of the individual soul or self is illusory.

The Muslim concept, like that of the Christian, holds that the soul comes into existence at the same time as the body; thereafter, it has a life of its own, its union with the body being a temporary condition.

THE PROBLEM OF EVIL

In theology and the philosophy of religion, the problem of evil arises for any view that affirms the following three propositions: God is almighty, God is perfectly good, and evil exists.

THE PROBLEM

An important statement of the problem of evil was formulated by the Scottish philosopher David Hume when he asked "Is [God] willing to prevent evil, but not able? then is he impotent. Is he able, but not willing? then is he malevolent. Is he both able and willing? whence then is evil?" (*Dialogues Concerning Natural Religion*, 1779). Since well before Hume's time, the problem has been the basis of a positive argument for atheism: If God exists, then he is omnipotent and perfectly good; a perfectly good being would eliminate evil as far as it could; there is no limit to what an omnipotent being can do; therefore, if God exists, there would be no evil in the world; there is evil in the world; therefore, God does not exist. In this argument and in the problem of evil itself, evil is understood to encompass both moral evil (caused by free human actions) and natural evil (caused by natural phenomena such as disease, earthquakes, and floods).

Most thinkers, however, have found this argument too simple, since it does not recognize cases in which eliminating one evil causes another to arise or in which the existence of a particular evil entails some good state of affairs that morally outweighs it. Moreover, there may be logical limits to what an omnipotent being can or cannot do. Most skeptics, therefore, have taken the reality of evil as evidence that God's existence is unlikely rather than impossible. Often the reality of evil is treated as canceling out whatever evidence there may be that God exists—e.g., as set forth in the argument from design, which is based on an analogy between the apparent design discerned in the cosmos and the design involved in human artifacts. Thus, Hume devotes much of the earlier parts of his *Dialogues* to attacking the argument from design, which was popular in the 18th century. In later parts of the work, he discusses the problem of evil and concludes by arguing after all that the mixed evidence available supports the existence of a divine designer of the world, but only one who is morally neutral and not the God of traditional theistic religions.

THEISTIC RESPONSES

Religious believers have had recourse to two main strategies. One approach is to offer a theodicy, an account of why God chooses to permit evil in the world (and why he is morally justified in so choosing)—e.g., that it is a necessary consequence of sin or that, as Gottfried Wilhelm

Leibniz claimed, this is the "best of all possible worlds." The other approach is to attempt a more limited "defense," which does not aim to explain God's purposes but merely to show that the existence of at least some evil in the world is logically compatible with God's goodness, power, and wisdom. Many philosophers and theologians have rejected accounts of the first kind as inherently implausible or as foolhardy attempts to go beyond the bounds of human knowledge to discern God's inscrutable purposes.

A variety of arguments have been offered in response to the problem of evil, and some of them have been used in both theodicies and defenses. One argument, known as the free will defense, claims that evil is caused not by God but by human beings, who must be allowed to choose evil if they are to have free will. This response presupposes that humans are indeed free, and it fails to reckon with natural evil, except insofar as the latter is increased by human factors such as greed or thoughtlessness. Another argument, developed by the English philosopher Richard Swinburne, is that natural evils can be the means of learning and maturing. Natural evils, in other words, can help cultivate virtues such as courage and generosity by forcing humans to confront danger, hardship, and need. Such arguments are commonly supplemented by appeals to belief in a life after death, not just as reward or compensation but as the state in which the point of human suffering and the way in which God brings good out of evil will be made clear. Since many theodicies seem limited (because one can easily imagine a better world), and since many thinkers have not been convinced by the argument that the reality of evil establishes atheism, it is likely that future discussions will attempt to balance the reality of evil against evidence in favour of the existence of God.

HANNAH ARENDT

(b. Oct. 14, 1906, Hannover, Ger.—d. Dec. 4, 1975, New York, N.Y., U.S.)

Hannah Arendt was a German-born U.S. political scientist and philosopher known for her critical writing on Jewish affairs and her study of totalitarianism. She studied philosophy at the Universities of Marburg, Freiburg, and Heidelberg, receiving a doctorate from the latter in 1928. While at Marburg she began a romantic relationship with her teacher Martin Heidegger. Following the Nazi takeover of Germany in 1933, Arendt, who was Jewish, fled to Paris, where she became a social worker, and then to New York City in 1941. Her major work, *Origins of Totalitarianism* (1951), traced totalitarianism to 19th-century anti-Semitism, imperialism, and the disintegration of the traditional nation-state. Her highly controversial book *Eichmann in Jerusalem* (1963) argued that the Nazi war criminal Adolf Eichmann was not inwardly wicked or depraved but merely "thoughtless"; his role in the extermination of the Jews thus epitomized the fearsome "banality of evil" that had swept across Europe at the time. Resuming contact with Heidegger in 1950, she claimed that his involvement with the Nazis had been the "mistake" of a great philosopher. She taught at the University of Chicago (1963–67) and thereafter at the New School for Social Research in New York City.

JUST WAR

Jus ad bellum, as it is phrased in Latin, refers to the notion that the resort to armed force is justified under certain conditions and to the notion that the use of such force (*jus in bello*) should be limited in certain ways. Just war is a

Western concept and should be distinguished from the Islamic concept of *jihad* (Arabic: "striving"), or holy war, which in Muslim legal theory is the only type of just war.

Rooted in Classical Roman and biblical Hebraic culture and containing both religious and secular elements, just war first coalesced as a coherent body of thought and practice during the Middle Ages as a by-product of canon law and theology, the ideas of *jus naturale* (Latin: "natural law") and *jus gentium* (Latin: "law of nations") from Roman law, established practices of statecraft, and the chivalric code. The canonists drew together existing Christian traditions on the justification of war and on noncombatant immunity, ideas later developed by various Christian theologians; and the chivalric code contributed further to the idea of noncombatant immunity and also added restraints on the means of war. Rationales for war based on Christian ethics can be found in the writings of theologians, such as Augustine (354–430) and Thomas Aquinas (1224/25–74), whose *Summa Theologiae* (1265/66–73) outlined the justifications for war and discussed the acts it is permissible to commit in wartime. Secular theorists include the Roman jurist and philosopher Marcus Tullius Cicero (106–43 BCE), who argued that legitimate wars must be openly declared, have a just cause, and be conducted justly. The Dutch jurist Hugo Grotius (1583–1645) maintained in *De Jure Belli ac Pacis* (1625; *On the Law of War and Peace*) that war is justifiable only if a country faces imminent danger and the use of force is both necessary and proportionate to the threat.

Most scholars agree that, to be considered just, a war must meet several *jus ad bellum* requirements. The four most important conditions are: (1) the war must be declared openly by a proper sovereign authority (e.g., the governing authority of the political community in question); (2) the war must have a just cause (e.g., defense of the common good or a response to grave injustice); (3) the warring state must have just intentions (i.e., it must wage the war for justice rather than for self-interest); and (4) the aim of the war must be the establishment of a just peace. Since the end of World War II it has become customary to add three other conditions: (1) there must be a reasonable chance of success; (2) force must be used as a last resort; and (3) the expected benefits of war must outweigh its anticipated costs.

Since the Peace of Westphalia (1648), which ended the Thirty Years' War, there has been a concerted effort in international law to develop binding laws of war and military codes of conduct. Since the 1860s these have increasingly taken the form of written rules governing the conduct of war, including rules of engagement for national military forces, the Geneva Conventions (1864–1949) and their protocols (1977), and various treaties, agreements, and declarations limiting the means allowable in war. Contemporary moral debate often has centred on *jus in bello* issues—especially the question of whether the use of nuclear weapons is ever just. The Hague Convention (1899 and 1907) and the Geneva Conventions attempted to regulate conflict and the treatment of prisoners of war and civilians by imposing international standards. Three principles established by the conventions generally govern conduct during war: (1) targets should include only combatants and legitimate military and industrial complexes; (2) combatants should not use unjust methods or weapons (e.g., torture and genocide); and (3) the force used should be proportionate to the end sought.

Since the end of the Cold War, several international military interventions were undertaken to put an end to perceived human rights abuses (e.g., in Somalia and in

JIHAD

In Islam, jihad, meaning "struggle" or "battle," is the religious duty of Muslims to strive to realize the will of Allāh (God).

Islam distinguishes four ways by which the duty of jihad can be fulfilled: by the heart, the tongue, the hand, and the sword. The first consists in a spiritual purification of one's own heart by doing battle with the devil and overcoming his inducements to evil. The Prophet Muhammad referred to this as the "greater jihad," the war with one's inner self. The jihads of the tongue and of the hand are accomplished in large measure by supporting what is right and correcting what is wrong. The fourth way to fulfill one's duty is to wage war physically against unbelievers and enemies of the Islamic faith. Muhammad called this actual physical combat the "lesser jihad," a defensive measure when the faith was in danger.

The lesser jihad has been taken to mean "holy war" and has been invoked to justify offensive combat. Throughout Islamic history, wars against non-Muslims, even though with political overtones, were termed jihads to reflect their religious flavour. This was especially true in the 18th and 19th centuries in Muslim Africa south of Sahara, where religiopolitical conquests were seen as jihads, most notably the jihad of Usman dan Fodio, which established the Sokoto caliphate (1804) in what is now northern Nigeria. The Afghan War in the late 20th and early 21st centuries was also viewed by many of its participants as a jihad, first against the Soviet Union and Afghanistan's Marxist government and, later, against the United States. During that time, Islamic extremists used the theory of jihad to justify violent attacks against Muslims whom the extremists accused of apostasy (Arabic *riddah*).

Yugoslavia in the 1990s). As a result of the increased attention paid to human rights abuses and the significant growth in international human rights law, the traditional notion that a head of state enjoys sovereign immunity for human rights abuses committed by the armed forces of his country has been challenged. Correspondingly, since the 1990s many just-war theorists have argued that the need to end and punish such abuses constitutes a just cause for the use of military force and that the intention to do so well expresses the just-war aim of responding to serious injustice and reestablishing peace. As yet, however, there is no consensus among just-war theorists on these matters, and their implications for international law remain to be seen.

NATURAL LAW

The philosophical concept of natural law is a system of right or justice held to be common to all humans and derived from nature rather than from the rules of society, or positive law.

There have been several disagreements over the meaning of natural law and its relation to positive law. Aristotle (384–322 BCE) held that what was "just by nature" was not always the same as what was "just by law," that there was a natural justice valid everywhere with the same force and "not existing by people's thinking this or that," and that appeal could be made to it from positive law. However, he drew his examples of natural law primarily from his observation of the Greeks in their city-states, who subordinated women to men, slaves to citizens, and "barbarians" to Hellenes. In contrast, the Stoics conceived of an entirely egalitarian law of nature in conformity with the logos (reason) inherent in the human mind. Roman jurists paid lip service to this notion, which was reflected in the writings of St. Paul (*c.* 10–67 CE), who described a law "written in the hearts" of the Gentiles (Romans 2:14–15).

Augustine of Hippo embraced Paul's notion and developed the idea of man's having lived freely under natural law before his fall and subsequent bondage under sin and positive law. In the 12th century, Gratian, an Italian monk and father of the study of canon law, equated natural law with divine law—that is, with the revealed law of the Old and the New Testament, in particular the Christian version of the Golden Rule.

Thomas Aquinas propounded an influential systematization, maintaining that, though the eternal law of divine reason is unknowable to us in its perfection as it exists in God's mind, it is known to us in part not only by revelation but also by the operations of our reason. The law of nature, which is "nothing else than the participation of the eternal law in the rational creature," thus comprises those precepts that humankind is able to formulate—namely, the preservation of one's own good, the fulfillment of "those inclinations which nature has taught to all animals," and the pursuit of the knowledge of God. Human law must be the particular application of natural law.

Other scholastic thinkers, including the Franciscan philosophers John Duns Scotus (1266–1308) and William of Ockham (*c.* 1285–1347/49) and the Spanish theologian Francisco Suárez (1548–1617), emphasized divine will instead of divine reason as the source of law. This "voluntarism" influenced the Roman Catholic jurisprudence of the Counter-Reformation in the 16th and early 17th centuries, but the Thomistic doctrine was later revived and reinforced to become the main philosophical ground for the papal exposition of natural right in the social teaching of Pope Leo XIII (1810–1903) and his successors.

In an epoch-making appeal, Hugo Grotius (1583–1645) claimed that nations were subject to natural law. Whereas his fellow Calvinist Johannes Althusius (1557–1638) had proceeded from theological doctrines of predestination to elaborate his theory of a universally binding law, Grotius insisted on the validity of the natural law "even if we were to suppose . . . that God does not exist or is not concerned with human affairs." A few years later Thomas Hobbes (1588–1679), starting from the assumption of a savage "state of nature" in which each man was at war with every other—rather than from the "state of innocence" in which man had lived in the biblical Garden of Eden—defined the right of nature (*jus naturale*) to be "the liberty each man hath to use his own power for the preservation of his own nature, that is to say, of life," and a law of nature (*lex naturalis*) as "a precept of general rule found out by reason, by which a man is forbidden to do that which is destructive of his life." He then enumerated the elementary rules on which peace and society could be established. Thus, Grotius and Hobbes stand together at the head of that "school of natural law" that, in accordance with the tendencies of the Enlightenment, tried to construct a whole edifice of law by rational deduction from a hypothetical "state of nature" and a "social contract" of consent between rulers and subjects. John Locke (1632–1704) departed from Hobbesian pessimism to the extent of describing the state of nature as a state of society, with free and equal men already observing the natural law. In France Charles-Louis de Secondat Montesquieu (1689–1755) argued that natural laws were presocial and superior to those of religion and the state, and Jean-Jacques Rousseau (1712–78) postulated a savage who was virtuous in isolation and actuated by two principles "prior to reason": self-preservation and compassion (innate repugnance to the sufferings of others).

The confidence in appeals to natural law displayed by 17th- and 18th-century writers such as Locke and the authors of the American Declaration of Independence evaporated in the early 19th century. The philosophy of Immanuel Kant (1724–1804), as well as the utilitarianism of Jeremy Bentham (1748–1832), served to weaken the belief that "nature" could be the source of moral or legal norms. In the mid-20th century, however, there was a revival of interest in natural law, sparked by the widespread belief that the Nazi regime of Adolf Hitler, which ruled Germany from 1933 to 1945, had been essentially lawless, even though it also had been the source of a significant amount of positive law. As in previous centuries, the need to challenge the unjust laws of particular states inspired the desire to invoke rules of right and justice held to be natural rather than merely conventional. However, the 19th century's skepticism about invoking nature as a source of moral and legal norms remained powerful, and contemporary writers almost invariably talked of human rights rather than natural rights.

JEAN-JACQUES ROUSSEAU
(b. June 28, 1712, Geneva, Switz.—d. July 2, 1778, Ermenonville, France)

Jean-Jacques Rousseau was a Swiss-born philosopher, writer, and political theorist whose treatises and novels inspired the leaders of the French Revolution and the Romantic generation. At age 16 Rousseau fled Geneva to Savoy, where he became the steward and later the lover of the baronne de Warens. At age 30, having furthered his education and social position under her influence, he moved to Paris, where he joined Denis Diderot at the centre of the Philosophes; he wrote on music and economics for Diderot's *Encyclopédie*. His first major work, the *Discourse on the Arts and Sciences* (1750), argued that man is good by nature but has been corrupted by society and civilization; Rousseau's belief in the natural goodness of man set him apart from Roman Catholic writers who, like him, were hostile to the idea of progress. He also wrote music; his light opera *The Cunning-Man* (1752) was widely admired. In 1752 he became involved in an influential dispute with Jean-Philippe Rameau over the relative merits of French and Italian music; Rousseau championed the latter. In the *Discourse on the Origin and Foundations of Inequality Among Men* (1754), he argued against Thomas Hobbes that human life before the formation of societies was healthy, happy, and free and that vice arose as the result of social organization and especially the introduction of private property. Civil society, he held, comes into being only to ensure peace and to protect property, which not everyone has; it thus represents a fraudulent social contract that reinforces inequality. In the *Social Contract* (1762), which begins with the memorable line, "Man was born free, but he is everywhere in chains," Rousseau argues that a civil society based on a genuine social contract rather than a fraudulent one would provide people with a better kind of freedom in exchange for their natural independence, namely, political liberty, which he understands as obedience to a self-imposed law created by the "general will." In 1762 the publication of *Émile*, a treatise on education, produced outrage, and Rousseau was forced to flee to Switzerland. He began showing signs of mental instability *c.* 1767, and he died insane. His *Confessions* (1781–88), which he modeled on the work of the same title by Augustine, is among the most famous autobiographies.

PUNISHMENT

The infliction of some kind of pain or loss upon a person for a misdeed (i.e., the transgression of a law or command) is punishment. It may take forms ranging from capital punishment, flogging, forced labour, and mutilation of the body to imprisonment and fines. Deferred punishments consist of penalties that are imposed only if an offense is repeated within a specified time.

In some premodern societies, punishment was largely vindictive or retributive, and its prosecution was left to the individuals wronged (or to their families). In quantity and quality such punishment bore no special relation to the character or gravity of the offense. Gradually there arose the idea of proportionate punishment, such as was reflected in the biblical dictum "an eye for an eye." Eventually punishment by individuals came under the control of the community; later, with the development of codes of law, the state took over the punitive function for the maintenance of public order. Under such a system, the state is viewed as the entity wronged by the crime, and the exaction of punishment by individuals acting on their own behalf (as in cases of lynching) is illegal.

THEORIES AND OBJECTIVES OF PUNISHMENT

Punishment has been a subject of debate among philosophers, political leaders, and lawyers for centuries. Various theories of punishment have been developed, each of which attempts to justify the practice in some form and to state its proper objectives.

Modern punishment theories date from the 18th century, when the humanitarian movement in Europe emphasized the dignity of the individual, as well as his rationality and responsibility. The quantity and severity of punishments were reduced, the prison system was improved, and the first attempts were made to study the psychology of crime and to distinguish between classes of criminals. During most of the 19th and 20th centuries, individuals who broke the law were viewed as the product of social conditions, and accordingly punishment was considered justified only insofar as (1) it protected society by acting as a deterrent or by temporarily or permanently removing one who has injured it or (2) it aimed at the moral or social regeneration of the criminal. By the latter half of the 20th century, however, many people in Western countries objected to this view of punishment, believing that it placed too little responsibility on offenders for their actions, undervalued the additional deterrent effect derivable from severe, as compared with moderate, punishment, and ignored society's ostensible right to retribution.

Retribution

The retributive theory of punishment holds that punishment is justified by the moral requirement that the guilty make amends for the harm they have caused to society. Retributive theories generally maintain, as did the Italian criminologist Cesare Beccaria (1738–94), that the severity of a punishment should be proportionate to the gravity of the offense. Some retributive theories hold that punishment should never be imposed to achieve a social objective (such as law-abiding behaviour in the future by the offender or by others who witness his example), while others allow social objectives to be pursued as secondary goals. Many (but not all) retributive theories also claim that punishment should not be inflicted on a person unless he is found guilty of a specific offense (thus, they would prohibit collective punishment and the taking of hostages from the general population).

Although retributive theorists do not base their justification of punishment on its possible deterrent or reformative effects, many of them agree that punishment can perform a salutary educational function. The enactment and implementation of the criminal law—including particularly the imposition of sentences—provides a concrete example of society's values and thereby reinforces them. Citizens whose moral values are reinforced by court judgments may feel more strongly committed to them than previously; by contrast, they may question or feel less constrained by values that the courts visibly ignore. Without this kind of reinforcement, some retributivists argue, the legitimacy of the legal system itself may be undermined, leading eventually to general moral decline and the dissolution of society.

Retributivists also contend that punishment of offenders by the state satisfies the community's natural demand for justice and helps to prevent victims of crime and those close to them from seeking revenge through direct violence. A variation of this idea is that punishment is a kind of expiation: offenders should undergo punishment in their own interests to discharge their guilt and to make themselves acceptable to society again.

Utilitarian Theories

According to utilitarian theories, punishment is justified by its deterrence of criminal behaviour and by its other beneficial consequences for individuals as well as for society. Among several utilitarian theories recognized by criminologists, some stress general deterrence and some individual deterrence.

General Deterrence

The approach based on general deterrence aims to dissuade others from following the offender's example. Less concerned with the future behaviour of the offender himself, general deterrence theories assume that, because most individuals are rational, potential offenders will calculate the risk of being similarly caught, prosecuted, and sentenced for the commission of a crime. Deterrence theory has proven difficult to validate, however, largely because the presence of many intervening factors makes it difficult to prove unequivocally that a certain penalty has prevented someone from committing a given crime. Nevertheless, there have been occasional examples showing that some sentences can have a strong deterrent effect. Laws designed to prevent driving under the influence of alcohol (e.g., by setting a maximum legal level of blood alcohol content) can have a temporary deterrent effect on a wide population, especially when coupled with mandatory penalties and a high probability of conviction.

Proponents of capital punishment have claimed that it serves as an effective deterrent against murder. Research in the United States, however, has shown that some jurisdictions that use the death penalty have higher murder rates than those that do not. There are several interpretations of this pattern. Some argue that use of the death penalty is a response to, but not a cause of, high murder rates, while some maintain that it has a brutalizing effect on society that increases the incidence of murder by instilling a lower regard for human life.

Another form of deterrence, known by the term *denunciation*, utilizes public condemnation as a form of community moral education. In this approach, a person found guilty of a crime is denounced—that is, subjected to shame and public criticism. Although denunciation is closely associated with general deterrence through fear—and many courts have imposed sentences designed to achieve both objectives simultaneously—there is an important distinction between them. Education through denunciation is generally aimed at discouraging law-abiding citizens from committing criminal acts. Its object is to reinforce their rejection of law-breaking behaviour. Most people do not steal because they believe that stealing is dishonest; a sentence imposed on a thief reinforces that view. General deterrence through fear is aimed at those who avoid law-breaking behaviour not on moral grounds but on the basis of a calculation of the potential rewards and penalties involved.

Individual Deterrence

Individual deterrence is directed at the person being punished: it aims to teach him not to repeat the behaviour. It is also the rationale of much informal punishment, such as parental punishment of children. Theoretically, the effectiveness of individual deterrence can be measured by examining the subsequent conduct of the offender. Such studies often have been misleading, however, because in most cases the only basis for proving that the offender repeated his crime is a further conviction. Because a high proportion of crimes do not result in convictions, many offenders who are not reconvicted after being punished may have committed additional crimes. Furthermore, the general pattern of "aging out" of crime (i.e., the fact that criminal behaviour peaks in the late teens and early 20s and declines rapidly thereafter) contributes to the difficulty of measuring the effectiveness of particular deterrence strategies.

Theories of deterrence and retribution share the idea that punishments should be proportionate to the gravity of the crime, a principle of practical importance. If all punishments were the same, there would be no incentive to commit the lesser rather than the greater offense. The offender might as well use violence against the victim of a theft if the penalty for armed robbery were no more severe than that for larceny.

Incapacitation

Incapacitation refers to the act of making an individual "incapable" of committing a crime—historically by execution or banishment, and in more modern times by execution or lengthy periods of incarceration. Most instances of incapacitation involve offenders who have committed repeated crimes (multiple recidivists) under what are known as habitual offender statutes, which permit longer-than-normal sentences for a given offense. Incapacitation is also utilized, for example, in cases involving offenders who are deemed dangerous (such as those guilty of murder) and likely to commit grave and violent crimes unless restrained. Given the difficulty of identifying such offenders with certainty, the principle of incapacitation is controversial. It has also been difficult to reconcile with other principles, especially those advocating equal retribution.

A particularly controversial example of incapacitation is the so-called "chemical castration" of sex offenders with hormonal drugs that supposedly reduce or eliminate the sex drive. In 1996 the U.S. state of California adopted a law requiring this treatment for those convicted of sex offenses against children. The results were mixed, however, as the drug therapies achieved their intended purpose principally when they were used on a voluntary basis in connection with psychological treatments intended to help the offender understand and control his actions. That is, the drugs alone usually did not make the offender "incapable" of committing sex crimes.

Rehabilitation

The most recently formulated theory of punishment is that of rehabilitation—the idea that the purpose of punishment is to apply treatment and training to the offender so that he is made capable of returning to society and functioning as a law-abiding member of the community. Established in legal practice in the 19th century, rehabilitation was viewed as a humane alternative to retribution and deterrence, though it did not necessarily result in an offender receiving a more lenient penalty than he would have received under a retributive or deterrent philosophy. In many cases rehabilitation meant that an offender would be released on probation under some condition; in other cases it meant that he would serve a relatively longer period in custody to undergo treatment or training. One widely used instrument of rehabilitation in the United States was the indeterminate sentence, under which the length of detention was governed by the degree of reform the offender exhibited while incarcerated.

Although rehabilitation was widely criticized in the United States in the 1970s, it gained greater acceptance once research in the 1980s and 1990s demonstrated that a carefully implemented rehabilitation program could reduce recidivism. Critics nonetheless objected to rehabilitation and sentencing programs that gave significant discretion to the prison administrator, who could decide to release or further detain an offender depending on his assessment of the offender's progress (which could itself be vaguely defined). At issue were cases in which this authority led to gross abuses, such as the lengthy detention of an offender guilty of only a minor crime, simply because of his inability or refusal to adopt a subservient attitude toward prison officials or other persons in positions of authority.

PUNISHMENT IN ISLAMIC LAW

Starting in the 19th century, most Muslim countries adopted Western criminal codes patterned after French,

Swiss, or English systems of justice. Traditional Islamic law (Sharī'ah) divides crimes into two general categories. Several serious offenses, known as *ḥadd* crimes, are specifically mentioned, along with their appropriate penalties, in the Qur'an; the *ḥadd* punishment for theft, for example, was amputation of a hand. In practice, however, many such punishments are mitigated by social and political constraints. Thus, a person who is caught stealing might negotiate a lenient punishment by offering to pay for the item in question, often at a much higher price.

Most other offenses in Islamic law are called *ta'zīr* crimes (discretionary crimes), and their punishment is left to the discretion of the *qāḍī* (judge), whose options are often limited to traditional forms (imprisonment or corporal punishment) but who may also feel obliged to enforce

A woman in the predominantly Muslim city of Banda Aceh, Indon., undergoing a caning. AP

punishments dictated by local customs and mores. The imposition of fines is a traditional punishment that has grown more common in some areas.

Murder within Islamic societies has traditionally been treated not as a crime against the people but as a dispute between family or tribal groups. The murdered man's kin might demand the death of the malefactor (they might even carry out the execution themselves), but they may also settle for *diyah* (wergild; literally, "man payment") at a rate determined by social convention. Such arrangements reflect the general belief in Islamic societies that the life of the individual belongs to the group rather than to the individual himself or to society as a whole.

Within many Islamic countries the extra-judicial killing of persons by members of their own families for real or perceived moral infractions has been relatively common. Such "honour killings" are in fact violations of both civil and Islamic law, but perpetrators frequently use religious reasons to defend their actions, thereby giving the crime a veneer of justification. Murders of this type are seldom punished, particularly when they involve the alleged sexual transgressions of a female, but when punishment is mandated, the sentences are generally light.

PUNISHMENT IN ASIAN SOCIETIES

After the Communists took power in China in 1949, the chief goal of criminal punishment in the country became reform. This policy was founded, according to authoritative Chinese criminal-law textbooks, on the historical mission of the proletariat to reform society and humanity. The notion that an offender incurs a debt to society that can be paid merely by serving a prison term was alien to Chinese penology. Because the state was keenly interested in changing the offender's thinking, imprisonment was generally accompanied by labour and political study.

The primacy of reform over deterrence changed in the 1970s, when China began to decentralize sectors of its economy. The resulting economic liberalization was accompanied by substantial increases in crime, to which the government responded with a series of deterrence campaigns based on swift, certain, and public punishments. Notwithstanding these efforts, which had limited success, China's imprisonment rate remained moderate. The country applied the death penalty widely, executing thousands of people every year—far more than the combined annual sum of executions occurring in other countries.

Other Asian countries exhibited very different patterns. Japan maintained a very low crime rate and one of the lowest imprisonment rates in the world, though some

CESARE BECCARIA
(b. March 15, 1738, Milan—d. Nov. 28, 1794, Milan)

The Italian criminologist and economist Cesare Beccaria is notable for having written *Dei delitti e delle pene* (1764; Eng. trans. *Crime and Punishment*), a celebrated volume on the reform of criminal justice. He became an international celebrity in 1764 with the publication of *Crime and Punishment*, the first systematic statement of principles governing criminal punishment, in which he argued that the effectiveness of criminal justice depended more on the certainty of punishment than on its severity. The book greatly influenced criminal-law reform in western Europe. In later years, Beccaria lectured at Milan's Palatine School and served as a public official, dealing with such issues as monetary reform, labour relations, and public education.

moderate increases in the severity of punishments, including incarceration, created conditions of overcrowding in its prisons starting in the 1990s. Singapore maintained a severe criminal code and a very high imprisonment rate despite having a very low crime rate. Indonesia, the most populous country in Southeast Asia, also imposed harsh penalties for many crimes, including the death penalty for drug trafficking. South Korea had a low crime rate and a moderate imprisonment rate, and it placed some emphasis on thought reform in its prisons. In the early 21st century Hong Kong was unique in housing the largest proportion of female prisoners worldwide: more than 20 percent of the total prison population was female, compared with a global average of about 5 percent.

UTOPIA

A utopia is an ideal commonwealth whose inhabitants exist under seemingly perfect conditions. Hence *utopian* and *utopianism* are words used to denote visionary reform that tends to be impossibly idealistic.

The word first occurred in Sir Thomas More's *Utopia,* published in Latin as *Libellus . . . de optimo reipublicae statu, deque nova insula Utopia* (1516; "Concerning the highest state of the republic and the new island Utopia"); it was compounded by More from the Greek words for "not" (*ou*) and "place" (*topos*) and thus meant "nowhere." During his embassy to Flanders in 1515, More wrote Book II of *Utopia,* describing a pagan and communist city-state in which the institutions and policies were entirely governed by reason. The order and dignity of such a state was intended to provide a notable contrast with the unreasonable polity of Christian Europe, divided by self-interest and greed for power and riches, which More then described in Book I, written in England in 1516. The description of Utopia is put in the mouth of a mysterious traveler, Raphael Hythloday, in support of his argument that communism is the only cure against egoism in private and public life. More, in the dialogue, speaks in favour of mitigation of evil rather than cure, human nature being fallible. The reader is thus left guessing as to which parts of the brilliant jeu d'esprit are seriously intended and which are mere paradox.

Written utopias may be practical or satirical, as well as speculative. Utopias are far older than their name. Plato's *Republic* was the model of many, from More to H.G. Wells. A utopian island occurs in the *Sacred History* of Euhemerus (flourished 300 BCE), and Plutarch's life of Lycurgus describes a utopian Sparta. The legend of Atlantis inspired many utopian myths; but explorations in the 15th century permitted more realistic settings, and Sir Thomas More associated *Utopia* with Amerigo Vespucci. Other utopias that were similar to More's in humanist themes were the *I mondi* (1552) of Antonio Francesco Doni and *La città felice* (1553) of Francesco Patrizi. An early practical utopia was the comprehensive *La città del sole* (written c. 1602) of Tommaso Campanella. Francis Bacon's *New Atlantis* (published 1627) was practical in its scientific program but speculative concerning philosophy and religion. Christian utopian commonwealths were described in *Antangil* (1616) by "I.D.M.," *Christianopolis* (1619) by Johann Valentin Andreae, and *Novae Solymae libri sex* (1648) by Samuel Gott. Puritanism produced many literary utopias, both religious and secular, notably, *The Law of Freedom . . .* (1652), in which Gerrard Winstanley advocated the principles of the Diggers. *The Common-Wealth of Oceana* (1656) by James Harrington argued for the distribution of land as the condition of popular independence.

In France such works as Gabriel de Foigny's *Terre aust-rale connue* (1676) preached liberty. François Fénelon's *Télémaque* (1699) contained utopian episodes extolling the simple life. *L'An 2440* by Louis-Sébastien Mercier (1770; Eng. trans., 1772) anticipated Revolutionary doctrines. G.A. Ellis's *New Britain* (1820) and Étienne Cabet's *Voyage en Icarie* (1840) were related to experimental communities in the United States that revealed the limitations of purely economic planning. Consequently, Bulwer-Lytton, in *The Coming Race* (1871), invented an essence that eliminated economics altogether, and William Morris demonstrated his contempt for economics in *News from Nowhere* (1890). Two influential utopias, however, had an economic basis: *Looking Backward, 2000–1887* (1888) by Edward Bellamy and *Freiland* (1890; *A Visit to Freeland . . .*, 1894) by Theodor Herzka. H.G. Wells, in *A Modern Utopia* (1905), returned to speculation.

Many utopias are satires that ridicule existent conditions rather than offering practical solutions for them. In this class are Swift's *Gulliver's Travels* (1726) and Samuel Butler's *Erewhon* (1872). In the 20th century, when the possibility of a planned society became too imminent, a number of bitterly anti-utopian, or dystopian, novels appeared. Among these are *The Iron Heel* (1907) by Jack London, *My* (1924; *We*) by Yevgeny Zamyatin, *Brave New World* (1932) by Aldous Huxley, and *Nineteen Eighty-four* (1949) by George Orwell. *The Story of Utopias* (1922) by Lewis Mumford is an excellent survey.

Concurrent with the literature, there have also been many attempts by religious groups and political reformers to establish utopian communities, especially in the Americas. In the two centuries between 1663 (when some Dutch Mennonites established the first such communitarian colony in what is now Lewes, Del.) and 1858, some

138 settlements were begun in North America. The first to outlast the lifetime of its founder was the Ephrata Community established in Pennsylvania in 1732 by some German Pietists. Other German Pietist settlements were founded by George Rapp (Harmony in Pennsylvania, Harmony [or Harmonie] in Indiana, and Economy in Pennsylvania), by the Amana group (in Iowa), and by the Shakers (18 villages in eight states). Some of them pursued celibacy. Other communal religious sects still flourish; among the largest are the Hutterites, chiefly in the United States and Canada but having colonies also in Paraguay and England.

One of the first secular communities was New Harmony, founded in 1825 when the British manufacturer Robert Owen purchased Harmony, Ind., from the Rappites. It was a cooperative rather than communist society. Although it foundered, it sponsored the first kindergarten, the first trade school, the first free library, and the first community-supported public school in the United States.

The ideas of the French social reformer Charles Fourier had a strong influence upon American reformers in the 1840s, particularly upon the leaders of Brook Farm in Massachusetts. Between 1841 and 1859, about 28 Fourierist colonies were established in the United States. The Icarians, followers of Cabet, established ill-fated communities in Illinois (Nauvoo, formerly settled by Mormons), Missouri, Iowa, and California.

A unique venture was the Oneida Community founded in Putney, Vt., by John Humphrey Noyes in 1841 and moved to Oneida, N.Y., in 1848. The group practiced "complex marriage," in which all husbands and wives were shared. Noyes said that Oneida was the continuation of Brook Farm without its mistakes. He was convinced that socialism was impossible without religion, and that the "extended"

SIR THOMAS MORE

(b. Feb. 7, 1478, London, Eng.—d. July 6, 1535, London; canonized
May 19, 1935; feast day June 22)

The English statesman and humanist Sir Thomas More
(also known as Saint Thomas More) was beheaded for
refusing to accept King Henry VIII as head of the Church
of England. He is recognized as a saint by the Roman
Catholic Church.

More studied at Oxford and was successful as a lawyer
from 1501. He served as an undersheriff of London (1510–
18) and endeared himself to Londoners as a fair judge and
consultant. He wrote the notable *History of King Richard
III* (1513–18) and the renowned *Utopia* (1516), which was an
immediate success with humanists, including Desiderius
Erasmus. In 1517 More was named to the king's council,
and he became Henry VIII's secretary and confidant. In
1523 he was elected speaker of the House of Commons. He
wrote *A Dialogue Concerning Heresies* (1529) to refute hereti-
cal writings. After the fall of Cardinal Wolsey (1529), More
succeeded him as lord chancellor, but he resigned in 1532
when he could not affirm Henry's divorce from Catherine
of Aragon. He also refused to accept the Act of Supremacy.
In 1534 More was charged with high treason and imprisoned in the Tower of London, where he wrote his *Dialogue
of Comfort Against Tribulation*. In 1535 he was tried and sentenced to death by hanging, which the king commuted to
beheading.

family system would dissolve selfishness and demonstrate
the practicality of this way of life. Children remained with
their mothers until they could walk but were then placed
in a common nursery.

After the American Civil War the enthusiasm for secular utopian experiments waned. There were some new settlements in the 1890s, following the publication of such Utopian tracts as Laurence Gronlund's *The Coöperative Commonwealth* (1884) and Bellamy's *Looking Backward,* but the impulse had run its course and these latter movements were soon gathered into the fold of political socialism. The creation of utopian religious communities continued into the 20th century, but they too were usually short-lived. The religious colonies, in almost all instances, were established and maintained by a single powerful personality who was believed by his disciples to have a singular gift of prophecy or wisdom. Most of these colonies flourished during the lifetime of the original leader and then declined slowly after his death.

MONOTHEISM

The belief in the existence of one god or in the oneness of God is called monotheism; as such, it is distinguished from polytheism, the belief in the existence of many gods, and from atheism, the belief that there is no god. Monotheism characterizes the traditions of Judaism, Christianity, and Islam, and elements of the belief are discernible in many other religions.

In the three great monotheistic religions, the essence and character of God are believed to be unique and fundamentally different from those of gods found in other religions. God is viewed as the creator of the world and of humanity. Moreover, he has not abandoned his creation but continues to lead it through his power and wisdom. God has created not only the natural world but also the ethical order to which humanity ought to conform. God is holy and is the source of the highest good.

AMARNA STYLE

Amarna style is the name given to the revolutionary style of Egyptian art created by Amenhotep IV, who took the name Akhenaton during his reign (1353–36 bce) in the 18th dynasty. Akhenaton's alteration of the artistic and religious life of ancient Egypt was drastic, if short-lived. His innovations were centred upon a new religion based on the worship of Aton, or the sun's disk, which Akhenaton elevated above all others in the Egyptian pantheon. The artistic elements that Akhenaton introduced in the decoration of the Aton temples and on other monuments of his reign, both at Karnak and at his new capital of Akhetaton (Tell el-Amarna), are referred to collectively as the Amarna style.

Unlike other Egyptian deities, usually portrayed face-to-face with the pharaoh in their anthropomorphic or animal form, the Aton was shown in its natural state as a sun disk in the heavens with pendant rays; each ray ended in a tiny hand. In such portrayals Akhenaton was placed at ground level, bathed in the sunlight descending from the disk and often accompanied by his queen, Nefertiti, and one or more of their daughters.

A new artistic idiom, for both wall relief and sculpture, was devised to represent the human body. Faces were depicted with a hanging jaw, pronounced facial folds, and narrow, slitted eyes, while the body itself consisted of a thin, attenuated neck, sloped shoulders, a heavy paunch, large hips and thighs, and rather spindly legs. The princesses are usually shown with greatly elongated skulls. Several theories, none thoroughly convincing, have been propounded to explain these features as the naturalistic depiction of Akhenaton's own physical deformation caused perhaps by disease.

Other innovations include the portrayal of the royal family in less formal, intimate contexts, even on private offering stelae, where Akhenaton and Nefertiti dandle their daughters on their laps, exchanging kisses and embracing them affectionately in a manner otherwise unknown in Egyptian art. The human body was depicted in more realistic detail, with the toes on the right and left feet carefully distinguished for the first time, earplug holes shown in the earlobes, and neck wrinkles visible. The vast wall expanses of the new Aton temples invited experimentation in large-scale composition, devoted not only to the ubiquitous offering scenes but to religious ceremonies such as the king's Karnak jubilee and detailed architectural depictions of the royal palace and the Aton temples. The peripheral regions of these compositions were peopled by the common citizens and soldiers of Akhenaton's court, often captured in informal poses, as well as scenes of the Egyptian riverfront and desert landscape, enlivened by animals and birds of the Nile River valley and its uplands.

Akhenaton seems to have been the guiding hand behind these stylistic changes, as much as the Aton religion itself; indeed, the two are irrevocably intertwined. A dedicatory text of the master sculptor Bek described him as "one whom his majesty himself instructed." The Amarna period also produced a number of sculptures of exquisite refinement, including the painted portrait bust of Nefertiti found in the workshop of the sculptor Thutmose, perhaps the most famous embodiment of female beauty from the ancient Middle East.

The term *Amarna style* obscures the fact that within these broad outlines, there exists a great variety of individual approaches, ranging from sublime beauty to what appears to be a severe caricature of the human form. The exaggerated tendencies in both sculpture and relief are more evident at the Karnak temples, built during the early years of Akhenaton's reign and obviously decorated in haste by a large number of craftsmen. Scholars have noted that during the later years at Akhetaton, these features are for the most part mitigated in a more naturalistic, less extreme portrayal of the human body. Some have even postulated that this "mature" style reflects a concomitant softening of the more radical elements of the Aton religion on the part of Akhenaton. Whatever the truth, the Amarna style represents a series of related artistic endeavours and experiments over the course of the reign. Despite the later abandonment of the Aton cult and the systematic destruction of its temples at Karnak and Akhetaton, a number of stylistic features were retained by later artisans of the Ramesside period. The most important was perhaps a confidence in effectively designing large-scale compositions on temple walls, in particular the battle scenes of Seti I and Ramses II, and the festival reliefs at the temples of Karnak and Luxor.

He is supreme and unique in both his being and his worth. Such a monotheistic belief system results in the rejection of all other belief systems as false religions, and this rejection partly explains the exceptionally aggressive or intolerant stance of monotheistic religions throughout history.

Evidence in the Hebrew scripture indicates that the Israelites practiced monolatry (i.e., the worship of one god without denying the existence of other gods). However, Israel's enthusiastic confession of Yahweh as the one God and its rejection of other gods make it more appropriate to label the religion of Israel as monotheistic, and thus also the hellenistic and rabbinic Judaism that developed from it.

The Islamic interpretation of monotheism is more literal and uncompromising than that of any other religion. Allāh is confessed as being one, eternal, unbegotten, unequaled, and beyond partnership of any kind.

The trinitarian creed of Christianity, on the other hand, sets it apart from the two other classical monotheistic religions. Although the Bible of Christians includes no assertions about God that are specifically trinitarian, it does invoke the name of the Father, Son, and Holy Spirit in triadic liturgical formulas. The early church, in reflecting upon the reality of God as related to Jesus, developed a theological language about the Trinity, speaking of three Persons that are one in substance.

Historians of religion have given much attention to the reform of Egyptian religion as effected by the pharaoh Akhenaton (Amenhotep IV) in the 14th century BCE. It is generally agreed that Akhenaton's theology, if not full monotheistic, in any case strongly tended toward monotheism.

*C*hapter 5:
POLITICS
AND THE LAW

I deas that have proved turning points in politics and the law include the notions of due process, equal protection, international law, and intellectual property law. Also discussed in this chapter are the ideas of democracy, neutrality, the social contract, absolutism, and nationalism.

NEUTRALITY

Neutrality is the legal status arising from the abstention of a state from all participation in a war between other states, the maintenance of an attitude of impartiality toward the belligerents, and the recognition by the belligerents of this abstention and impartiality. Under international law this legal status gives rise to certain rights and duties between the neutral and the belligerents.

The laws concerning the rights and duties of neutrality are contained, for the most part, in the Declaration of Paris of 1856, Hague Convention V, 1907 (neutrality in land war), and Hague Convention XIII, 1907 (neutrality in maritime war). One of the first recommendations of the last convention was that, when war breaks out between certain powers, each nation wishing to remain impartial should normally issue either a special or general declaration of neutrality. Such a declaration, however, is not required by international law. A neutral state may, during the course of the hostilities, repeal, change, or modify its position of neutrality, provided that such alterations are applied without bias to all belligerents.

The most important of the rights that result from a state of neutrality is the right of territorial integrity. Belligerents may not use a neutral's territory as a base of operations or engage in hostilities therein. This right applies not only to neutral territory and water but extends to air space above that territory as well. Under the Hague Rules of Air Warfare, 1923 (which never became legally binding), neutrals have the right to defend their air space from passage of belligerent aircraft. The emergence of ballistic missiles and space satellites as tools of warfare, however, has raised questions regarding the extent of a state's upper boundary.

A neutral also has the right to maintain diplomatic communications with other neutral states and with the belligerents; the right to demand compliance with its domestic regulations designed to secure its neutrality; and the right to require belligerents not to interfere with the commercial intercourse of its citizens, unless such interference is warranted by international law.

The events of World Wars I and II foreshadowed a breakdown of some of the basic concepts of neutrality. With the German invasion of Belgium, the Italian invasion of Greece, the British occupation of Iceland, and the passage by the United States of the Lend-Lease Act (1941), the traditional rules of neutrality appeared no longer viable. By the middle of the 20th century new developments in the law of neutrality were evident. (1) The total character of modern war, with its use of economic as well as mechanized means of warfare, has sharply reduced the traditional area of freedom of the neutral. (2) Under the provisions of the Charter of the United Nations, neutrality, as a permissive legal status, disappears for those members that the Security Council "calls upon" or requires in specific instances to take military or other measures of coercion against an aggressor (Articles 41, 48). (3) The socialization of national economies may result in a lessening of neutral trade; many business enterprises that could formerly trade with belligerents as private traders could no longer legally do so as state enterprises.

HAGUE CONVENTIONS

The Hague Conventions are a series of international treaties that issued from international conferences held at The Hague in the Netherlands in 1899 and 1907.

The first such conference was convened at the invitation of Count Mikhail Nikolayevich Muravyov, the minister of foreign affairs of Tsar Nicholas II of Russia. In his circular of Jan. 11, 1899, Count Muravyov proposed specific topics for consideration: (1) a limitation on the expansion of armed forces and a reduction in the deployment of new armaments, (2) the application of the principles of the Geneva Convention of 1864 to naval warfare, and (3) a revision of the unratified Brussels Declaration of 1874 regarding the laws and customs of land warfare. The conference met from May 18 to July 29, 1899; 26 nations were represented. Only two American countries participated, the United States and Mexico.

Although the conference of 1899 failed to achieve its primary objective, the limitation on armaments, it did adopt conventions defining the conditions of a state of belligerency and other customs relating to war on land and sea. Further, three declarations were accepted—one prohibiting the use of asphyxiating gases, another prohibiting the use of expanding bullets (dumdums), and another prohibiting the discharges of projectiles or explosives from balloons. Last, and most important, was the adoption of the Convention for the Pacific Settlement of International Disputes, creating the Permanent Court of Arbitration.

The conference of 1907, though first proposed by U.S. president Theodore Roosevelt, was officially convened by Nicholas II. This conference sat from June 15 to Oct. 18, 1907, and was attended by the representatives of 44 states. Again the proposal for the limitation of armaments was not

Members of the Permanent Court of Arbitration, established at The Hague in 1899 to settle international disputes by judicial means. Library of Congress, Washington, D.C.

accepted. The conference did, however, adopt several conventions relating to such matters as the employment of force for the recovery of contract debts; the rights and duties of neutral powers and persons in war on land and sea; the laying of automatic submarine contact mines; the status of enemy merchant ships; bombardment by naval forces in wartime; and the establishment of an international prize court. The conference of 1907 renewed the declaration prohibiting the discharge of projectiles from balloons but did not reaffirm the declarations prohibiting asphyxiating gas and expanding bullets. The final acts of the conference were the unanimous acceptance by the delegates of the principle of compulsory arbitration and the stating of a number of *voeux* (resolutions), the first of which was the recommendation that another conference be summoned in eight years, thus establishing the concept that the best way to handle international problems was through a series of successive conferences.

Although the conference scheduled for 1915 failed to meet because of the outbreak of World War I, the conference idea strongly influenced the creation of the more highly organized League of Nations after the war.

DUE PROCESS

A course of legal proceedings according to rules and principles that have been established in a system of jurisprudence for the enforcement and protection of private rights is known as due process. In each case, due process contemplates an exercise of the powers of government as the law permits and sanctions, under recognized safeguards for the protection of individual rights.

Principally associated with one of the fundamental guarantees of the United States Constitution, due process derives from early English common law and constitutional history. The first concrete expression of the due process idea embraced by Anglo-American law appeared in the 39th article of Magna Carta (1215) in the royal promise that "No freeman shall be taken or (and) imprisoned or disseised or exiled or in any way destroyed . . . except by the legal judgment of his peers or (and) by the law of the land." In subsequent English statutes, the references to "the legal judgment of his peers" and "laws of the land" are treated as substantially synonymous with due process of law. Drafters of the U.S. federal Constitution adopted the due process phraseology in the Fifth Amendment, ratified in 1791, which provides that "No person shall . . . be deprived of life, liberty, or property, without due process of law." Because this amendment was held inapplicable to state actions that might violate an individual's constitutional rights, it was not until the ratification of the Fourteenth Amendment in 1868 that the several states became subject to a federally enforceable due process restraint on their legislative and procedural activities.

The meaning of due process as it relates to substantive enactments and procedural legislation has evolved over decades of controversial interpretation by the Supreme Court. Today, if a law may reasonably be deemed to promote the public welfare and the means selected bear a reasonable relationship to the legitimate public interest, then the law has met the due process standard. If the law seeks to regulate a fundamental right, such as the right to travel or the right to vote, then this enactment must meet a stricter judicial scrutiny, known as the compelling interest test. Economic legislation is generally upheld if the state can point to any conceivable public benefit resulting from its enactment.

In determining the procedural safeguards that should be obligatory upon the states under the due process clause of the Fourteenth Amendment, the Supreme Court has exercised considerable supervision over the administration of criminal justice in state courts, as well as occasional influence upon state civil and administrative proceedings. Its decisions have been vigorously criticized, on the one hand, for unduly meddling with state judicial administration and, on the other hand, for not treating all of the specific procedural guarantees of the first 10 amendments as equally applicable to state and to federal proceedings.

Some justices have adhered to the proposition that the framers of the Fourteenth Amendment intended the entire Bill of Rights to be binding on the states. They have asserted that this position would provide an objective basis for reviewing state activities and would promote a desirable uniformity between state and federal rights and sanctions. Other justices, however, have contended that states should be allowed considerable latitude in conducting their affairs, so long as they comply with a fundamental fairness standard. Ultimately, the latter position substantially prevailed, and due process was recognized as embracing only those principles of justice that are "so rooted in the traditions and conscience of our people as to be ranked as fundamental." In fact, however, almost all of the Bill of Rights has by now been included among those fundamental principles.

DEMOCRACY

Democracy is, literally, rule by the people. The term is derived from the Greek *demokratia*, which was coined from *demos* ("people") and *kratos* ("rule") in the middle of the 5th century BCE to denote the political systems then existing in some Greek city-states, notably Athens.

HISTORY

Since the time of the ancient Greeks, both the theory and the practice of democracy have undergone profound changes. For thousands of years the kind of association in which democracy was practiced, the tribe or the city-state, was small enough to be suitable for some form of democracy by assembly, or "direct democracy." Much later, beginning in the 18th century, as the typical association became the nation-state or country, direct democracy gave way to representative democracy—a transformation so sweeping that, from the perspective of a citizen of ancient Athens, the governments of gigantic associations such as France or the United States might not have appeared democratic at all. Representative democracy, in turn, would require a set of political institutions radically different from those of all earlier democracies.

Another important change has concerned the prevailing answers to the question of who among the members of an association should enjoy full citizenship? Until fairly recently, most democratic associations limited the right to participate in government to a minority of the adult population—indeed, sometimes to a very small minority. Beginning in the 20th century, this right was extended to nearly all adults. Accordingly, a contemporary democrat could reasonably argue that Athens, because it excluded so many adults from the *demos*, was not really a democracy—even though the term *democracy* was invented and first applied in Athens.

Despite these and other important changes, it is possible to identify a considerable number of early political systems that involved some form of "rule by the people," even if they were not fully democratic by contemporary standards. Indeed, evidence suggests that democratic government, in a broad sense, existed in several areas of the world well before the turn of the 5th century.

During the Classical period (corresponding roughly to the 5th and 4th centuries BCE), Greece was not a country in the modern sense but a collection of several hundred independent city-states, each with its surrounding countryside. In 507 BCE, under the leadership of Cleisthenes, the citizens of Athens began to develop a system of popular rule that would last nearly two centuries. For the Greeks, the political association most appropriate to democratic government was the polis, or city-state. But in 321, Athens was subjugated by its more powerful neighbour to the north, Macedonia, which introduced property qualifications that effectively excluded many ordinary Athenians from the demos. In 146 BCE what remained of Athenian democracy was extinguished by the conquering Romans.

Like Athens, Rome was originally a city-state. Although it expanded rapidly by conquest and annexation far beyond its original borders to encompass all the Mediterranean world and much of western Europe, its government remained, in its basic features, that of a moderately large city-state. Indeed, throughout the Republican era (until roughly the end of the first century BCE), Roman assemblies were held in the very small Forum at the centre of the city. The Romans called their system a *respublica*, or *republic*, from the Latin *res*, meaning thing or affair, and *publicus* or *publica*, meaning public—thus, a republic was the thing that belonged to the Roman people, the *populus romanus*. As the Romans adapted to the special features of their society, including its rapidly increasing size, they created a political structure so complex and idiosyncratic that later democratic leaders chose not to emulate it. The Romans used not only an extremely powerful Senate but also four assemblies. In all the assemblies, votes were counted by units (centuries or tribes) rather than by individuals; thus, insofar as a majority prevailed in voting, it would have been a majority of units, not of citizens.

After the western Roman Empire collapsed in 476, the Italian Peninsula broke up into a congeries of smaller political entities. About six centuries later, in northern Italy, some of these entities developed into more or less independent city-states and inaugurated systems of government based on wider—though not fully popular—participation and on the election of leaders for limited periods of time. Drawing on Latin rather than Greek, the Italians called their city-states republics, not democracies. But after about the mid-14th century, the conditions that had favoured the existence of independent city-states and wider participation in government—particularly their economic growth and the civic loyalty of their populations—gradually disappeared. Economic decline, corruption, factional disputes, civil wars, and wars with other states led to the weakening of some republican governments and their eventual replacement by authoritarian rulers, whether monarchs, princes, or soldiers.

Until the 17th century, democratic theorists and political leaders largely ignored the possibility that a legislature might consist neither of the entire body of citizens, as in Greece and Rome, nor of representatives chosen by and from a tiny oligarchy or hereditary aristocracy, as in the Italian republics. An important break in the prevailing orthodoxy occurred during and after the English Civil Wars (1642–51), when the Levelers and other radical followers of Puritanism demanded broader representation in Parliament, expanded powers for Parliament's lower house, the House of Commons, and universal manhood suffrage. As with many political innovations, representative government resulted less from philosophical speculation than from a search for practical solutions to a fairly self-evident problem.

By the end of the 18th century both the idea and the practice of democracy had been profoundly transformed by the creation, in the United States, of the world's first representative democracy. Political theorists and statesmen now recognized what the Levelers had seen earlier, that the nondemocratic practice of representation could be used to make democracy practicable in the large nation-states of the modern era. Representation, in other words, was the solution to the ancient dilemma between enhancing the ability of political associations to deal with large-scale problems and preserving the opportunity of citizens to participate in government.

In the 19th and 20th centuries the demos was gradually expanded to include all adult citizens. Although important issues remained unsettled—for example, should permanent legal foreign residents of a country be entitled to vote?—such an expanded demos became a new condition of democracy itself. By the mid-20th century, no system whose demos did not include all adult citizens could properly be called "democratic." So too, by the end of the 19th century, it was nearly universally accepted that the existence of independent and competitive political parties is an elementary standard that every democracy must meet. And although political theorists today continue to disagree about the best means to effect majority rule in democratic systems, it seems evident that majorities cannot legitimately abridge the fundamental rights of citizens. Nor should minorities ever be entitled to prevent the enforcement of laws and policies designed to protect these fundamental rights. In short, because democracy is not only a political system of "rule by the people" but necessarily also a system of rights, a government that infringes these rights is to that extent undemocratic.

CONTEMPORARY DEMOCRATIC SYSTEMS

Differences among democratic countries in historical experience, size, ethnic and religious composition, and other factors have resulted in significant differences in their political institutions. Some of the features with respect to which these institutions have differed are described below.

Whereas versions of the American presidential system were frequently adopted in Latin America, Africa, and elsewhere in the developing world (where the military sometimes converted the office into a dictatorship through a coup d'état), as European countries democratized they adopted versions of the English parliamentary system, which made use of both a prime minister responsible to parliament and a ceremonial head of state (who might be either a hereditary monarch, as in the Scandinavian countries, the Netherlands, and Spain, or a president chosen by parliament or by another body convoked specially for the purpose). A notable exception is France, which in its fifth constitution, adopted in 1958, combined its parliamentary system with a presidential one.

In most older European and English-speaking democracies, political authority inheres in the central government, which is constitutionally authorized to determine the limited powers, as well as the geographic boundaries, of subnational associations such as states and regions. Such unitary systems contrast markedly with federal systems, in which authority is constitutionally divided between the central government and the governments of relatively autonomous subnational entities. Democratic countries that have adopted federal systems include—in addition to the United States—Switzerland, Germany, Austria, Spain, Canada, and Australia. The world's most populous democratic country, India, also has a federal system.

Electoral arrangements vary enormously. Some democratic countries divide their territories into electoral districts, each of which is entitled to a single seat in the legislature, the seat being won by the candidate who gains the most votes—hence the terms *first past the post* in Britain and *winner take all* in the United States. As critics of this system point out, in districts contested by more than two candidates, it is possible to gain the seat with less than a strict majority of votes (50 percent plus one). As a result, a party that receives only a minority of votes in the entire country could win a majority of seats in the legislature. Systems of proportional representation are designed to ensure a closer correspondence between the proportion of votes cast for a party and the proportion of seats it receives. With few exceptions, Continental European countries have adopted some form of proportional representation, as have Ireland, Australia, New Zealand, Japan, and South Korea. Winner-take-all systems remain in the United States, Canada, and, for parliamentary elections, in Britain.

Because proportional representation does not favour large parties over smaller ones, as does the winner-take-all system, in countries with proportional representation there are almost always three or more parties represented in the legislature, and a coalition government consisting of two or more parties is ordinarily necessary to win legislative support for the government's policies. Thus the prevalence of proportional representation effectively ensures that coalition governments are the rule in democratic countries; governments consisting of only two parties, such as that of the United States, are extremely rare.

Because of differences in electoral systems and other factors, democratic countries differ with respect to whether laws and policies can be enacted by a single, relatively cohesive party with a legislative majority, as is ordinarily the case in Britain and Japan, or instead require consensus among several parties with diverse views, as in Switzerland, the Netherlands, Sweden, Italy, and elsewhere. Political scientists and others disagree about which of the two types of system, majoritarian or consensual, is more desirable. Critics of consensual systems argue that they allow a minority of citizens to veto policies they dislike and that they make the tasks of forming governments and passing legislation excessively difficult. Supporters contend that consensual arrangements produce comparatively wider public support for government policies and even help to increase the legitimacy and perceived value of democracy itself. Here again, it appears that a country's basic political institutions need to be tailored to its particular conditions and historical experience. The strongly majoritarian system of Britain would probably be inappropriate in Switzerland, whereas the consensual arrangements of Switzerland or the Netherlands might be less satisfactory in Britain.

EQUAL PROTECTION

In United States law, equal protection is the constitutional guarantee that no person or group will be denied the protection under the law that is enjoyed by similar persons or groups. In other words, persons similarly situated must be similarly treated. Equal protection is extended when the rules of law are applied equally in all like cases and when persons are exempt from obligations greater than those imposed upon others in like circumstances. The Fourteenth Amendment to the U.S. Constitution, one of three amendments adopted in the immediate aftermath of the American Civil War (1861–65), prohibits states from denying to any person "the equal protection of the laws."

For much of the post–Civil War period, the Supreme Court held that the postwar amendments had but one purpose: to guarantee "the freedom of the slave race . . . and the protection of the newly-made freeman and citizen from the oppressions of those who had formerly exercised unlimited domination over him." Thus, the equal protection clause of the Fourteenth Amendment was applied minimally— except in some cases of racial discrimination, such as the invalidation of literacy tests and grandfather clauses for voting. In other decisions—such as *Plessy* v. *Ferguson* (1896), which sanctioned racial segregation, and the decisions creating the doctrine of state action, which limited the enforcement of national civil rights legislation—the court diminished the envisioned protections. Indeed, for nearly 80 years after the adoption of the Fourteenth Amendment, the intent of the equal protection clause was effectively circumvented. As late as 1927, Justice Oliver Wendell Holmes, Jr., referred to equal protection as "the usual last resort of constitutional arguments." Not until the landmark *Brown v. Board of Education* (1954) decision did the court reverse its decision in *Plessy* and declare racial segregation unconstitutional.

Under Chief Justice Earl Warren in the 1960s, the concept of equal protection was dramatically transformed and applied to cases involving welfare benefits, exclusionary zoning, municipal services, and school financing. Equal protection became a prolific source of constitutional litigation. During the tenure of Chief Justices Warren E. Burger and William H. Rehnquist, the court added considerably to the list of situations that might be adjudicated under the doctrine of equal protection, including sexual discrimination, the status and rights of aliens, voting, abortion, and access to the courts. In *Bush v. Gore* (2000), which stemmed from the controversial presidential election of that year, the Supreme Court's ruling that a selective recount of ballots in the state of Florida violated the equal protection clause helped to preserve George W. Bush's narrow win in that state and in the electoral college.

BUSH v. *GORE*

The Supreme Court of the United States, in a 5–4 decision handed down on Dec. 12, 2000, reversed a Florida Supreme Court request for a selective manual recount of that state's U.S. presidential election ballots, and by so doing effectively awarded Florida's 25 votes in the electoral college — and thus the election itself — to Republican candidate George W. Bush.

On the evening of Nov. 7, 2000, a clear winner had yet to emerge in that day's U.S. presidential election between Bush and Democratic candidate and Al Gore. Print and broadcast media cited often contradictory exit-polling numbers, and the races in Oregon and New Mexico would remain too close to call for some days. Ultimately, the contest focused on Florida. Television news networks initially projected Gore the winner in Florida, but later declared that Bush had opened an insurmountable lead. Gore called Bush to concede the election, but in the early hours of the following morning it became apparent that the Florida race was much closer than Gore's staff had originally believed. Fewer than 600 votes separated the candidates, and that margin appeared to be narrowing. At about 3:00 AM, Gore called a stunned Bush to retract his concession.

According to Florida law, a machine recount of all votes cast was required because the margin of victory was less than 0.5 percent. In this race, the gap appeared to be roughly 0.01 percent. Both campaigns immediately dispatched teams of lawyers to Florida. Charges of conflict of interest were leveled by both sides—Bush's brother Jeb was the governor of the state and Secretary of State Katherine Harris was the cochair of Bush's Florida campaign, while state attorney general Bob Butterworth headed the Gore campaign. By November 10, the machine recount was complete, and Bush's lead stood at 327 votes out of six million cast. As court challenges were issued over the legality of hand recounts in select counties, news stories were filled with the arcane vocabulary of the election judge. County officials tried to discern voter intent through a cloud of "hanging chads" (incompletely punched paper ballots) and "pregnant chads" (paper ballots that were dimpled, but not pierced, during the voting process), as well as "overvotes" (ballots that

A canvassing board member shows a disputed ballot to an election observer at the Broward County Courthouse in Fort Lauderdale, Fla., Nov. 23, 2000. Rhoma Wise—AFP/Getty Images

recorded multiple votes for the same office) and "undervotes" (ballots that recorded no vote for a given office). Also at issue was the so-called butterfly ballot design used in Palm Beach County, which caused confusion among some Gore voters—prompting them to inadvertently cast their votes for third-party candidate Pat Buchanan, who received some 3,400 (some 20 percent of his total votes state-wide). A tug-of-war ensued between Harris, who initially sought to certify the state's election results on November 14, and the Florida Supreme Court, which ruled that hand recounts of questionable ballots should proceed in four counties and that the results must be included in the state's final count. In the month following the election, some 50 individual suits were filed concerning the various counts, recounts, and certification deadlines. On December 8, in a 4–3 decision, the Florida Supreme Court ruled that manual recounts should continue in all counties where a statistically significant number of undervotes were observed for the office of president.

The Bush campaign immediately filed suit, and the U.S. Supreme Court issued a writ of certiorari to take up the case the following day. On December 9, in a 5–4 decision, the U.S. Supreme Court ruled in the case of *Bush* v.

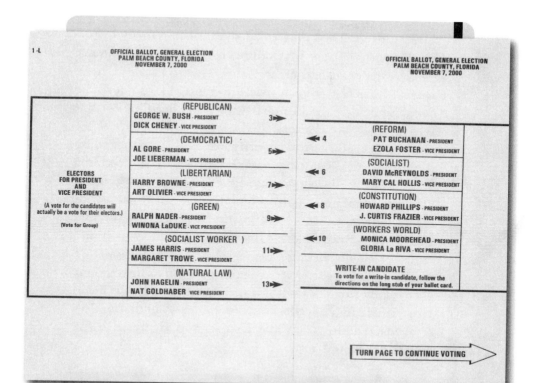

1-L

OFFICIAL BALLOT, GENERAL ELECTION
PALM BEACH COUNTY, FLORIDA
NOVEMBER 7, 2000

OFFICIAL BALLOT, GENERAL ELECTION
PALM BEACH COUNTY, FLORIDA
NOVEMBER 7, 2000

ELECTORS FOR PRESIDENT AND VICE PRESIDENT

(A vote for the candidates will actually be a vote for their electors.)

(Vote for Group)

(REPUBLICAN)
GEORGE W. BUSH - PRESIDENT
DICK CHENEY - VICE PRESIDENT   3 ➡

(DEMOCRATIC)
AL GORE - PRESIDENT
JOE LIEBERMAN - VICE PRESIDENT   5 ➡

(LIBERTARIAN)
HARRY BROWNE - PRESIDENT
ART OLIVIER - VICE PRESIDENT   7 ➡

(GREEN)
RALPH NADER - PRESIDENT
WINONA LaDUKE - VICE PRESIDENT   9 ➡

(SOCIALIST WORKER)
JAMES HARRIS - PRESIDENT
MARGARET TROWE - VICE PRESIDENT   11 ➡

(NATURAL LAW)
JOHN HAGELIN - PRESIDENT
NAT GOLDHABER - VICE PRESIDENT   13 ➡

⬅ 4   (REFORM)
PAT BUCHANAN - PRESIDENT
EZOLA FOSTER - VICE PRESIDENT

⬅ 6   (SOCIALIST)
DAVID McREYNOLDS - PRESIDENT
MARY CAL HOLLIS - VICE PRESIDENT

⬅ 8   (CONSTITUTION)
HOWARD PHILLIPS - PRESIDENT
J. CURTIS FRAZIER - VICE PRESIDENT

⬅ 10 (WORKERS WORLD)
MONICA MOOREHEAD - PRESIDENT
GLORIA La RIVA - VICE PRESIDENT

WRITE-IN CANDIDATE
To vote for a write-in candidate, follow the directions on the long stub of your ballot card.

TURN PAGE TO CONTINUE VOTING ➤

Sample ballot from Palm Beach County, Fla., for the 2000 U.S. presidential election.

Gore that the manual recounts must halt, and it agreed to hear oral arguments from both parties. On December 11, the two sides presented their cases, Bush's team asserting that the Florida Supreme Court had exceeded its authority by authorizing the recount of undervotes and Gore's team stating that the case, having already been decided at the state level, was not a matter for consideration at the federal level. The following day, in a 7–2 ruling, the U.S. Supreme Court overturned the Florida decision, holding that the various methods and standards of the recount process violated the equal protection clause of the U.S.

Constitution. The court ruled 5–4 on the remedy of the matter, with the majority holding that the Florida Supreme Court's decision had created new election law—a right reserved for the state legislature—and that no recount could be held in time to satisfy a federal deadline for the selection of state electors.

The decision of the majority was heavily criticized by the minority. Dissenting justices wrote that the recount process, while flawed, should be allowed to proceed, on the grounds that constitutional protection of each vote should not be subject to a timeline. Particularly notable was Justice Ruth Bader Ginsburg's dissent, which she ended with "I dissent" rather than the traditional "I respectfully dissent." With the termination of the recount process, Florida's 25 electoral votes were awarded to Bush. Gore officially conceded on December 13 and stated in a televised address, "While I strongly disagree with the court's decision, I accept it."

INTERNATIONAL LAW

The body of legal rules, norms, and standards that apply between sovereign states and other entities that are legally recognized as international actors is known as international law, public international law, or the law of nations. The term *international law* was coined by the English philosopher Jeremy Bentham (1748–1832).

DEFINITION AND SCOPE

According to Bentham's classic definition, international law is a collection of rules governing relations between states. It is a mark of how far international law has evolved that this original definition omits individuals and international organizations—two of the most dynamic and vital elements of modern international law. Furthermore, it is no longer accurate to view international law as simply a collection of rules; rather, it is a rapidly developing complex of rules and influential—though not directly binding—principles, practices, and assertions coupled with increasingly sophisticated structures and processes. In its broadest sense, international law provides normative guidelines as well as methods, mechanisms, and a common conceptual language to international actors—i.e., primarily sovereign states but also increasingly international organizations and some individuals. The range of subjects and actors directly concerned with international law has widened considerably, moving beyond the classical questions of war, peace, and diplomacy to include human rights, economic and trade issues, space law, and international organizations. Although international law is a legal order and not an ethical one, it has been influenced significantly by ethical principles and concerns, particularly in the sphere of human rights.

International law is distinct from international comity, which comprises legally nonbinding practices adopted by states for reasons of courtesy (e.g., the saluting of the flags of foreign warships at sea). In addition, the study of international law, or public international law, is distinguished from the field of conflict of laws, or private international law, which is concerned with the rules of municipal law—as international lawyers term the domestic law of states—of different countries where foreign elements are involved.

International law is an independent system of law existing outside the legal orders of particular states. It differs from domestic legal systems in a number of respects. For example, although the United Nations (UN) General Assembly, which consists of representatives of some 190 countries, has the outward appearances of a legislature, it has no power to issue binding laws. Rather, its resolutions serve only as recommendations — except in specific cases and for certain purposes within the UN system, such as determining the UN budget, admitting new members of the UN, and, with the involvement of the Security Council, electing new judges to the International Court of Justice (ICJ). Also, there is no system of courts with comprehensive jurisdiction in international law. The ICJ's jurisdiction in contentious cases is founded upon the consent of the particular states involved. There is no international police force or comprehensive system of law enforcement, and there also is no supreme executive authority. The UN Security Council may authorize the use of force to compel states to comply with its decisions, but only in specific and limited circumstances; essentially, there must be a prior act of aggression or the threat of such an act. Moreover, any such enforcement action can be vetoed by any of the council's five permanent members (China, France, Russia, the United Kingdom, and the United States). Because there is no standing UN military, the forces involved must be assembled from member states on an ad hoc basis.

International law is a distinctive part of the general structure of international relations. In contemplating responses to a particular international situation, states usually consider relevant international laws. Although considerable attention is invariably focused on violations of international law, states generally are careful to ensure that their actions conform to the rules and principles of international law, because acting otherwise would be regarded negatively by the international community. The rules of international law are rarely enforced by military means or even by the use of economic sanctions. Instead, the system is sustained by reciprocity or a sense of enlightened self-interest. States that breach international rules suffer a decline in credibility that may prejudice them in future relations with other states. Thus, a violation of a treaty by one state to its advantage may induce other states to breach other treaties and thereby cause harm to the original violator. Furthermore, it is generally realized that consistent rule violations would jeopardize the value that the system brings to the community of states, international organizations, and other actors. This value consists in the certainty, predictability, and sense of common purpose in international affairs that derives from the existence of a set of rules accepted by all international actors. International law also provides a framework and a set of procedures for international interaction, as well as a common set of concepts for understanding it.

HISTORICAL DEVELOPMENT

International law reflects the establishment and subsequent modification of a world system founded almost exclusively on the notion that independent sovereign states are the only relevant actors in the international system. The essential structure of international law was mapped out during the European Renaissance, though its origins lay deep in history and can be traced to cooperative agreements between peoples in the ancient Middle East. Among the earliest of these agreements were a treaty between the rulers of Lagash and Umma (in the area of Mesopotamia) in approximately 2100 BCE and an agreement between the Egyptian pharaoh Ramses II and Hattusilis III, the king of the Hittites, concluded in 1258 BCE. A number of pacts were subsequently negotiated by various Middle Eastern empires. The long and rich cultural traditions of ancient Israel, the Indian subcontinent, and China were also vital in the development of international law. In addition, basic notions of governance, of political relations, and of the interaction of independent units provided by ancient Greek political philosophy and the relations between the Greek city-states constituted important sources for the evolution of the international legal system.

Many of the concepts that today underpin the international legal order were established during the Roman Empire. The *jus gentium* (Latin: "law of nations"), for example, was invented by the Romans to govern the status of foreigners and the relations between foreigners and Roman citizens. In accord with the Greek concept of natural law, which they adopted, the Romans conceived of the *jus gentium* as having universal application. In the Middle Ages, the concept of natural law, infused with religious principles through the writings of the Jewish philosopher Moses Maimonides (1135–1204) and the theologian St. Thomas Aquinas (1224/25–1274), became the intellectual foundation of the new discipline of the law of nations, regarded as that part of natural law that applied to the relations between sovereign states.

After the collapse of the western Roman Empire in the 5th century CE, Europe suffered from frequent warring for nearly 500 years. Eventually, a group of nation-states emerged, and a number of supranational sets of rules were developed to govern interstate relations, including canon law, the law merchant (which governed trade), and various codes of maritime law—e.g., the 12th-century Rolls of Oléron, named for an island off the west coast of France, and the Laws of Wisby (Visby), the seat of the Hanseatic League until 1361. In the 15th century the arrival of Greek scholars in Europe from the collapsing Byzantine Empire and the introduction of the printing press spurred the development of scientific, humanistic, and individualist thought, while the expansion of ocean navigation by European explorers spread European norms throughout the world and broadened the intellectual and geographic horizons of western Europe. The subsequent consolidation of European states with increasing wealth and ambitions, coupled with the growth in trade, necessitated the establishment of a set of rules to regulate their relations. In the 16th century the concept of sovereignty provided a basis for the entrenchment of power in the person of the king and was later transformed into a principle of collective sovereignty as the divine right of kings gave way constitutionally to parliamentary or representative forms of government. Sovereignty also acquired an external meaning, referring to independence within a system of competing nation-states.

Early writers who dealt with questions of governance and relations between nations included the Italian lawyers Bartolo da Sassoferrato (1313/14–57), regarded as the founder of the modern study of private international law, and Baldo degli Ubaldi (1327–1400), a famed teacher, papal adviser, and authority on Roman and feudal law. The essence of the new approach, however, can be more directly traced to the philosophers of the Spanish Golden Age of the 16th and 17th centuries. Both Francisco de Vitoria (1486–1546), who was particularly concerned with the treatment of the indigenous peoples of South America by the conquering Spanish forces, and Francisco Suárez (1548–1617) emphasized that international law was founded upon the law of nature. In 1598 Italian jurist Alberico Gentili (1552–1608), considered the originator of the secular school of thought in international law, published *De jure belli libri tres* (1598; *Three Books on the Law of War*), which contained a comprehensive discussion of the laws of war and treaties. Gentili's work initiated a transformation of the law of nature from a theological concept to a concept of secular philosophy founded on reason. The Dutch jurist Hugo Grotius (1583–1645) has influenced the development of the field to an extent unequaled by any other theorist, though his reputation as the father of international law has perhaps been exaggerated. Grotius excised theology from international law and organized it into a comprehensive system, especially in *De Jure Belli ac Pacis* (1625; *On the Law of War and Peace*). Grotius emphasized the freedom of the high seas, a notion that rapidly gained acceptance among the northern European powers that were embarking upon extensive missions of exploration and colonization around the world.

The scholars who followed Grotius can be grouped into two schools, the naturalists and the positivists. The former camp included the German jurist Samuel von Pufendorf (1632–94), who stressed the supremacy of the law of nature. In contrast, positivist writers, such as Richard Zouche (1590–1661) in England and Cornelis van Bynkershoek (1673–1743) in the Netherlands, emphasized the actual practice of contemporary states over concepts derived from biblical sources, Greek thought, or Roman law. These new writings also focused greater attention on the law of peace and the conduct of interstate relations than on the law of war, as the focus of international law shifted away from the conditions necessary to justify the resort to force in order to deal with increasingly sophisticated interstate relations in areas such as the law of the sea and commercial treaties. The positivist school made use of the new scientific method and was in that respect consistent with the empiricist and inductive approach to philosophy that was then gaining acceptance in Europe. Elements of both positivism and natural law appear in the works of the German philosopher Christian Wolff (1679–1754) and the Swiss jurist Emmerich de Vattel (1714–67), both of whom attempted to develop an approach that avoided the extremes of each school. During the 18th century, the naturalist school was gradually eclipsed by the positivist tradition, though, at the same time, the concept of natural rights—which played a prominent role in the American and French revolutions—was becoming a vital element in international politics. In international law, however, the concept of natural rights had only marginal significance until the 20th century.

Positivism's influence peaked during the expansionist and industrial 19th century, when the notion of state sovereignty was buttressed by the ideas of exclusive domestic jurisdiction and nonintervention in the affairs of other states—ideas that had been spread throughout the world by the European imperial powers. In the 20th century, however, positivism's dominance in international law was undermined by the impact of two world wars, the resulting growth of international organizations—e.g., the League of Nations, founded in 1919, and the UN, founded in 1945—and the increasing importance of human rights. Having become geographically international through the colonial expansion of the European powers, international law became truly international in the first decades after World War II, when decolonization resulted in the establishment of scores of newly independent states. The varying political and economic interests and needs of these states, along with their diverse cultural backgrounds, infused the hitherto European-dominated principles and practices of international law with new influences.

The development of international law—both its rules and its institutions—is inevitably shaped by international political events. From the end of World War II until the 1990s, most events that threatened international peace and security were connected to the Cold War between the Soviet Union and its allies and the U.S.-led Western alliance. The UN Security Council was unable to function as intended, because resolutions proposed by one side were likely to be vetoed by the other. The bipolar system of alliances prompted the development of regional organizations—e.g., the Warsaw Pact organized by the Soviet Union and the North Atlantic Treaty Organization (NATO) established by the United States—and encouraged the proliferation of conflicts on the peripheries of the two blocs, including in Korea, Vietnam, and Berlin. Furthermore, the development of norms for protecting human rights proceeded unevenly, slowed by sharp ideological divisions.

The Cold War also gave rise to the coalescence of a group of nonaligned and often newly decolonized states, the so-called "Third World," whose support was eagerly sought by both the United States and the Soviet Union. The developing world's increased prominence focused attention upon the interests of those states, particularly as they related to decolonization, racial discrimination, and economic aid. It also fostered greater universalism in international politics and international law. The ICJ's statute, for example, declared that the organization of the court must reflect the main forms of civilization and the principal legal systems of the world. Similarly, an informal agreement among members of the UN requires that nonpermanent seats on the Security Council be apportioned to ensure equitable regional representation; 5 of the 10 seats have regularly gone to Africa or Asia, two to Latin America, and the remainder to Europe or other states. Other UN organs are structured in a similar fashion.

The collapse of the Soviet Union and the end of the Cold War in the early 1990s increased political cooperation between the United States and Russia and their allies across the Northern Hemisphere, but tensions also increased between states of the north and those of the south, especially on issues such as trade, human rights, and the law of the sea. Technology and globalization—the rapidly escalating growth in the international movement in goods, services, currency, information, and persons—also became significant forces, spurring international cooperation and somewhat reducing the ideological barriers that divided the world, though globalization also led to increasing trade tensions between allies such as the United States and the European Union (EU).

Since the 1980s, globalization has increased the number and sphere of influence of international and regional organizations and required the expansion of international law to cover the rights and obligations of these actors. Because of its complexity and the sheer number of actors it affects, new international law is now frequently created through processes that require near-universal consensus. In the area of the environment, for example, bilateral negotiations have been supplemented— and in some cases replaced—by multilateral ones, transmuting the process of individual state consent into community acceptance. Various environmental agreements and the Law of the Sea treaty (1982) have been negotiated through this consensus-building process. International law as a system is complex. Although in principle it is "horizontal," in the sense of being founded upon the concept of the equality of states—one of the basic principles of international law—in reality some states continue to be more important than others in creating and maintaining international law.

INTERNATIONAL LAW AND MUNICIPAL LAW

In principle, international law operates only at the international level and not within domestic legal systems—a perspective consistent with positivism, which recognizes international law and municipal law as distinct and independent systems. Conversely, advocates of natural law maintain that municipal and international law form a single legal system, an approach sometimes referred to as monism. Such a system, according to monists, may arise either out of a unified ethical approach emphasizing universal human rights or out of a formalistic, hierarchical approach positing the existence of one fundamental norm underpinning both international law and municipal law.

A principle recognized both in international case law (e.g., the *Alabama* claims case between the United States and the United Kingdom following the American Civil War) and in treaties (e.g., Article 27 of the 1969 Vienna Convention on the Law of Treaties) is that no municipal rule may be relied upon as a justification for violating international law. The position of international law within municipal law is more complex and depends upon a country's domestic legislation. In particular, treaties must be distinguished from customary international law. Treaties are written agreements that are signed and ratified by the parties and binding on them. Customary international law consists of those rules that have arisen as a consequence of practices engaged in by states.

The Constitution of the United States stipulates (Article VI, Section 2) that treaties "shall be the supreme Law of the Land." Treaties are negotiated by the president but can be ratified only with the approval of two-thirds of the Senate (Article II)—except in the case of executive agreements, which are made by the president on his own authority. Further, a treaty may be either self-executing or non-self-executing, depending upon whether domestic legislation must be enacted in order for the treaty to enter into force. In the United States, self-executing treaties apply directly as part of the supreme law of the land without the need for further action. Whether a treaty is deemed to be self-executing depends upon the intention of the signatories and the interpretation of the courts. In *Sei Fujii* v. *State of California* (1952), for example, the

California Supreme Court held that the UN Charter was not self-executing because its relevant principles concerning human rights lacked the mandatory quality and certainty required to create justiciable rights for private persons upon its ratification; since then the ruling has been consistently applied by other courts in the United States. In contrast, customary international law was interpreted as part of federal law in the *Paquette Habana* case (1900), in which the U.S. Supreme Court ruled that international law forbade the U.S. Navy from selling, as prizes of war, Cuban fishing vessels it had seized. Domestic legislation is supreme in the United States even if it breaches international law, though the government may be held liable for such a breach at the international level. In order to mitigate such a possibility, there is a presumption that the U.S. Congress will not legislate contrary to the country's international obligations.

The United Kingdom takes an incorporationist view, holding that customary international law forms part of the common law. British law, however, views treaties as purely executive, rather than legislative, acts. Thus, a treaty becomes part of domestic law only if relevant legislation is adopted. The same principle applies in other countries where the English common law has been accepted (e.g., the majority of Commonwealth states and Israel). Although the incorporationist view regards customary law as part of the law of the land and presumes that municipal laws should not be inconsistent with international law, municipal laws take precedence over international law in cases of conflict. Those common-law countries that have adopted a written constitution generally have taken slightly different positions on the incorporation of international law into municipal law. Ireland's constitution, for example, states that the country will not be bound by any treaty involving public funds without the consent of the national legislature, and in Cyprus treaties concluded in accordance with its constitution have a status superior to municipal law on the condition of reciprocity.

In most civil-law countries, the adoption of a treaty is a legislative act. The relationship between municipal and international law varies, and the status of an international treaty within domestic law is determined by the country's

JEREMY BENTHAM
(b. Feb. 15, 1748, London, Eng.—d. June 6, 1832, London)

The British moral philosopher and legal theorist Jeremy Bentham was the earliest expounder of utilitarianism. A precocious student, he graduated from Oxford at age 15. In his *An Introduction to the Principles of Morals and Legislation*, he argued that humankind was governed by two sovereign motives, pain and pleasure. The object of all legislation, therefore, must be the "greatest happiness of the greatest number"; and since all punishment involves pain and is therefore evil, it ought only to be used "so far as it promises to exclude some greater evil." His work inspired much reform legislation, especially regarding prisons. He was also an exponent of the new laissez-faire economics of Adam Smith and David Ricardo. Though a vocal advocate of democracy, he rejected the notions of the social contract, natural law, and natural rights as fictional and counterproductive ("Rights is the child of law; from real law come real rights; but from imaginary laws, from 'law of nature,' come imaginary rights"). He helped found the radical *Westminster Review* (1823). In accordance with his will, his clothed skeleton is permanently exhibited at University College, London.

constitutional provisions. In federal systems, the application of international law is complex, and the rules of international law are generally deemed to be part of the federal law. Although a treaty generally becomes operative only when it has been ratified by a national legislature, EU countries have agreed that regulations and decisions emanating from EU institutions are directly applicable and enforceable without the need for enabling legislation—except for legislation permitting this form of lawmaking, which is adopted upon the country's entry into the union (e.g., Britain's adoption of the European Communities Act in 1972).

SOCIAL CONTRACT

An actual or hypothetical compact, or agreement, between the ruled and their rulers, that defines the rights and duties of each is a social contract. In primeval times, according to the theory, individuals were born into an anarchic state of nature, which was happy or unhappy according to the particular version. They then, by exercising natural reason, formed a society (and a government) by means of a contract among themselves.

Although similar ideas can be traced back to the Greek Sophists, social-contract theories had their greatest currency in the 17th and 18th centuries and are associated with such names as the Englishmen Thomas Hobbes and John Locke and the Frenchman Jean-Jacques Rousseau. What distinguished these theories of political obligation from other doctrines of the period was their attempt to justify political authority on grounds of individual self-interest and rational consent. They attempted to demonstrate the value and purposes of organized government by comparing the advantages of civil society with the disadvantages of the state of nature, a hypothetical condition characterized by a complete absence of governmental authority. The purpose of this comparison was to show why and under what conditions government is useful and ought therefore to be accepted by all reasonable people as a voluntary obligation. These conclusions were then reduced to the form of a social contract, from which it was supposed that all the essential rights and duties of citizens could be logically deduced.

Theories of the social contract differed according to their purpose: some were designed to justify the power of the sovereign; on the other hand, some were intended to safeguard the individual from oppression by an all-too-powerful sovereign.

According to Hobbes (*Leviathan*, 1651), the state of nature was one in which there were no enforceable criteria of right and wrong. Each person took for himself all that he could; human life was "solitary, poor, nasty, brutish and short." The state of nature was therefore a state of war, which could be ended only if individuals agreed (in a social contract) to give their liberty into the hands of a sovereign, who was thenceforward absolute, on the sole condition that their lives were safeguarded by sovereign power.

Locke (in the second of *Two Treatises of Government*, 1690) differed from Hobbes insofar as he described the state of nature as one in which the rights of life and property were generally recognized under natural law, the inconveniences of the situation arising from insecurity in the enforcement of those rights. He therefore argued that the obligation to obey civil government under the social contract was conditional upon the protection not only of the person but also of private property. If a sovereign violated these terms, he could be justifiably overthrown.

Rousseau (in *Du contrat social,* 1762) held that in the state of nature man was unwarlike and somewhat undeveloped in his reasoning powers and sense of morality and responsibility. When, however, people agreed for mutual protection to surrender individual freedom of action and establish laws and government, they then acquired a sense of moral and civic obligation. In order

THOMAS HOBBES
(b. April 5, 1588, Westport, Wiltshire, Eng.—d. Dec. 4, 1679, Hardwick Hall, Derbyshire)

The English philosopher and political theorist Thomas Hobbes expounded his ideas in several works, the best known of which is *Leviathan* (1651).

The son of a vicar who abandoned his family, Hobbes was raised by his uncle. After graduating from the University of Oxford he became a tutor and traveled with his pupil in Europe, where he engaged Galileo in philosophical discussions on the nature of motion. He later turned to political theory, but his support for absolutism put him at odds with the rising antiroyalist sentiment of the time. He fled to Paris in 1640, where he tutored the future King Charles II of England. In Paris he wrote his best-known work, *Leviathan*, in which he attempted to justify the absolute power of the sovereign on the basis of a hypothetical social contract in which individuals seek to protect themselves from one another by agreeing to obey the sovereign in all matters. Hobbes returned to Britain in 1651 after the death of Charles I. In 1666 Parliament threatened to investigate him as an atheist. His works are considered important statements of the nascent ideas of liberalism as well as of the longstanding assumptions of absolutism characteristic of the times.

to retain its essentially moral character, government must thus rest on the consent of the governed, the *volonté générale* ("general will").

The more perceptive social-contract theorists, including Hobbes, invariably recognized that their concepts of the social contract and the state of nature were unhistorical and that they could be justified only as hypotheses useful for the clarification of timeless political problems.

ABSOLUTISM

Absolutism is the political doctrine and practice of unlimited, centralized authority and absolute sovereignty, as vested especially in a monarch or dictator. The essence of an absolutist system is that the ruling power is not subject to regularized challenge or check by any other agency, be it judicial, legislative, religious, economic, or electoral. King Louis XIV (1643–1715) of France furnished the most familiar assertion of absolutism when he said, "L'état, c'est moi" ("I am the state"). Absolutism has existed in various forms in all parts of the world, including in Nazi Germany under Adolf Hitler and in the Soviet Union under Joseph Stalin.

The most commonly studied form of absolutism is absolute monarchy, which originated in early modern Europe and was based on the strong individual leaders of the new nation-states that were created at the breakup of the medieval order. The power of these states was closely associated with the power of their rulers; to strengthen both, it was necessary to curtail the restraints on centralized government that had been exercised by the church, feudal lords, and medieval customary law. By claiming the absolute authority of the state against such former restraints, the monarch as head of state claimed his own absolute authority.

Portrait of King Louis XIV, by Charles Le Brun, c. *1655.* © Photos.com/ Jupiterimages

By the 16th century monarchical absolutism prevailed in much of western Europe, and it was widespread in the 17th and 18th centuries. Besides France, whose absolutism was epitomized by Louis XIV, absolutism existed in a variety of other European countries, including Spain, Prussia, and Austria.

The most common defense of monarchical absolutism, known as "the divine right of kings" theory, asserted that kings derived their authority from God. This view could justify even tyrannical rule as divinely ordained punishment, administered by rulers, for human sinfulness. In its origins, the divine-right theory may be traced to the medieval conception of God's award of temporal power to the political ruler, while spiritual power was given to the head of the Roman Catholic Church. However, the new national monarchs asserted their authority in all matters and tended to become heads of church as well as of state, as did King Henry VIII when he became head of the newly created Church of England in the 16th century. Their power was absolute in a way that was impossible to achieve for medieval monarchs, who were confronted by a church that was essentially a rival centre of authority.

More pragmatic arguments than that of divine right were also advanced in support of absolutism. According to some political theorists, complete obedience to a single will is necessary to maintain order and security. The most elaborate statement of this view was made by the English philosopher Thomas Hobbes in *Leviathan* (1651). A monopoly of power also has been justified on the basis of a presumed knowledge of absolute truth. Neither the sharing of power nor limits on its exercise appear valid to those who believe that they know—and know absolutely—what is right. This argument was advanced by Vladimir Ilich Lenin to defend the absolute authority of the Communist Party in Russia after the Bolshevik Revolution in 1917.

LOUIS XIV

(b. Sept. 5, 1638, Saint-Germain-en-Laye, France—d. Sept. 1, 1715, Versailles)

Known as the Sun King, Louis XIV of France (1643–1715) reigned during one of France's most brilliant periods. He was the symbol of absolute monarchy of the Neoclassical age. He succeeded his father, Louis XIII, at age four, under the regency of his mother, Anne of Austria. In 1648 the nobles and the Paris Parlement, who hated the prime minister, Cardinal Mazarin, rose against the crown and started the Fronde. In 1653, victorious over the rebels, Mazarin gained absolute power, though the king was of age. In 1660 Louis married Marie-Thérèse of Austria (1638–83), daughter of Philip IV of Spain. When Mazarin died in 1661, Louis astonished his ministers by informing them that he intended to assume responsibility for ruling the kingdom. A believer in dictatorship by divine right, he viewed himself as God's representative on earth. He was assisted by his able ministers, Jean-Baptiste Colbert and the marquis de Louvois. Louis weakened the nobles' power by making them dependent on the crown. A patron of the arts, he protected writers and devoted himself to building splendid palaces, including the extravagant Versailles, where he kept most of the nobility under his watchful eye. In 1667 he invaded the Spanish Netherlands in the War of Devolution (1667–68) and again in 1672 in the Third Dutch War. The Sun King was at his zenith; he had extended France's northern and eastern borders and was adored at his court. In 1680 a scandal involving his mistress, the marchioness de Montespan (1641–1707), made him fearful for his reputation, and he openly renounced pleasure. The queen died in 1683, and he secretly married the pious marchioness de Maintenon. After trying to convert French Protestants by force, he revoked the Edict of Nantes in 1685. Fear of his expansionism led to alliances against France during the War of the Grand Alliance (1688–97) and the War of the Spanish Succession (1701–14). Louis died at age 77 at the end of the longest reign in European history.

NATIONALISM

The ideology of nationalism is based on the premise that the individual's loyalty and devotion to the nation-state surpass other individual or group interests.

Nationalism is a modern movement. Throughout history people have been attached to their native soil, to the traditions of their parents, and to established territorial authorities; but it was not until the end of the 18th century that nationalism began to be a generally recognized sentiment molding public and private life and one of the great, if not the greatest, single determining factors of modern history. Because of its dynamic vitality and its all-pervading character, nationalism is often thought to be very old; sometimes it is mistakenly regarded as a permanent factor in political behaviour. Actually, the American and French revolutions may be regarded as its first powerful manifestations. After penetrating the new countries of Latin America it spread in the early 19th century to central Europe and from there, toward the middle of the century, to eastern and southeastern Europe. At the beginning of the 20th century nationalism flowered in the ancient lands of Asia and Africa. Thus the 19th century has been called the age of nationalism in Europe, while the 20th century has witnessed the rise and struggle of powerful national movements throughout Asia and Africa.

THE IDENTIFICATION OF STATE AND PEOPLE

Nationalism, translated into world politics, implies the identification of the state or nation with the people—or at least the desirability of determining the extent of the state according to ethnographic principles. In the age of nationalism, but only in the age of nationalism, the principle was generally recognized that each nationality should form a state—its state—and that the state should include all members of that nationality. Formerly states, or territories under one administration, were not delineated by nationality. Men did not give their loyalty to the nation-state but to other, different forms of political organization: the city-state, the feudal fief and its lord, the dynastic state, the religious group, or the sect. The nation-state was nonexistent during the greater part of history, and for a very long time it was not even regarded as an ideal. In the first 15 centuries of the Christian Era, the ideal was the universal world-state, not loyalty to any separate political entity. The Roman Empire had set the great example, which survived not only in the Holy Roman Empire of the Middle Ages but also in the concept of the *res publica christiana* ("Christian republic" or community) and in its later secularized form of a united world civilization.

As political allegiance, before the age of nationalism, was not determined by nationality, so civilization was not thought of as nationally determined. During the Middle Ages civilization was looked upon as determined religiously; for all the different nationalities of Christendom as well as for those of Islam there was but one civilization—Christian or Muslim—and but one language of culture—Latin (or Greek) or Arabic (or Persian). Later, in the periods of the Renaissance and of Classicism, it was the ancient Greek and Roman civilizations that became a universal norm, valid for all peoples and all times. Still later, French civilization was accepted throughout Europe as the valid civilization for educated people of all nationalities. It was only at the end of the 18th century that, for the first time, civilization was considered to be determined by nationality. It was then that the principle was put forward that a man could be educated only in his own mother tongue, not in languages of other civilizations and other times, whether they were classical languages or the literary creations of other peoples who had reached a high degree of civilization.

CULTURAL NATIONALISM

From the end of the 18th century on, the nationalization of education and public life went hand in hand with the nationalization of states and political loyalties. Poets and scholars began to emphasize cultural nationalism first. They reformed the mother tongue, elevated it to the rank of a literary language, and delved deep into the national past. Thus they prepared the foundations for the political claims for national statehood soon to be raised by the people in whom they had kindled the spirit.

Before the 18th century there had been evidences of national feeling among certain groups at certain periods, especially in times of stress and conflict. The rise of national feeling to major political importance was encouraged by a number of complex developments: the creation of large, centralized states ruled by absolute monarchs who destroyed the old feudal allegiances; the secularization of life and of education, which fostered the vernacular languages and weakened the ties of church and sect; the growth of commerce, which demanded larger territorial units to allow scope for the dynamic spirit of the rising middle classes and their capitalistic enterprise. This large, unified territorial state, with its political and economic centralization, became imbued in the 18th century with a new spirit—an emotional fervour similar to that of religious movements in earlier periods. Under the influence of the new theories of the sovereignty of the people and the rights of man, the people replaced the king as the centre of the nation. No longer was the king the nation or the state; the state had become the people's state, a national state, a fatherland. State became identified with nation, as civilization became identified with national civilization.

That development ran counter to the conceptions that had dominated political thought for the preceding 2,000 years. Hitherto man had commonly stressed the general and the universal and had regarded unity as the desirable goal. Nationalism stressed the particular and parochial, the differences, and the national individualities. Those tendencies became more pronounced as nationalism developed. Its less attractive characteristics were not at first apparent. In the 17th and 18th centuries the common standards of Western civilization, the regard for the universally human, the faith in reason (one and the same everywhere) as well as in common sense, the survival of Christian and Stoic traditions—all of these were still too strong to allow nationalism to develop fully and to disrupt society. Thus nationalism in its beginning was thought to be compatible with cosmopolitan convictions and with a general love of humankind, especially in western Europe and North America.

European Nationalism

The countries of Europe were early adherents to notions of nationalism. The first full manifestation of modern nationalism occurred in 17th-century England, in the Puritan revolution.

English Puritanism and Nationalism

England had become the leading nation in scientific spirit, in commercial enterprise, in political thought and activity.

Swelled by an immense confidence in the new age, the English people felt upon their shoulders the mission of history, a sense that they were at a great turning point from which a new true reformation and a new liberty would start. In the English revolution an optimistic humanism merged with Calvinist ethics; the influence of the Old Testament gave form to the new nationalism by identifying the English people with ancient Israel.

The new message, carried by the new people not only for England but for all humankind, was expressed in the writings of John Milton, in whose famous vision the idea of liberty was seen spreading from Britain, "celebrated for endless ages as a soil most genial to the growth of liberty" to all the corners of the earth.

> *Surrounded by congregated multitudes, I now imagine that . . . I behold the nations of the earth recovering that liberty which they so long had lost; and that the people of this island are . . . disseminating the blessings of civilization and freedom among cities, kingdoms and nations.*

English nationalism then was thus much nearer to its religious matrix than later nationalisms that rose after secularization had made greater progress. The nationalism of the 18th century shared with it, however, its enthusiasm for liberty, its humanitarian character, its emphasis upon the individual and his rights and upon the human community as above all national divisions. The rise of English nationalism coincided with the rise of the English trading middle classes. It found its final expression in John Locke's political philosophy, and it was in that form that it influenced American and French nationalism in the following century.

American nationalism was a typical product of the 18th century. British settlers in North America were influenced partly by the traditions of the Puritan revolution and the ideas of Locke and partly by the new rational interpretation given to English liberty by contemporary French philosophers. American settlers became a nation engaged in a fight for liberty and individual rights. They based that fight on current political thought, especially as expressed by Thomas Jefferson and Thomas Paine. It was a liberal and humanitarian nationalism that regarded America as in the vanguard of humankind on its march to greater liberty, equality, and happiness for all. The ideas of the 18th century found their first political realization in the Declaration of Independence and in the birth of the American nation. Their deep influence was felt in the French Revolution.

FRENCH NATIONALISM

Jean-Jacques Rousseau had prepared the soil for the growth of French nationalism by his stress on popular sovereignty and the general cooperation of all in forming the national will, and also by his regard for the common people as the true depository of civilization.

The nationalism of the French Revolution was more than that: it was the triumphant expression of a rational faith in common humanity and liberal progress. The famous slogan "liberty, equality, fraternity" and the Declaration of the Rights of Man and of the Citizen were thought valid not only for the French people but for all peoples. Individual liberty, human equality, fraternity of all peoples: these were the common cornerstones of all liberal and democratic nationalism. Under their inspiration new rituals were developed that partly took the place of the old religious feast days, rites, and ceremonies: festivals and flags, music and poetry, national holidays and patriotic sermons. In the most varied forms, nationalism permeated all manifestations of life. As in America, the rise of French nationalism produced a new phenomenon in the art of warfare: the nation in arms. In America and in France, citizen armies, untrained but filled with a new fervour, proved superior to highly trained professional armies that fought without the incentive of nationalism. The revolutionary French nationalism stressed free individual decision in the formation of nations. Nations were constituted by an act of self-determination of their members. The plebiscite became the instrument whereby the will of the nation was expressed. In America as well as in revolutionary France, nationalism meant the adherence to a universal progressive idea, looking toward a common future of freedom and equality, not toward a past characterized by authoritarianism and inequality.

Napoleon's armies spread the spirit of nationalism throughout Europe and even into the Near East, while at the same time, across the Atlantic, it aroused the Latin Americans. But Napoleon's yoke of conquest turned the nationalism of the Europeans against France. In Germany the struggle was led by writers and intellectuals, who rejected all the principles upon which the American and the French revolutions had been based as well as the liberal and humanitarian aspects of nationalism.

THE 1848 REVOLUTIONARY WAVE

German nationalism began to stress instinct against reason; the power of historical tradition against rational attempts at progress and a more just order; the historical differences between nations rather than their common aspirations. The French Revolution, liberalism, and equality were regarded as a brief aberration, against which the eternal foundations of societal order would prevail.

That German interpretation was shown to be false by the developments of the 19th century. Liberal nationalism reasserted itself and affected more and more people: the rising middle class and the new proletariat. The revolutionary wave of 1848, the year of "the spring of the peoples," seemed to realize the hopes of nationalists such as Giuseppe Mazzini, who had devoted his life to the unification of the Italian nation by democratic means and to the brotherhood of all free nations. Though his immediate hopes were disappointed, the 12 years from 1859 to 1871 brought the unification of Italy and Romania, both with the help of Napoleon III, and of Germany; at the same time the 1860s saw great progress in liberalism, even in Russia and Spain. The victorious trend of liberal nationalism, however, was reversed in Germany by Bismarck. He unified Germany on a conservative and authoritarian basis and defeated German liberalism. The German annexation of Alsace-Lorraine against the will of the inhabitants was contrary to the idea of nationalism as based upon the free will of man. The people of Alsace-Lorraine were held to be German by objective factors, by race, independent of their will or of their allegiance to any nationality of their choice.

In the second half of the 19th century, nationalism disintegrated the supranational states of the Habsburgs and the Ottoman sultans, both of which were based upon prenational loyalties. In Russia, the penetration of nationalism produced two opposing schools of thought. Some nationalists proposed a westernized Russia, associated with the progressive, liberal forces of the rest of Europe. Others stressed the distinctive character of Russia and Russianism, its independent and different destiny based upon its autocratic and orthodox past. These Slavophiles, similar to and influenced by German romantic thinkers, saw Russia as a future saviour of a West undermined by liberalism and the heritage of the American and French revolutions.

One of the consequences of World War I was the triumph of nationalism in central and eastern Europe. From the ruins of the Habsburg and Romanov empires emerged the new nation-states of Austria, Hungary, Czechoslovakia, Poland, Yugoslavia and Romania. Those states in turn, however, were to be strained and ravaged by their own internal nationality conflicts and by nationalistic disputes over territory with their neighbours.

Russian nationalism was in part suppressed after Lenin's victory in 1917, when the Bolsheviks took over the old empire of the tsars. But the Bolsheviks also claimed the leadership of the world Communist movement, which was to become an instrument of the national policies of the Russians. During World War II Stalin appealed to nationalism and patriotism in rallying the Russians against foreign invaders. After the war he found nationalism one of the strongest obstacles to the expansion of Soviet power in eastern Europe. National Communism, as it was called, became a divisive force in the Soviet bloc. In 1948 Josip Broz Tito, the Communist leader of Yugoslavia, was denounced by Moscow as a nationalist and a renegade; nationalism was a strong factor in the rebellious movements in Poland and Hungary in the fall of 1956; and subsequently its influence was also felt in Romania and Czechoslovakia and again in Poland in 1980.

ASIAN AND AFRICAN NATIONALISM

Nationalism began to appear in Asia and Africa after World War I. It produced such leaders as Kemal Atatürk in Turkey, Sa'd Pasha Zaghlūl in Egypt, Ibn Sa'ūd in the Arabian peninsula, Mahatma Gandhi in India, and Sun Yat-sen in China. Atatürk succeeded in replacing the medieval structure of the Islamic monarchy with a revitalized and modernized

Kemal Atatürk in 1923. UPI/Bettmann Newsphotos

secular republic in 1923. Demands for Arab unity were frustrated in Africa and Asia by British imperialism and in Africa by French imperialism. Yet Britain may have shown a gift for accommodation with the new forces by helping to create an independent Egypt (1922; completely, 1936) and Iraq (1932) and displayed a similar spirit in India, where the Indian National Congress, founded in 1885 to promote a liberal nationalism inspired by the British model, became more radical after 1918. Japan, influenced by Germany, used modern industrial techniques in the service of a more authoritarian nationalism.

THE NEW NATIONS

The progress of nationalism in Asia and Africa is reflected in the histories of the League of Nations after World War I and of the United Nations after World War II. The Treaty of Versailles, which provided for the constitution of the League of Nations, also reduced the empires of the defeated Central Powers, mainly Germany and Turkey. The league distributed Germany's African colonies as mandates to Great Britain, France, Belgium, and South Africa, and its Pacific possessions to Japan, Australia, and New Zealand under various classifications according to their expectations of achieving independence. Among the League's original members, there were only five Asian countries (China, India, Japan, Thailand, and Iran) and two African countries (Liberia and South Africa), and it added only three Asian countries (Afghanistan, Iraq, and Turkey) and two African countries (Egypt and Ethiopia) before it was dissolved in 1946. Of the mandated territories under the League's control, only Iraq, Lebanon, and Syria achieved independence during its lifetime.

Of the original 51 members of the United Nations in 1945, eight were Asian (China, India, Iraq, Iran, Lebanon, Saudi Arabia, Syria, and Turkey) and four were African (the same as in the League). By 1980, 35 years after its founding, the United Nations had added more than 100 member nations, most of them Asian and African. Whereas Asian and African nations had never totalled even one-third of the membership in the League, they came to represent more than one-half of the membership of the United Nations. Of these new Asian and African nations, several had been created, entirely or in part, from mandated territories.

After World War II, India, Pakistan, Ceylon (Sri Lanka), Burma, and Malaya (Malaysia) in Asia, and Ghana in Africa achieved independence peacefully from the British Commonwealth, as did the Philippines from the United States. Other territories had to fight hard for their independence in bitter colonial wars, as in French Indochina (Vietnam, Laos, Cambodia) and French North Africa (Tunisia, Algeria). Communism recruited supporters from within the ranks of the new nationalist movements in Asia and Africa, first by helping them in their struggles against Western capitalist powers, and later, after independence was achieved, by competing with Western capitalism in extending financial and technical aid. Chinese nationalism under Chiang Kai-shek during World War II was diminished with the takeover of the Chinese Communists. But Chinese Communism soon began to drift away from supranational Communism, as the European Communist countries had earlier. By the late 1960s Russian and Chinese mutual recriminations revealed a Chinese nationalism in which Mao Zedong had risen to share the place of honour with Lenin. As Chinese Communism turned further and further inward, its influence on new Asian and African nations waned.

Political and Religious Differences

Ambitions among new Asian and African nations clashed. The complex politics of the United Nations illustrated the problems of the new nationalism. The struggle with Dutch colonialism that brought the establishment of Indonesia continued with the UN mediation of the dispute over West Irian (Irian Jaya). In the Suez crisis of 1956, UN forces intervened between those of Egypt and Israel. Continuing troubles in the Middle East, beginning with the establishment of Israel and including inter-Arab state disputes brought on by the establishment of the United Arab Republic, concerned the UN. Other crises involving the UN included: the India-Pakistan dispute over Jammu and Kashmir; the Korean partition and subsequent war; the four-year intervention in the Congo; the struggle of Greece and Turkey over newly independent Cyprus; and Indonesian and Philippine objection to the inclusion of Sarawak and Sabah (North Borneo) in newly formed Malaysia.

Many new nations, all sharing the same pride in independence, faced difficulties. As a result of inadequate preparation for self-rule, the first five years of independence in the Congo passed with no semblance of a stable government. The problem of widely different peoples and languages was exemplified in Nigeria, where an uncounted population included an uncounted number of ethnic groups (at least 150, with three major divisions) that used an uncounted number of languages (more than 100 language and dialect clusters). The question of whether the predominantly Muslim state of Jammu and Kashmir should go with Muslim Pakistan or Hindu India lasted for more than 20 years after the India Independence Act became effective in 1949. Desperate economic competition caused trouble, as in Israel where the much-needed waters of the Jordan River kept it in constant dispute with its water-hungry Arab neighbours.

In Europe the spirit of nationalism appeared to wane after World War II with the establishment of international economic, military, and political organizations such as NATO, the European Coal and Steel Community, Euratom, and the Common Market. But the policies pursued by France under Pres. Charles de Gaulle and the problem of a divided Germany showed that the appeal of the nation-state was still very much alive.

PURITANISM AND THE ESTABLISHMENT OF THE HOLY COMMONWEALTH

The religious reform movement in the late 16th and 17th centuries that sought to "purify" the Church of England of remnants of the Roman Catholic "popery" that the Puritans claimed had been retained after the religious settlement reached early in the reign of Queen Elizabeth I is known as Puritanism.

Puritans became noted in the 17th century for a spirit of moral and religious earnestness that informed their whole way of life, and they sought through church reform to make their lifestyle the pattern for the whole nation. Their efforts to transform the nation contributed both to civil war in England and to the founding of colonies in America as working models of the Puritan way of life.

Puritanism may be defined primarily by the intensity of the religious experience that it fostered. Puritans believed that it was necessary to be in a covenant relationship with God in order to redeem one from one's sinful condition, that God had chosen to reveal salvation through preaching, and that the Holy Spirit was the energizing instrument of salvation. Calvinist theology and polity proved to be major influences in the formation of Puritan teachings. This naturally led to the rejection of much that was characteristic of Anglican ritual at the time, these being viewed as "popish idolatry." In its place the Puritans emphasized preaching that drew on images from scripture and from everyday experience. Still, because of the importance of preaching, the Puritans placed a premium on a learned ministry. The moral and religious earnestness that was characteristic of Puritans was combined with the doctrine of predestination inherited from Calvinism to produce a "covenant theology," a sense of themselves as elect spirits chosen by God to live godly lives both as individuals and as a community.

King Henry VIII separated the Church of England from the Roman Catholic Church in 1534, and the cause of Protestantism advanced rapidly under Edward VI (reigned 1547–53). During the reign of Queen Mary (1553–58), however, England returned to Roman Catholicism, and many Protestants were forced into exile. Many of the exiles found their way to Geneva, where John Calvin's church provided a working model of a disciplined church. Out of this experience also came the two most popular books of Elizabethan England—the Geneva Bible and John Foxe's *Book of Martyrs*—which provided justification to English Protestants to view England as an elect nation chosen by God to complete the work of the Reformation. Thus, Elizabeth's accession in 1558 was enthusiastically welcomed by these Protestants; but her early actions while reestablishing Protestantism disappointed those who sought extensive reform, and this faction was unable to achieve its objectives in the Convocation, the primary governing body of the church.

Many of these Puritans—as they came to be known during a controversy over vestments in the 1560s—sought parliamentary support for an effort to institute a presbyterian form of polity for the Church of England. Other Puritans, concerned with the long delay in reform, decided upon a "reformation without tarrying for any." These "Separatists" repudiated the state church and formed voluntary congregations based on a covenant with God and among themselves. Both groups, but especially the Separatists, were repressed by the establishment. Denied the opportunity to reform the established church, English Puritanism turned to preaching, pamphlets, and a variety of experiments in religious expression and in social behaviour and organization. Its successful growth also owed much to patrons among the nobility and in Parliament and its control of colleges and professorships at Oxford and Cambridge.

Puritan hopes were again raised when the Calvinist James VI of Scotland succeeded Elizabeth as James I of

Depiction of an English Puritan family, 16th century. The Granger Collection, New York

England in 1603. But at the Hampton Court Conference in 1604 he dismissed the Puritans' grievances with the phrase "no bishop, no king." Puritans remained under pressure. Some were deprived of their positions; others got by with minimal conformity; and still others, who could not accept compromise, fled England. The pressure for conformity increased under Charles I (1625–49) and his archbishop, William Laud. Nevertheless, the Puritan spirit continued to spread, and when civil war broke out between Parliament and Charles in the 1640s, Puritans seized the opportunity to urge Parliament and the nation to renew its covenant with God. Parliament called together a body of clergy to advise it on the government of the church, but this body—the Westminster Assembly—was so badly divided that it failed to achieve reform of church government and discipline. Meanwhile, the New Model Army, which had defeated the royalist forces, feared that the Assembly and Parliament would reach a compromise with King Charles that would destroy their gains for Puritanism, so it seized power and turned it over to its hero, Oliver Cromwell. The religious settlement under Cromwell's Commonwealth allowed for a limited pluralism that favoured the Puritans. A number of radical Puritan groups appeared, including the Levelers, the Diggers, the Fifth Monarchy Men, and the Quakers (the only one of lasting significance).

After Cromwell's death in 1658, conservative Puritans supported the restoration of King Charles II and a modified episcopal polity. However, they were outmaneuvered by those who reinstituted Laud's strict episcopal pattern. Thus, English Puritanism entered a period known as the Great Persecution. English Puritans made a final unsuccessful attempt to secure their ideal of a comprehensive church during the Glorious Revolution, but England's religious solution was defined in 1689 by the Toleration Act, which continued the established church as episcopal but also tolerated dissenting groups.

The Puritan ideal of realizing the Holy Commonwealth by the establishment of a covenanted community was carried to the American colony of Virginia by Thomas Dale, but the greatest opportunity came in New England. The original pattern of church organization in the Massachusetts Bay colony was a "middle way" between presbyterianism and Separatism, yet in 1648 four New England Puritan colonies jointly adopted the Cambridge Platform, establishing a congregational form of church government.

The New England Puritans fashioned the civil commonwealth according to the framework of the church. Only the elect could vote and rule. When this raised problems for second-generation residents, they adopted the Half-Way Covenant, which permitted baptized, moral, and orthodox persons to share the privileges of church membership. Other variations of the Puritan experiment were established. These included one in Rhode Island by Roger Williams, who was banished from the Massachusetts Bay colony, and one in Pennsylvania by the Quaker William Penn.

INTELLECTUAL-PROPERTY LAW

Intellectual-property law concerns the legal regulations governing an individual's or an organization's right to control the use or dissemination of ideas or information. Various systems of legal rules exist that empower persons and organizations to exercise such control. Copyright law confers upon the creators of "original forms of expression" (e.g., books, movies, musical compositions, and works of art) exclusive rights to reproduce, adapt, and publicly perform their creations. Patent law enables the inventors of new products and processes to prevent others from making, using, or selling their inventions. Trademark law empowers the sellers of goods and services to apply distinctive words or symbols to their products and to prevent their competitors from using the same or confusingly similar insignia or phrasing. Finally, trade-secret law prohibits rival companies from making use of wrongfully obtained confidential commercially valuable information (e.g., soft-drink formulas or secret marketing strategies).

THE EMERGENCE OF INTELLECTUAL-PROPERTY LAW

Until the middle of the 20th century, copyright, patent, trademark, and trade-secret law commonly were understood to be analogous but distinct. In most countries they were governed by different statutes and administered by disparate institutions, and few controversies involved more than one of these fields. It also was believed that each field advanced different social and economic goals. During the second half of the 20th century, however, the lines between these fields became blurred. Increasingly, they were considered to be closely related, and eventually they became known collectively as "intellectual-property law." Perceptions changed partly as a result of the fields' seemingly inexorable growth, which frequently caused them to overlap in practice. In the 1970s, for example, copyright law was extended to provide protection to computer software. Later, during the 1980s and '90s, courts in many countries ruled that software also could be protected through patent law. The result was that the developers of software programs could rely upon either or both fields of law to prevent consumers from copying, and rivals from selling, identical or closely similar programs.

Copyright, patent, trademark, and trade-secret law also have overlapped dramatically in the area of so-called "industrial design," which involves the creation of objects that are intended to be both useful and aesthetically pleasing. Contemporary culture is replete with examples of such objects — e.g., eyeglass frames, lamps, doorknobs, telephones, kitchen appliances, and automobile bodies. In many countries the work of the creators of these objects is protected by at least three systems of rules: copyright protection for "useful objects" (a variant of ordinary copyright law); design-patent law (a variant of ordinary patent law); and "trade-dress" doctrine (a variant of trademark law). These rules stop short of protecting "functional" features, which are understood to include the shapes of objects when those shapes are determined by the objects' practical uses. Nevertheless, the rules combine to create strong impediments to the imitation of nonfunctional design features.

The integration of copyright, patent, trademark, and trade-secret law into an increasingly consolidated body of intellectual-property law was reinforced by the emergence in many jurisdictions of additional types of legal protection for ideas and information. One such protection is the "right of publicity," which was invented by courts in the

United States to enable celebrities to prevent others from making commercial use of their images and identities. Similarly, the European Union has extended extensive protections to the creators of electronic databases. Computer chips, the shapes of boat hulls, and folklore also have been covered by intellectual-property protections.

INTERNET DOMAIN NAMES

In the 1990s the exclusive right to use Internet domain names—unique sequences of letters (divided, by convention, into segments separated by periods) that correspond to the numerical "Internet Protocol Addresses" that identify each of the millions of computers connected to the Internet—became a highly contested issue. Domain-name labels enable "packets" of information transmitted over the Internet to be delivered to their intended destinations. The mnemonic character of domain names (e.g., http://www.britannica.com) also assists consumers in locating Internet-based businesses. As commercial activity on the Internet grew, evocative domain names became increasingly valuable, and struggles over them multiplied, especially as a result of the activities of so-called "cybersquatters," who registered popular domain names with the aim of selling them to businesses at huge profits. The task of allocating domain names throughout the world and of resolving disputes over them has been largely assumed by a private organization, the Internet Corporation for Assigned Names and Numbers (ICANN). With the assistance of the World Intellectual Property Organization (WIPO), ICANN promulgated a Uniform-Domain-Name-Dispute-Resolution Policy to resolve domain-name controversies and has licensed several arbitration services to interpret and enforce it. In 1999 the United States established a similar national system, known as the

"Anticybersquatting Consumer Protection Act," which is administered by the federal courts. Under the law, individuals can be fined up to $100,000 for registering a domain name in "bad faith." Defenders of the law contended that it was crucial to protect the commercial value of trademarks and to shield businesses from extortion. Critics argued that the legislation was too broad and could be used by companies to suppress consumer complaints, parody, and other forms of free speech.

THE WORLD TRADE ORGANIZATION AND INTELLECTUAL-PROPERTY LAW

The Agreement on Trade-Related Aspects of Intellectual Property Rights (commonly known as TRIPS) has contributed greatly to the expansion of intellectual-property law. Negotiated as part of the Uruguay Round (1986–94) of the General Agreement on Tariffs and Trade (GATT), the TRIPS Agreement obligates members of the World Trade Organization (WTO) to establish and enforce minimum levels of copyright, patent, and trademark protection within their jurisdictions. Countries that fail to do so are subject to various WTO-administered trade sanctions.

The leaders of some developing countries contend that the TRIPS Agreement reflects and perpetuates a form of Western imperialism. Noting that most owners of intellectual property (e.g., the copyrights on popular movies and music, the patents on pharmaceutical products, and the trademarks of multinational food and clothing companies) reside in developed countries, these officials argue that strengthening intellectual-property rights unfairly raises the prices paid by consumers in the developing world. Accordingly, developing countries generally have been slow to implement TRIPS. Some economists, however, maintain that the long-term effect of the agreement will be to benefit developing countries by stimulating local innovation and encouraging foreign investment. Despite the existence of TRIPS, global rates of piracy of software, music, movies, and electronic games remain high, in part because many countries in Africa and Latin America have not met the deadlines imposed by the agreement for revamping their intellectual-property laws. Other countries, particularly in Asia, have formally complied with the agreement by passing new laws but have not effectively enforced them.

ECONOMIC AND ETHICAL ISSUES

The tightening of laws governing intellectual property has been paralleled by a steady increase in the economic and cultural importance of intellectual-property rights. The entertainment industry has long been heavily dependent on intellectual property; the fortunes of record companies and movie studios are closely tied to their ability to enforce their copyrights on their products. Similarly, pharmaceutical companies have used the monopoly power created by their patent rights to charge high prices for their products, which has enabled them both to cover the enormous costs of developing new drugs and to make considerable profits. Other, newer industries have become equally or even more dependent on intellectual-property rights. The developers and distributors of computer software, for example, insist that their ability to remain in business is dependent on their power to prevent the unauthorized reproduction of their creations. Intellectual-property protection is widely thought to be even more important to the rapidly growing biotechnology industry, where the development of new techniques of genetic engineering or new life-forms employing such techniques can be extremely expensive.

Biotechnology firms argue that, if they were unable to prevent rivals from imitating their creations, they would not be able to recoup their costs and thus would have no incentive to invest in the research and development necessary for scientific breakthroughs. Companies selling goods and services over the Internet have made similar claims concerning the importance of their domain names.

The strengthening of intellectual-property rights has not met with unanimous approval. Some critics argue that it is immoral for pharmaceutical companies to use their patent rights to set prices for their AIDS drugs at levels that cannot be afforded by most of the people in Africa and Latin America who are afflicted by the disease. Others point out that many patented drugs are developed by using the genetic material of plants found in tropical regions and the knowledge of indigenous groups concerning the plants' medicinal powers. Current patent law, however, awards the exclusive right to market and profit from such drugs to the pharmaceutical companies, leaving uncompensated the countries and indigenous groups whose contributions were essential to the finished products.

THEORETICAL DEBATES

The growth and increasing importance of intellectual-property rights have stimulated a vigorous debate among scholars concerning the justification for and the appropriate contours of this body of law. The debate has largely centred around the advancement and criticism of four theories. The first and most prominent of these is an outgrowth of utilitarianism. Utilitarians argue that the primary problem with intellectual products is that they can be copied easily and that they are "nonrivalrous"—i.e., consumption of them by one person does not prevent their consumption by others. These seemingly benign characteristics result in the danger that, unless the creators of intellectual products are given legal control over their reproduction, there will be little incentive to create them, because creators will be unable to recover their original production costs. Somewhat more specifically, utilitarians urge lawmakers to craft intellectual-property regulations carefully in order to strike an optimal balance between the socially desirable tendency of such laws to stimulate the creation of inventions and works of art and their partially offsetting tendency to curtail the widespread public enjoyment of these products.

A second theory was inspired by the writings of the 17th-century English philosopher John Locke, and specifically by his account of the origin of property rights. Proponents of this theory argue that a person who labours upon unowned resources has a natural right to the fruits of his efforts, and the state has a duty to respect and enforce that natural right. Theories in this vein are considered especially strong when applied to items such as books, music, and simple inventions, which are created primarily through intellectual labour and which are commonly fashioned from raw materials (facts and ideas) that lie in the public domain.

A third theory grew more loosely out of the writings of the 18th- and 19th-century German philosophers Immanuel Kant and Georg Wilhelm Friedrich Hegel and out of a sentiment, common in western Europe, that artists and authors should enjoy certain "moral rights." This approach is premised on the notion that private-property rights are crucial to the satisfaction of fundamental human needs, among which is the need for creative expression. Intellectual-property rights are thus justified either because they protect artifacts through which authors, artists, and inventors have expressed their "wills" or because they create social and economic conditions conducive to creativity.

A fourth, less-well-defined theory contends that intellectual-property rights can and should be shaped so as to help foster the achievement of a just and aesthetically sophisticated culture. Advocates of this approach emphasize the capacity of copyright, patent, and trademark systems—if properly crafted and limited—to promote a vibrant democracy and a participatory and pluralist civil society.

Each theory has its critics, who either doubt the premises of the argument in support of the theory or contest their application to the law. Together the proponents and critics of the four perspectives have generated a cacophonous debate in journals of law, economics, and philosophy. On occasion, lawmakers have been moved by this debate. In the 1990s scholars of all four stripes denounced the growth in the United States of the right of publicity. Utilitarians argued that the lures of fame and money already provided more than sufficient incentives to induce people to become renowned and thus that no additional creative activity would be stimulated by protecting celebrities against commercial uses of their identities. Labour theorists argued that celebrities were already more than fairly rewarded for their creative efforts; personality theorists noted that a strengthened right of privacy would more effectively prevent illegitimate encroachments upon celebrities' senses of self than the commercially oriented right of publicity; and social planning theorists contended that the right of publicity impeded "semiotic democracy" (in which the many would actively participate in defining cultural meaning). Some appellate courts responded to this chorus of criticism by limiting the scope of the right.

Another example of scholarly influence involves the proliferation of patents on methods of doing business. Patents of this sort were rarely granted in any jurisdiction before 1998, when an influential U.S. court decision led to a surge in applications for and grants of business-method patents (e.g., the manner in which a company takes orders placed over the Internet or how a company determines the profile of computer users). Scholars have been nearly unanimous in denouncing this development, and in part this opposition led the Patent and Trademark Office to revise its procedures to limit the availability of such patents. Several European Union countries also were hesitant about following the lead of the United States. Such points of contact between scholars and legislators have been rare, however, as the development of intellectual-property law has been largely unaffected by the views of scholars.

TRENDS

Despite the strengthening of intellectual-property laws, the growing economic and cultural importance of intellectual-property rights, and a widespread view that such rights are socially desirable, the future of intellectual property remains in some doubt. Intellectual-property rights are threatened principally by the proliferation of technologies that facilitate the violation of copyright and patent rules. At the beginning of the 21st century, the sector most affected by these technologies was the music industry, as the combination of compression technologies and "peer-to-peer" copying systems led to widespread unauthorized copying and distribution of digital music. One such system, known as Napster, acquired 70 million subscribers before courts in the United States compelled its closure. From the ashes of Napster sprang many other

TRADEMARK

A trademark is a visible sign or device used by a business enterprise to identify its goods and distinguish them from those made or carried by others. Trademarks may be words or groups of words, letters, numerals, devices, names, the shape or other presentation of products or their packages, colour combinations with signs, combinations of colours, and combinations of any of the enumerated signs.

By indicating the origin of goods and services, trademarks serve two important purposes. They provide manufacturers and traders with protection from unfair competition (one person representing or passing for sale his goods as the goods of another), and they provide customers with protection from imitations (assuring them of a certain expected quality). In terms of the protection of the rights of trademark holders, the law in most countries extends beyond the rule of unfair competition, for a trademark is considered the property of the holder; and, as such, unauthorized use of the trademark constitutes not only misrepresentation and fraud but also a violation of the holder's private property rights.

In most countries, registration is a prerequisite for ownership and protection of the mark. In the United States, however, the trademark right is granted by the mere use of the mark; registering the mark provides the owner only with certain procedural advantages and is not a prerequisite for legal protection.

It is not necessary for the mark to be in use before a registration application is filed, although most countries require applicants to have a bona fide intent to use the mark after registration. Formerly, the United States was one of the few countries requiring actual use prior to registration. Under the Trademark Law Revision Act of 1988, the United

States permits registration upon application attesting to an intent to use the trademark in the near future.

In many countries, ownership of a trademark is not acknowledged until the mark has been registered and gone uncontested for a given period of time, so as to afford protection to a prior user of the mark. Even after that period has passed, the prior user may move to have the registration canceled. After a certain number of years (from three to seven, depending on the country), the registration and ownership become uncontestable.

For a mark to be registered, it must be distinctive. In many cases a mark, when first brought into use, may not have been distinctive, but over time the public may have attached a secondary meaning to it, forming a specific association between the mark and the product, thus making the mark distinctive, hence registrable.

When a question of infringement (unauthorized use) of a trademark arises, the primary legal question addressed in court is whether the accused infringer's use of the mark is likely to confuse the purchasing public. In most countries, including the United States, protection against infringement extends to goods or services similar to those covered by the registration. In countries following British law (some 66 nations), an infringement action can, however, be brought only for the precise goods identified in the registration.

For a long time the rights of a trademark could not be transferred separately from the business to which it was attached. Now, however, because trademarks are deemed property, they may be sold, inherited, or leased, as long as such a transfer of rights does not deceive the public. In most countries a public notice of such a transfer must be given. A common form of transfer is international licensing, whereby a trademark holder allows the use of his mark in a foreign country for a fee. Often in such instances the foreign licensee must meet certain product quality requirements so that his use of the mark does not deceive the consumer.

There are some instances in which the right of trademark may be lost. The two most serious reasons for loss of trademark are the failure to use a registered trademark and the use of a trademark that becomes a generic term. In many countries if a trademark is not used within a certain number of years, the rights of protection of the mark are forfeited. In the United States when a trademark becomes a generic term in the public's mind (such as Aspirin, Kleenex, or Linoleum) the courts may decide that the trademark holder no longer has rights of protection. In other countries the courts are not concerned if the mark is considered generic, and the original trademark holder retains all rights and privileges of the mark.

Although each nation has its own trademark law, there are increasingly multinational efforts to ease registration and enforcement practices. The first international agreement was the Paris Convention for the Protection of Industrial Property of 1883, which has been regularly revised ever since. It sets minimum standards for trademark protection and provides similar treatment for foreign trademark holders as for nationals. Approximately 100 countries are party to the Paris Convention. Uniform trademark laws have been enacted by the African Intellectual Property Organization in 13 French-speaking African countries, the Andean Common Market in Colombia, Ecuador, and Peru, in the Benelux and Scandinavian countries, and under the Central American Treaty on Industrial Property (Costa Rica, El Salvador, Guatemala, and Nicaragua). In addition, nearly 30 countries (mostly European but including Morocco, Algeria, Vietnam, and North Korea) adhere to the Madrid Agreement, which provides for a single application process through filing in a central office located in Geneva.

less-centralized, and thus less legally vulnerable, file-sharing systems. Partly as a result, sales of authorized copies of recorded music began to decline, and the recording industry attempted to develop procedures to enable it to profit from Internet file sharing.

Analogous developments threaten copyrights on movies, books, and software. Similarly, the owners of patent rights or other intellectual-property rights on new plant varieties complain that the unauthorized replication of their inventions is common. The creators of these materials have sought (and often have secured) legislative reinforcements of their legal positions, but those reinforcements often are not sufficient to stem violations.

To combat the threat and to provide themselves with effective protection, many developers have turned to technological shields or to alternative sources of revenue. Encryption systems for music, movies, and software, "terminator genes" that prevent the natural reproduction of genetically engineered plants, and government prizes and subsidies for artistic or technical advances may eventually partially replace intellectual-property law in some areas. Nevertheless, the system of intellectual-property rules is likely to play an evolving and vital role in economic and social life in the 21st century.

Glossary

abscissa The distance from the vertical axis measured parallel to the horizontal axis.

anesthesia A pharmacologically induced reversible state of amnesia, analgesia, loss of consciousness, loss of skeletal muscle reflexes and decreased stress response.

chromosome An organized structure of DNA and protein that is found in cells. It is a single piece of coiled DNA containing many genes, regulatory elements and other nucleotide sequences.

cosmology The field of study that brings together the natural sciences, particularly astronomy and physics, in a joint effort to understand the physical universe as a unified whole.

cytochemistry The biochemistry of cells, especially that of the macromolecules responsible for cell structure and function.

deoxyribonucleic acid (DNA) A nucleic acid that contains the genetic instructions used in the development and functioning of all known living organisms and some viruses.

diffraction The phenomena which occur when a wave encounters an obstacle. It is described as the apparent bending of waves around small obstacles and the spreading out of waves past small openings.

dissonance A combination of tones contextually considered to suggest unrelieved tension and require resolution.

ecology The interdisciplinary scientific study of the distribution and abundance of organisms and their interactions with their environment.

enzymes Biomolecule that increases the rate of chemical reactions. Nearly all known enzymes are proteins.

geocentric system Any theory of the structure of the solar system (or the universe) in which Earth is assumed to be at the centre of all.

geophysics The major branch of the Earth sciences that applies the principles and methods of physics to the study of the Earth.

hypothesis A suggested explanation for an observable phenomenon or of a reasoned proposal predicting a possible causal correlation among multiple phenomena.

inertia The resistance of mass (any physical object) to a change in its state of motion.

infinitesimal A quantity less than any finite quantity yet not zero.

metabolism The set of chemical reactions that occur in living organisms to maintain life. These processes allow organisms to grow and reproduce, maintain their structures, and respond to their environments.

methodology The analysis of the principles of methods, rules, and postulates employed by a discipline.

microbiology The study of microorganisms, or microbes, a diverse group of minute, simple life-forms that include bacteria, archaea, algae, fungi, protozoa, and viruses.

mutation Changes to the sequence of the genetic material of an organism.

naturalist A person who studies natural history.

nucleotides Molecules that, when joined together, make up the structural units of RNA and DNA.

pangenesis A theory of heredity in which gemmules containing hereditary information are incorporated into the reproductive cells.

parallax The difference in direction of a celestial object as seen by an observer from two widely separated points.

protozoology The study of protozoans, which are single-celled organisms possessing a well-defined nucleus.

stratigraphy The scientific discipline concerned with the description of rock successions and their interpretation in terms of a general time scale.

tillite Sedimentary rock that consists of consolidated masses of unweathered blocks and glacial till (unsorted and unstratified rock material deposited by glacial ice) in a rock flour.

tonality The principle of organizing musical compositions around a central note, the tonic.

uniformitarianism In geology, the doctrine that existing processes acting in the same manner and with essentially the same intensity as at present are sufficient to account for all geologic change.

urbanologist A sociologist who specializes in the problems of cities and urban life.

utilitarianism A theory that an action is right if it promotes happiness and wrong otherwise.

*F*or Further Reading

Arendt, Hannah. *The Portable Hannah Arendt*. New York, NY: Penguin Books, 2003.

Augustine of Hippo. *The Confessions of St. Augustine*. Grand Rapids, MI: Revell, 2005.

Bowker, John, ed. *The Cambridge Illustrated History of Religions* (Cambridge Illustrated Histories), Cambridge, UK: University of Cambridge Press, 2002.

Darwin, Charles. *The Origin of Species: 150th Anniversary Edition*. New York, NY: New American Library, 2003.

Fazio, Michael, et al. *A World History of Architecture*. New York, NY: McGraw-Hill Professional, 2008.

Flint, Anthony. *Wrestling with Moses: How Jane Jacobs Took on New York's Master Builder and Transformed the American City*. New York, NY: Random House, 2009.

Freud, Sigmund. *Civilization and Its Discontents*. New York, NY: W. W. Norton & Company, 2005.

Garber, Steven B. *Biology: A Self-Teaching Guide*. Hoboken, NJ: John Wiley & Sons, Inc., 2002.

Gay, Peter. *Modernism: The Lure of Heresy*. New York, NY: W.W. Norton & Co. 2007.

Gifford, Don. *Ulysses Annotated: Notes for James Joyce's Ulysses*. Berkeley, CA: University of California Press, 2008.

Grimme, Karin H., and Norbert Wolf. *Impression* (Taschen Basic Genre Series). Koln, Germany: Taschen, 2007.

Jodidio, Philip, ed. *Green Architecture*. Koln, Ger.: Taschen, 2008.

Oreskes, Naome, ed. *Plate Tectonics: An Insider's History of the Modern Theory of the Earth*. Boulder, CO: Westview Press, 2003.

Piaget, Jean, and Bärbel Inhelder. *The Psychology of the Child*. New York, NY: Basic Books, 2000.

Rogers, John J.W., and M. Santosh. *Continents and Supercontinents*. New York, NY: Oxford University Press, 2004.

Sandler, Irving. *Abstract Expressionism and the American Experience: A Reevaluation*. Manchester Center, VT: Hudson Hills Press, 2009.

Shubin, Neil. *Your Inner Fish: A Journey into the 3.5-Billion-Year History of the Human Body*. New York, NY: Pantheon Books, 2008.

Wolf, Norbert. *Expressionism* (Taschen Basic Art). Koln, Germany: Taschen, 2004.

Zimmerman, Barry E. *Killer Germs: Microbes and Diseases that Threaten Humanity*. New York, NY: McGraw-Hill, 2003.

Index

H